My Love Affair with the French

A Personal History

by

Fannie Lillian Miles Bellamy

DORRANCE PUBLISHING CO., INC.
PITTSBURGH, PENNSYLVANIA 15222

ISBN # 0-8059-6646-3
Printed in the United States of America

First Printing

For information or to order additional books, please write:
Dorrance Publishing Co., Inc.
701 Smithfield Street
Third Floor
Pittsburgh, Pennsylvania 15222
U.S.A.
1-800-788-7654
Or visit our web site and on-line catalog at www.dorrancepublishing.com

To Mama and my father

Mama, circa 1930

My father, circa 1933

Acknowledgments

I am indebted to my family, George Robert who took care of me in first grade, and Eliza Etta and Willoughby who have always been there for me through happy and sad times. I express my gratitude to Uncle Flood and Aunt Luella who were there for Mama and me after my father's death. I am appreciative of the companionship of Little Frank, Johnnie, and Jackie who were more like siblings than a nephew and nieces. Thanks to my best friends Thelma Calbert, Annette Coward, Yvonne Jackson, and especially Charletta Woodward who has spent so much time with me on the byways and highways of France.

I would also like to thank my teachers and coworkers and my students past and present.

I am especially appreciative of my immediate family, my husband Paul, my daughter and traveling companion Nikki, my son Paul III, and my son-in-law Dave. They give me much to write about.

There are many others I would wish to acknowledge, if only space permitted. I can only ask for their understanding, and to tell them they are in my thoughts always. Two people deserve recognition for their influence on my life, and I wish to mention them here: Dorothy Hamilton Hall and Clara Hamilton Peterson. Both of these women, the smartest women I have ever known, are the epitomes of modesty and kindness. Their greatest gifts to me are their constant reminders of Mama.

Finally, I would like to thank my editor, Robert Middlemiss, author, lecturer, and teacher for his advice and his editing of this manuscript.

Chapter 1

How dear to this heart are the scenes of my childhood,
When fond recollection recalls them to view;
The orchard, the meadow, the deep-tangled wildwood,
And every loved spot, which my infancy knew.
                    Samuel Woodworth, *The Old Oaken Bucket*

I love the French. It's a compelling and lasting love affair. I'll tell you why, and for that, I must go back into the past. I was born Fannie Lillian Miles on December 11, 1935, in a very small town, Drakes Branch, Virginia. We had one bank, one drug store that housed the doctor's office, three general stores, one owned by a black man and two owned by whites. There was one deli-like store where they sold cheese, some meats, and canned goods, and we had Miss Minnie's Millinery Shop. My brother George Robert worked for Miss Minnie for ten cents an hour. Mr. Cousins's tailoring shop was in the center of Main Street, next door to Hamilton's Department Store. Mr. Cousins was a black man. I know he did a lot of work for the white people, but I can't recall if he also serviced blacks. Mama never gave him any work because she never got any clothes repaired or cleaned. I made most of my clothes on the secondhand treadle machine Mama bought from Mrs. Paulette. The black man who had the barbershop only cut white men's hair. His shop was also in the center of Main Street, catching a lot of trade. Earl Younger cut black men's hair in his home. His mother took in washing from the white folk. Her work was just like the work of a Chinese laundry man. The only car dealer was Pettus Pontiac, so the Pontiac was the people's car of choice.

People had an interesting way of distinguishing between the educated and not so well educated, particularly for black women. Mama always described Alma Cousins as having finished "normal school." That is, she

1

went as far as she could go in the educational system in Charlotte County. So the neighborhood kids called this friend of Mama, Mrs. Cousins. Every one else was Miss So and So.

When I went off to college and beyond, people would ask, "Where are you from?" When I would say, "Drakes Branch," they would look at me, "What did you say? What's that?" Later, I began using the name of the adjoining town, Keysville, and then explain Drakes was about two hours from the capital of Richmond. "You've heard of Richmond, Virginia, haven't you?" Well, Drakes Branch is located in Charlotte County about eighty miles from Richmond and sixty miles from Danville.

A family by the name of Drakes lived on the heights west of the railroad, and there is a branch that runs from the heights parallel to Main Street. Pipes were laid and water from the headwaters was brought into the railroad tanks by gravity. Later a station was built where the water flows into Twitty Creek. The creek is a tributary of the Roanoke River that runs from south to north. The watering spot was named Drakes' Branch. The apostrophe was later dropped.

A year ago when I went back to Drakes, a historical plaque had been placed near the site where our railroad station used to be. According to some history buff, Confederate President Jefferson Davis, members of his cabinet, and a guard from the Confederate Navy were sent to protect the Confederate Treasury as it passed through Drakes Branch on its way to Danville on April 2, 1864. In June 1864, to deny General Robert E. Lee the use of the South Side Rail Road and the Richmond and Danville Rail Road, General Ulysses S. Grant sent General August V. Kautz south of Petersburg on a cavalry raid to destroy tracks and rolling stock. The main Union forces arrived at Drakes Depot about nine o'clock in the morning on June 25 and stayed for about two hours. The Federals destroyed the tracks from there to present day Randolph, Virginia.

Perhaps, some day, I'll go back and try to find out more of the history of my town. I didn't learn anything about the history in any textbook. It pulls at me now and again, usually when I am down, or maybe proud and excited about something, and I want to share my town's history with some of the people I grew up with.

Drakes, as Mama would say, is only a stone's throw from Appomattox Court House. This town is where General Robert E. Lee surrendered to the Federal General Ulysses S. Grant on April 9, 1865.

I was named after a maternal aunt I never met. She died before I was born. In fact, my three maternal aunts May Gray, Gay Nell, and Fannie Mae all died at the age of twenty-two. Mama was born July 18, 1902. Like her sisters, she also became deathly ill at the age of twenty-two, but she survived, along with her only brother, Flood. Lillian was the name of my paternal grandmother, about whom I know nothing.

2

I have only a fleeting image of my maternal grandmother, Eliza. There are no pictures of her that I am aware of. I have a mental picture of a very tall lady in a long black dress and coat wearing a bonnet. She learned midwifery from her mother, who probably learned it from her mother. A midwife assists women who are in childbirth. Drakes Branch covers a wide area, so she used a horse and buggy to cover fifteen to twenty miles in all directions. She lived in a house with one big room on the lower level and one room of the exact same size on the top level. Her kitchen was out back, and was completely separated from the rest of the house. Later a room was added. It required you to go through the front porch to reach it. This room was called "the little room." It served as the living or sitting room.

The little room was my favorite because it contained our most valuable possessions—a new studio couch, a coffee table, and the piano where Mama kept my father's shotgun. Uncle Flood took us to a Keysville furniture store to buy them. A studio couch was a sofa that opened up into a double bed. The coffee table had a glass top. Mama had leaned on it with her elbow and broken it as we sat on the bed of the truck riding home. A doily always covered the corner of the coffee table to hide the broken corner. There was no glass company in Drakes Branch to repair it. The "little room" had no central heating or electricity either.

Several years later Mama tore down the outdoor kitchen and had one built that was attached to the rest of the house. This room became my second favorite. For this room Mama bought a newfangled oil stove that had hidden burners and resembled an electric range. She also added a mahogany server and cupboard. This room also held the large 1930s, battery-run radio with a built-in aerial and loudspeaker. A battery did not last very long and soon after purchasing a new one, I would have to put my ear to the sound panel to hear *Amos and Andy*, *Our Miss Brooks*, and *Edgar Bergen and Charlie McCarthy*.

My grandmother's well had gone dry, so until Mama had another well dug, we would get water from our neighbor's water pump every couple of days. Rainwater was caught in two large barrels that were used for washing clothes. The drinking water was kept in two buckets on a side table. A dipper always stood in one of the buckets.

My maternal grandmother delivered all of her grandchildren, including me. Sometimes I look at her handwriting on my birth certificate and think about her. I try to imagine her in her bonnet, driving her buggy as she made her rounds. She was born three years after the Civil War ended. There is one question on my birth certificate that asks if eye drops were put in my eyes. My grandmother's answer is, "No, I didn't have any." Luckily, there was nothing wrong with my eyes as I have always had twenty-twenty vision, that is, until I became a *dame d'un certain age* as old age set in.

I do recall the night my grandmother died because of the scar on my right leg that came from a hot glass lamp-chimney. The night my grandmother died, Mama was taking me upstairs to bed. She was carrying an oil lamp in her left hand and me on her right side. She was balancing both the lamp and me. The hot chimney fell off the lamp and landed on my right thigh. A blister formed the length of the chimney, and as I grew in height, the scar did too. Today it reaches from my right knee to my torso. I can see the bulging blister on my little leg as clearly today as the day it happened. I was three years old at the time. How odd it is, the way we remember family: the writing on a birth certificate, a scar on a leg.

There is another very deep scar on my right leg from my simple and adventurous childhood. When I was about eight or nine years old and tired of having cold feet at night, I heated a flat iron, I wrapped it in a towel, and put it in my bed. When I awakened the next morning, I discovered the tip of the iron had burned a deep hole in my leg. I never used this method of keeping my feet warm again.

My grandmother delivered most of the children around Drakes Branch and most of Charlotte County. She lived the typical life of a midwife. Anytime, night or day, she would heed the call and assist in a delivery. The only doctor in town was old Doctor Watkins, a white man. He seemed not to age. He was old but he never got any older. For as long as I knew him he never changed. After my grandmother died, there was another midwife by the name of Mrs. Keating who delivered the black children in the area, and in emergencies white babies as well.

The memory of my father is almost as vague as the memory of my grandmother. People would tell me he was very smart and brave, and that he had a very bad temper. I'm told I'm like my father in many ways—having above average intelligence, being impetuous, stubborn, and prone to express my honest opinion. He once rode his horse through a white man's store because the man had cheated him out of some money owed him. I never understood why he was not lynched. That was still the punishment for being uppity and out of line in the thirties and forties.

The states of Alabama, Arkansas, Florida, Georgia, Louisiana, Mississippi, South Carolina, Tennessee, Texas, and Kentucky were historically the states with the greatest number of lynchings. Lynching is usually thought of as being put to death by hanging; this type of hanging is named after Charles Lynch, a Virginia farmer who organized a band of patriots to punish British sympathizers during the Revolutionary War. Oddly, Virginia is the southern state with the fewest number of lynchings.

In the late eighteenth century lynching referred to flogging and tarring and feathering. I often heard old ladies speaking of people they knew who were tarred and feathered. God knows, there were enough chickens running around to provide the feathers. Perhaps the white man thought somehow my father would get away from the vigilantes and his punishment then would be worse than having a horse come through his front door destroying everything in sight.

4

There wasn't a jail in my hometown. Anyone who broke the law was dealt with by mob violence. Lynching, too, would have been the punishment for my half brother, William James Miles, Jr. who punched a white boy in the white boy's father's general store. The argument was over a pair of shoes. A group of white men came looking for my brother straight away. My father stood in the front doorway with his double-barrel shotgun and said, "I'm going to shoot the breeches off at least one of you." No one in the group of about ten moved a step closer. At the time my brother was hiding under the bed of his dying mother. Somehow, my father got Willie out of town on the six o'clock train heading north. He ended up in Baltimore living with relatives. I never got to know my brother Willie James. The whites in Drakes must have thought that my father really possessed some supernatural powers.

Both whites and blacks in my town believed in the power of magical forces. One of the ironies of country people is their justification of witchcraft by reciting biblical texts. Both Catholics and Protestants quote Exodus XXII. 18, "Thou shall not suffer a witch to live." There are many other references to witchcraft such as in Leviticus, Deuteronomy, Samuel, Kings, and Samuel.

Most of the people in Drakes were Baptist and often took the teachings of the Bible literally. Conjuration and demonic possession rather than witchcraft were the terms I heard most often. Certain people were supposedly possessed by the devil and they had the power to do extraordinary things. Aunt Luella spoke of being ridden by the devil as she slept. Some of Mama's friends believed in haunts or poltergeists who do little tricks at night, like breaking things, pulling off bedclothes, sounding out footsteps, and moving things around. Hearing these ghoulish stories is probably why I turn the security system onto instant response when Paul is out of town and I am home alone.

The prominent belief was that Miss Emma was a conjurer who was capable of stealing a lock of hair, nailing it to a tree, and causing great pain for the owner. My Great Aunt Mary Coleman believed that her being conjured had caused her uncontrollable shaking. An odd birthmark was considered a devil's mark, but most people have some unexplainable blemish which could be considered a devil's mark. Warts, moles, and various kinds of nevus, spots of elevations of red, purple, or black were common back then. There was an old wives' tale that frogs caused warts. I never knew exactly how this could happen, but I stayed clear of frogs. Miss Bessie's grandchild had a big black birthmark on her forehead, but she was no child of the devil. I loved playing with both of Miss Bessie's granddaughters when they came down from Baltimore to spend the summer with her.

There were other minor superstitions such as: *Never open an umbrella in the house; seven years of bad luck if you broke a mirror; walking under a leaning ladder would certainly bring bad luck; if the right ear itched, then something good was being said about the person; if the left eye twitched or fluttered, bad luck was on its way; if the nose itched, someone would be coming; if it rained while the sun was out, then the devil was beating his wife; if one stepped on a line in the sidewalk, that was bad luck; if one spilled salt, a few grains must be thrown over the shoulder or who knew what would happen; and never, never let a black cat cross your path.*

All of these sayings I heard repeated over and over by Mama and people in the community. Some of them Mama repeated more often than others. Her itching nose always brought guests to our house. I am wary when either of my eyes flutters. I believe in ESP, for so often when I think of a friend, I'll get a call or some form of communication from that friend. Of course, if I dream of snakes of any kind, something tragic will happen.

The folk around Drakes firmly believed in the innate ability of fortunetellers and astrologers to predict the future. I never heard anyone, black or white, speak of the greatest astrologer who ever lived, *Michel de Notredame*. He is widely known by his latin name, *Nostradamus*. He was born in St. Remy, France, and studied medicine at Montpellier University. He gained fame as an astrologer after he published his prophecies in verse form, titled *Centuries*, in 1559. There was a renewed interest in Nostradamus in the 1930s because it was thought that he predicted a number of antichrists. Among them were Adolph Hitler, Stalin, and perhaps he was even seeing images of Saddam Hussein. Nostradamus foretold the terrible wars of the twentieth century, space travel (including the moon landing), submarines, nuclear energy, the Kennedy assassination and the AIDS epidemic, earthquakes, political scandals, and social upheavals. As a physician, he gained fame for healing victims of the Black Plague that was spreading across Europe. He died in December 1503, just as he had predicted he would. In 1791, during the French Revolution, looters broke into his tomb and opened his casket. Again, just as Nostradamus had predicted, the looters met with gruesome deaths.

The black people in Drakes may not have been familiar with Nostradamus, but they were well read in Greek mythology. There was Laocoon who warned the Trojans, "I fear the Greeks, even when bringing gifts," and Cassandra, the daughter of King Priam, who had the gift of prophecy, but whom no one believed. *Never look a gift horse in the mouth.*

I am not sure how my father's family arrived in this small town. The French, not recognizing my French as being either Parisian or provincial, always ask if I am from Haiti, Guadeloupe, or Martinique. Historical research tells me that *Miles* is an English surname derived from the first name of a father. My English friends, John and Diane, showed Paul and me a Plymouth telephone book that had a whole list of Miles and Bellamys. They took us for a tour of Plymouth, England. Both the British and American flags are at the exact spot where the ship set sail. There is a museum dedicated to the sailing of the Mayflower in 1620. Both Paul's ancestors and my ancestors may have crossed the Atlantic; however, it is much more likely that they landed at Jamestown in 1607 or thereabouts. When John and Diane came over for Nikki and Dave's wedding, they took an extended vacation to the Boston area. They wanted to see where the Mayflower landed and Plymouth Rock, where some of their ancestors may have come to the shores of America.

We returned to the Butler home in Basingstoke, England, by way of Dartmoor, site of the famous prison that was originally set up to accommodate French prisoners. During the war of 1812, many American prisoners died there as well. We had driven two cars to Plymouth. Diane, Mark, and I were in one car and John, Simon, and Paul were following us. The moor is always a wild and desolate place. On that particular foggy and dreary day we saw no one and only a few sheep and goats. The Butlers wanted to show us the famous Dartmoor Prison up close, but all we could see was the gate that Diane kept passing, turning around, backing up, so we could get a closer look. Each time she would slow down almost to a stop, so we could see the outline of the prison. Mark finally told his *Mum*, "There is a sign. *No stopping in front of the gate!*" We continued on our way with only glimpses of that grim gate.

I met John, Diane and their children during a home stay in the late eighties. Our families have been friends ever since. They have visited us numerous times, and we have visited them. In 1995, we spent the week between Christmas and New Year's in their town of Basingstoke. During the day John, Diane, Mark, and Simon would take us around Basingstoke. We spent an old-fashioned Christmas with the Butlers, reminiscing about my Christmases in Drakes during my childhood.

During the day we visited the historical sites in the area. Evenings, we were busy in Diane's kitchen. Diane prepared main courses consisting of turkey, chicken, or beef with two or three side dishes. Cakes and puddings had been made several days before our arrival, and like the French there were *aperitifs* and *digestifs*. An appropriate wine was served with lunch and dinner. The evenings were spent playing games with the boys. Paul and I learned a new and interesting card game called, "A Penny In, A Penny Out." Emily, the teenage daughter, was often out on a date.

There are many places of interest in and around Basingstoke. Not far from the town is a historical site dating back to the Norman invasion. We also visited the town of Winchester, supposedly the site of King Arthur's Court. The King's legendary Round Table is displayed there. There is also the famous Winchester Cathedral where Jane Austen and other notables are buried. The setting for the children's novel *Watership Down* is also outside of Basingstoke. A New Year's party at Diane's cousin's home in London topped off our visit.

My friend Micheline, who is still fighting the Hundred Year War between France and England, swears that we are really French. She provided me with a list of the names and telephone numbers of all the Bellamys living in Paris proper. I just have not had time to call any of the "Paris Bellamys." Nikki and I once stopped for lunch at *Pizza Bellamy* and the owner declared we were his long lost relatives.

The name *Miles* is of English and Germanic origin. I have turned up no evidence connecting my family to the Germans. A few years ago Nikki and I ran into a professor as we entered the gate of Oxford University. His last name was *Miles*. We were in a bit of a hurry, so we had no time to compare ancestry. He directed us to the university bookstore where Nikki could locate the whereabouts of an author whose research she had used in her dissertation.

I am very fond of Dr. Volker Brandt, the German doctor who delivered both Nikki and Pauly. There are also German teachers from my college days that I would not mind having as long lost relatives.

Nevertheless, later research identifies my family ancestry on my father's side as being in North Carolina as early as 1806. A William Miles was born around 1837, and he fought in the Civil War for the Confederate States of America. He enlisted in Wytheville, Virginia. After the Civil War he worked as a farmer in North Carolina. There was also a Nelson Appleton Miles (1839-1925), who was an army officer who rose to the rank of lieutenant general in the United States Army in 1901. A Miles was also listed in the Andersonville Prison Camp that housed northern prisoners. I looked up the name of Miles as we toured the site while traveling through the southeastern states.

I have no proven link of any one man to my father, except possibly the man in North Carolina, who bears the same name as my father. There were no other blacks or whites that I know of in Drakes Branch or in Saxe, where my father was supposedly born, with the surname Miles.

It is also a mystery to me as to how any family in Charlotte County could have owned slaves. Most of the white people I knew were as poor as the blacks. In fact, the blacks possessed more land than the whites. Mama had more land than the people she worked for. It must have been true that each freed slave in Charlotte County was given at least two acres of land and a mule.

According to county records, my grandmother Eliza got her house and land in 1924 with a highest bid of $400.00. She was born three years after the *Proclamation*, so her mother was a slave. Black people didn't talk about slavery and neither did the white. Well-off families, like the Canadas, Paynes, and Watkins, may have had plantations that once used slave labor. There was only one sentence about it in the history textbook, which told how "happy the slaves were to be slaves in America, and especially to have escaped from their barbaric existence in Africa."

After consulting *Freedman's Bank Records*, available in both book and on computer disk, I have come up with a couple of William Miles, but no information that is pertinent to my father. Perhaps my father really did end up in Drakes Branch by way of Haiti or some other French-speaking country in the Caribbean. I have a burning desire to know more about my father.

When I was growing up, the Blacks in Drakes were referred to as Negroes or colored. I did not like either term, largely because the whites mispronounced the word Negro. I can't think of any reason why I should refer to myself as colored, although on my birth certificate my grandmother stated that both of my parents were colored.

I once read an article in a magazine about a woman who was studying art in Milan, Italy, with other Americans. For a traditional United States Thanksgiving celebration, the director decided that the chef would prepare a traditional Thanksgiving celebration. The American students were asked to help the chef with the preparation. One of the black students decided on corn bread stuffing. When she went into the chef's kitchen she saw that the chef wasn't too keen on having a female in the kitchen. She responded, to his displeasure—"I want to prepare a dish that is representative of my people!"

"What people are they?" asked the chef.

"African Americans," replied the student.

"All Americans come from some place else," answered the chef.

When I am in France or any French-speaking country, no one ever asks me if I am African American. The questions are always *"Etes-vous américaine?"* or *"D' où venez-vous?"* Or they just know I am an American. I once asked a Frenchman how he knew that Nikki and I were from the United States as opposed to being from Africa. He said, *"C'est simple! Votre contenance!"* (It's easy. Your countenance.)

I was happy when *Black* became our identification of choice in the 1960's, so I am sticking with "black" to refer to others like myself. Black is beautiful! When people look at my family and me, they instantly know that some of our ancestors came from Africa, and some must have come from England, France, or some other European country. I don't know any African Americans who are full-blooded Africans. What we call ourselves in America really doesn't matter, we are judged by the color of our skin.

My dad didn't really practice any witchcraft or voodoo, but he was like Toussaint L'Ouverture. He didn't deliver a nation, but he sure delivered his family from evil. There was no other black that would stand up to the whites like my father and live to tell about it. The whites in Drakes must have believed he was capable of destroying them, if not by his double-barrel shotgun then by his knowledge of voodoo. My father had very dark skin and like many Haitians appeared to have no white blood in him.

Voodoo is the name given to the religious beliefs and practice of magic of certain African tribes and parts of the West Indies, especially Haiti. It has also spread to parts of the United States. Voodoo is a West African word meaning god or spirit. According to voodooism, the spirits of the dead live in the world of ghosts, but can visit the world of the living to bless or curse people. If a man makes a wax or any doll-like image of his enemy and sticks pins into it, he is practicing voodooism to injure his enemy.

My father's religion was Presbyterian. I think it was God's miracle that he could torment the whites the way he did and live to die of natural causes. Another explanation may be that the whites simply admired the fearlessness of this black man. I would be satisfied just to know about the two people whose love produced my father.

How strange were those times. The cruelty and malice toward Blacks, the swirling forces of witchcraft and superstition, which governed some of the ugliness. And yet, existing side by side, were the kindnesses and caring that could be shown, starting in their spontaneity and good will. And through it all, my father stood tall and did not compromise, and my mother offered her goodness to anyone in need and sought solace in her prayers and in God. Strong people living, flourishing, contributing, in strange and violent days.

I have only vague memories of my father but I have the truths told to me by others who knew him. What kind of an adult would I have become, if I had grown up with Mama and my father together? I'll never know. Mama used to say that my father would come back for visits after his death. Once we were returning home after a visit to one of her friends. We saw a figure of a tall man dressed in black who turned and looked at us from a distance. He stared at us but said nothing. "That's your father, Mr. Miles," Mama said. At the time I was about eight or nine years old. I believed her at the time.

I also had a picture of my father that I cherished. It disappeared when I went off to school. In this picture he was dressed in a dark suit, just like that man on the lonely road leading from Miss Gracie's to our home. Now, I am not so sure if the man we saw was my father, because I would have to believe that the spirits of the dead return in observable forms. But I have always believed that my father is watching over me.

All of my close friends, except for Elaine Watkins, had a living father. From what others have told me my father was a very brave, honest, intelligent, and hard-working man. It was very sad that he died so young. He was only forty-two. I know my parents' courage in pitting themselves against adversity to overcome many obstacles helped to shape me. There is no other explanation for my being able to venture from the tiny isolated southwestern Virginia town of Drakes Branch and go off on so many strange and wonderful adventures far, far beyond my place of birth.

My brother, Willie James, never came home until our father's funeral. The white boy he had punched and other white men came looking for him at our old farmhouse. They were sure he would be returning to Drakes for our father's funeral. He did return, but when the family heard the whites were searching for him, he returned quickly to Baltimore before father's funeral.

I was five and a half when my father died in the spring of 1941. He was a farmer most of his life, and during the Great Depression of the 1930s he worked his farm where he was able to grow enough food to feed his family.

Our farm, with its house where I was born, was located about a mile from the center of town a very short distance from the main road leading to town.

The first floor consisted of one big room that served as a living room and our parents' bedroom. A large fireplace heated this room. The fireplace was also used for cooking and baking. Sweet potatoes, Irish potatoes, and a type of pancake called a hoecake were baked in the ashes. The kitchen was off to the right and a smaller bedroom used for guests was in the back. A bedroom for all the children was above the living room and our parent's bedroom. There was no heat in the upstairs bedroom, so each bed was covered in winter with a very heavy quilt. My grandmother and her friends made them. Neighbors got together as a means of socializing and helping each other with the quilts. Mama and I used Grandma's quilts until we left our home in Drakes.

The kitchen contained a table and chairs and a wood-burning range. There was also a green upright oil stove for cooking. Water was gotten from a well a few steps from the back door. The outhouse, or toilet, was a couple of yards from the house. I don't remember too much about the outhouse, but like my grandmother's outhouse, it probably contained two round holes, a big one for adults and a small one for children. The outhouse at my grandmother's was located at the bottom of an incline. It flooded after each rain.

When Mama and I moved into her house another outhouse was built on higher ground and closer to our living quarters. The Sears Catalog was used as toilet paper as in the previous one, and lime was used to control the smell. Should the hole fill up, a couple of men would dig another one with a little house surrounding it. Only the white people who lived within the town limits had inside plumbing. All the other people, black and white, had outdoor "plumbing."

Our new outhouse lasted throughout my elementary and high school years. My greatest fear in using the outhouse was opening the door and finding a big black snake or even a moccasin dangling from the rafters.

Recently, my Bennett classmate Geneva Averett told me the story of her cousins shutting her up in the pitch-black darkness of an outhouse. She was visiting an aunt who lived on a farm outside of Greensboro, North Carolina. These children were brave even to go near an outhouse after dark. We had a portable pot referred to as a "slop jar," but called a "chamber pot" in polite society. So Mama and I never went near our outdoor toilet after dark.

The Europeans are much more open when discussing or referring to natural body functions. I thought it was really funny when I saw a sign on a public restroom in Switzerland indicating I was about to enter a "pissoir."

Not only were snakes all around the outside of the house, they also came inside. One evening Mama called me upstairs to show me the skin of a snake stretched across the ceiling of the bedroom. The skin meant that a snake had hibernated in our house all winter. We had been sleeping with my worst enemy. Of all the towns in Charlotte County, Drakes had to have been the most populated with black snakes.

Mama's deadly encounter with a cluster of black snakes reminds me of the story by the French writer Alphonse Daudet, *Sept à Un Coup, Seven at a Blow*. This story tells of a little tailor who goes through the village boasting that he has killed seven at a blow. The town folk think that the little tailor has killed seven dangerous men rather than seven troublesome flies. What a hero he became! One Sunday morning, Mama was reading the newspaper, as she usually did, in front of the kitchen window. She looked up and saw a big black snake crawling out of a clump of bushes onto the path leading to the back door. She jumped up, ran outside, and grabbed the hoe that she always kept close by. She killed the big snake with one swift blow, almost cutting him in half. She put him on a pile of debris for burning and returned to her reading. Each time she looked up from her paper she saw another black snake coming from the same clump of bushes. By the end of the morning she had killed a total of eight black snakes with one blow each.

I too have killed my share of black snakes. I would run like the wind from a moccasin or green snake. We knew that the black snakes were harmless, and they balanced nature by killing rodents such as mice and rats. Evidently, the black snakes in Drakes did not have a natural enemy other than Mama and me. If we were not their sworn enemy, our house and yard would have been overrun with hordes of snakes.

Mama put our icebox underneath the kitchen because it would begin leaking all over the place by mid-week. Our kitchen was built on high pillars because the front of the house rested on a sloping hill. A fifty-pound block of ice never lasted from one Saturday until the next. *The Iceman Cometh* only once a week. One evening I went down the six or seven steps to get ice from the box. As I rounded the stairs, I saw a big moccasin snake stretched out in front of the icebox. I dropped the bucket and ice pick and scurried up the stairs, screaming at the top of my lungs. By the time Mama and I got back down the stairs, the snake had disappeared. A moccasin could be lethal, and it was probably an old wives' tale that a green snake was also just as poisonous. There were many green snakes around, but I knew of no one who had ever been bitten.

There were also many lizards around our house. There was one lizard in particular that always frightened the living daylights out of me, and I would get out of its way as fast as my little legs would carry me. This little red creature had the exact features of a dog. Our official name for it was "Red Dog." The story was that if this little lizard barked at you, you would drop dead on the spot. I now realize that if this little reptile barked at you, you would die of surprise. This was just another story like the tales of the bogeyman, created to frighten little kids like me.

While traveling in West Africa years later, I finally realized that I had had nothing to fear from the reptiles, bugs, and spiders around our house. In Liberia and Ghana, giant lizards crawled around my feet as I ate in the hotel restaurants. In the airport restroom in Abidjan, I saw a black bug that could have been created by Steven Spielberg for one of his horror movies.

Of all the ports along the West Africa Coast, Abidjan is the one I remember most. It is a large vigorous city, and the skyline reminded me of New York. It is a melting pot that blends together many ethnic communities such as Plateau, Adjamé, and Treichville. We stayed for a week at the Hôtel d' Ivoire at the edge of the Cocody Plateau, looking over the several lagoons over which the hotel is built. The forest begins right at the edge of the calm gray waters of the network of lagoons.

Several times we ventured from the city and walked through the forest to visit neighboring villages. I would continually look down as I walked, for fear of stepping on a snake. Those snakes on the outskirts of the modern city of Abidjan are far from harmless. I realized this when an American invited us into her home. She kept an anti-venom kit in her refrigerator. She lived within walking distance of the Hôtel d' Ivoire.

In 1976, my family and I visited three other countries in West Africa— Senegal, Liberia, and Ghana. These countries were relatively peaceful at the time. Since then Liberia's lower class, made up of various ethnic groups, murdered and annihilated the upper class. The upper class had controlled the government, industry, the educational system, and the financial institutions. We stayed for a week in a luxurious hotel owned by a European. Nikki and Pauly preferred swimming in the large swimming pool rather than going out on tours. The Liberians we came in contact with were the descendents of the freed slaves who had left America and relocated on the coast of Liberia, the land of the free. A few months after we left the country, President Tolbert, and all members of his cabinet were assassinated and buried in a common grave.

It was Paul's fraternity who sponsored this trip as part of the 1976 celebration of our country's birthday. His Liberian brothers were our hosts. All members of this chapter of the Alpha Phi Alpha Fraternity were killed, along with members of President Tolbert's ruling party. The upper class was completely wiped out. Monrovia, the capital city named after President Monroe, and the rest of the country is, to this day, in shambles. The economic base has also been destroyed.

When my family and I were in Monrovia we toured a rubber plantation owned and operated by Firestone, an American company. The rebels destroyed the Firestone Plantation along with the rest of the country. A Liberian representative of the Firestone Company gave Paul and his Alpha brothers a banquet of food and entertainment more elaborate than anything I had experienced. I voiced my concern about the broiled animal hanging from the spit. I wanted to make sure it wasn't a monkey. While we were being wined and dined by the Alpha Phi Alpha brothers and even President Tolbert himself, crowds of poor people could be seen staring at us through the windows. A chapter of my sorority Alpha Kappa Alpha (AKA) also entertained the

Alpha wives with a luncheon and fashion show. There was no middle class in Liberia, only the "haves" and "have-nots." Changes needed to be made, but was it necessary to kill all of the educated and wealthy people? Did Liberia, a country rich in gold, diamonds, and other natural resources, have to be destroyed?

Killing all descendents of American slaves did not solve Liberia's problems. The various ethnic groups began fighting among themselves. In 2003, a pre-election year, President Bush sent troops to Liberia. Rival factions were now attacking the government of the United States educated tyrant, Charles Taylor. President Bush stationed American forces off the coast of this West African country and demanded that Charles Taylor seek asylum elsewhere. The toppling of Charles Taylor will not solve all the problems of Liberia. The United Nations must find solutions to deal with countries like Afghanistan, Iraq, and Liberia. America cannot police all troubled nations of the world while at the same time keeping its own citizens out of harm's way from terrorists and others who hate this country.

The Ivory Coast (La Côte d'Ivoire), that once was the most stable country in Africa, is at the present time in the midst of a civil war. Much of the stability of the country for such a long time was due to the presence of the French and then President Houphouet Boigny. Since its independence in 1960, the Ivory Coast has had a very strong economy, based on coffee, cocoa, and mahogany. Today, unrest has struck this West Africa country. Rebels from the north have attempted to overthrow the government of President Gbagbo. Like the United States, the Ivory Coast is a nation shaped by immigrants, in this case, from troubled African nations like Liberia, Sierra Leone, and Burkina Faso. France continually sends troops to help stabilize the region, and to bring about a truce between rival ethnic and religious groups. Perhaps this truce will be a lasting one. It would be tragic to see this beautiful country destroyed like so many other African nations.

When we arrived in Ghana, several Ghanaians had just been executed for attempting a coup. Ghana was under military rule, but its citizens tolerated it. At the present time a president and a nineteen-member cabinet govern the country. Ghana is a small country on the west coast of Africa. It was the first member of the British Commonwealth to be governed by blacks. It has two universities. Portuguese traders founded the first white settlement in Ghana in the 1400s and named it the Gold Coast because of its gold deposits. The University of Ghana is near the capital city of Accra, where we stayed for almost a week. Kwame Nkrumah University is at Kumasi in the Ashanti region. Ghana is well endowed with natural resources, and has twice the per capita output of the poorer countries in West Africa. France has now included Ghana in its Solidarity and Propriety Zone (ZSP).

Since Ghana was our last stop on the tour of West Africa, we saved our shopping for the many shops and markets in Accra. There we were able to buy a few artifacts for our home. Our most interesting side trip was a visit to Cape Coast Castle where most of our ancestors were held before they were put on boats to become slaves in the Americas.

President Bush visited the island of Gorée off the coast of Senegal. Gorée was also an embarkation point of the slave trade. Our Pan Am flight first landed in Senegal. We saw this French speaking country only from the air and the airport. In Senegal we switched to *Air Afrique*. While on Gorée Island, President Bush gave a speech on slavery, which stopped short of apologizing for this particular sin of our nation. His apology would mean nothing anyway. Would it change the past? According to news reports, the ordinary citizens of the West African nations got nary a glimpse of our president.

We also visited the grave of W. E. B. DuBois. It overlooks the Atlantic from its site in Accra, Ghana. William Edward Burghardt DuBois was born in 1868 in Great Barrington, Massachusetts. He experienced little prejudice during his early years in New England, but while attending Fisk University he encountered the reality of race in America. After graduating from Fisk, he earned a Ph.D. from Harvard, the university that would not accept him as an undergraduate student. He became one of the great pioneer sociologists.

W. E. B. DuBois began his illustrious career as a teacher in a small community in Tennessee. Oddly enough, my first teaching position in Lake View, South Carolina, mirrors his experiences as a first-year teacher. Dr. DuBois disagreed vehemently with Booker T. Washington, who believed the success of black folk could be realized if they worked the land as their ancestors had done. Booker T. Washington believed that "the picture of a lone black boy poring over a French grammar amid the weeds and dirt of a neglected home soon seemed (to him) the acme of absurdities." If this statement is true, I also disagree with this great educator and scientist. Though I did not come from the weeds and dirt of a neglected home, I was "a lone black girl poring over French grammar and French literature." In his later years, DuBois became disillusioned with America, renounced his citizenship, and exiled himself in Ghana where he died in 1963. Today, his dream still has not been realized.

During our visit, Nikki and Pauly were able to gain insight into this vast continent of their ancestors and the new countries there. Paul and I learned much of the history that we should have learned from our U.S. school studies, and much, much more.

When my family lived on the farm our closest neighbors were the Hancocks. Their house was adjacent to ours and another family whose name I don't remember. Delores Hancock, who was one year younger than I, was my playmate. Almost directly behind the Hancocks were the Mosleys, one of the most educated black families in the community. The daughter of this family, Miss Mosley, was my first grade teacher.

In first grade she taught me to read from *Dick and Jane*. It had become a standard textbook in all Virginia schools in 1927. None of my teachers or anyone else had ever heard of phonics. I learned as everyone else did, by rote. The Dick and Jane series was the way we learned to read back then. There were colorful illustrations of the blond, blue-eyed children, Dick and Jane, and Spot, their black-and-white dog. Their parents had the same blond hair and blue eyes. As I look back, the only connection I had with the people in the story was Spot. He reminded me of my first dog, little black-and-white Toby.

Mama never told me that I should "act like the little white girl." Nor did she ever tell me to "act black." She did tell me that I was just like my father, "You always have your head struck in a book."

"Isn't that why you ordered these books?"

She would give me a big smile.

Mama had only a third-grade education. Her reader was much more difficult to read than *Dick and Jane*. It probably accounts for the fact that she could read and write really well. Willoughby and Eliza went to a church school just as our mother did. School started with devotions consisting of "The Lord's Prayer" and reading from a textbook called *The Peep of the Day*. Lesson I is entitled "Of the Body" and begins—

> *MY DEAR LITTLE CHILDREN: You have seen the sun in the*
> *sky. Who put the sun in the sky? God.*
> *Can you reach up so high? No.*
> *Who holds up the sun, that it does not fall? It is God.*
> *God lives in heaven; heaven is much higher than the sun.*
> *Can you see God? No.*
> *Yet He can see you, for God sees everything.*

In the 1940s and 1950s when George Robert and I were in school, there was no separation between school and religion. School started with the Lord's Prayer. Songs like *God Bless America* and *When the Saints Come Marching In* were part of morning devotions. Back then we also said the Pledge of Allegiance. There was no choice of sitting or standing. Other times during the day, if the classes were good, we would break into renditions of *Shoo Fly, When Johnnie Comes Marching Home*, and *Carry Me Back to Old Virginny*. In 1940, *Carry Me Back to Old Virginia* (Virginny) became the state song.

The black American composer and entertainer James Bland (1854-1911) wrote this song. Bland was born in Queens, New York, of freeborn parents. He was part of an all black group of minstrel performers from Georgia.

While Douglas Wilder was governor of Virginia (1990-1994), he objected to this song because of its romanticized view of slavery. The song was retired to "state song emeritus." An unsuccessful competition for a new song was held in 1998. I suppose Virginia doesn't have a state song anymore. When we sang this old song at Organ Hill, no thought was really given to

16

the meanings of individual words and phrases, especially the part referring to us as "darkies." We just wanted to get out of doing the monotonous work of reading, writing, and arithmetic.

The poem does show that James A. Bland was a talented poet and composer. Virginia is one of America's most beautiful states. He could have written about the beauty of my state, that he had visited, without pretending that a Virginia slave actually enjoyed laboring for his "old massa and missis," and was looking forward to meeting them in Heaven. His master and mistress believed that God would separate blacks and whites in Heaven. I suppose all whites that believe they are the chosen ones are looking forward to a "Hereafter" that God has prepared just for them.

Bland may have chosen to write in dialect much like the comedians, filmmakers, and poets of today who choose black dialect, or Ebonics today in preference to Standard English.

Nevertheless, our teacher taught most of us to sing in perfect pitch the words to *Carry Me Back to Old Virginny*. My children grew up in Virginia and they were never aware of what was once their state song. Now they are!

Pauly's first-grade teacher said that he was very good at his phonics lessons and drills, but he saw no connection between phonics and reading. He learned by rote as I did. He would say, "Mommy or Daddy, what is this word?" We would tell him. The next time he came across the word he would remember it, or if he didn't he would ask again. On the other hand, Nikki learned to read by using phonics. She was constantly showing me how she could sound out new words.

It's a mystery to me how so many black and white children reach high school not knowing how to read as well as a first grader did back then. Black children are disproportionally represented in special education classes in Virginia's Fairfax County and the United States as a whole. Often black children are in special education because they continually misbehave in class, and neither teacher nor parent has insisted that they behave, not since their preschool and kindergarten days.

Children learn to read in different ways—through phonics or by rote. Textbooks are not chosen to meet the needs of each and every child, but now at least they are realistic and pluralistic. They attempt to recognize the real world and not a highly selective one as shown in this passage from *Dick and Jane*.

Look
Look, look.
Oh, oh, oh.
Spot.
Come Dick.
Come and see.
Come and see Spot.

Look, Spot.
Oh. Look.
Look and see.
Oh, see.
Run Spot, run, run.
Oh, oh, oh.
Funny, funny, Spot.

I am constantly asking myself, *Why Can't Johnny Read?* Gordon Parks in one of his autobiographies, *A Choice of Weapons*, believes that the key to continued progress of black people is education. Education should be our weapon and not the continual laying of blame on what has happened to us in the past. August Wilson explores our heritage and experiences volitionally in his plays. In *Ma Rainey's Black Bottom*, when we can't defeat racism and the white man, we take our hatred out on each other and ourselves. We have not come to realize that when we hurt and kill each other, we are playing right into white bigotry. Children of my generation were determined to make the best of what our deplorable learning environment had to offer. Dick and Jane taught us all to read and write.

Parents must be involved in their children's education. Mama never told me I had to go to college. It was just something she expected, something that my brothers and sisters expected, and something I just expected to do. After all, they did not even have the luxury of attending a high school. I loved learning new things. I could not fathom leaving school after receiving my high school diploma. There was a whole new world out there that I had to explore.

There were no PTAs at Organ Hill Elementary or Central High School. Students came from all over the county, and back then most families didn't have a car. The only black families I knew who had a car were the Dusenburgs, the Cousins, and the Eubanks. While I was at Central High, there was one day each school year set aside for parents to visit with the teachers. Mama would have to find someone to take her to Charlotte Courthouse ten or fifteen miles away. She always found someone, usually Mr. Cousins. There were no coaches who told the boys who played basketball that this was their key to success. Boys and girls alike were told that learning to read and write would lead to success.

Dr. William E. Ward, an outstanding player on Central High's 1950-1953 basketball team, went on to study at Virginia State College and Clark University. He is now the longest serving mayor in the history of Chesapeake, Virginia. Before becoming mayor he was chair of the History Department at Norfolk State University. He is now Professor Emeritus. His résumé reads like that of a U. S. president rather than a mayor. Lee Malvo's trial was moved to his city. I am sure William Ward gladly accepted the challenge.

There will come a time, and very soon, when we will no longer see two different NBA teams, or even college teams, on the floor and all ten players are black. Teams and owners are now recruiting foreign players from Eastern Europe and even China. They are much more coachable and do not cause problems involving drugs, spousal abuse, gun charges, assault charges, infidelity, and paternity suits. There was no guidance counselor to guide us as to what we should do after high school. College bulletins were sent to my U. S. Government teacher, Mrs. Binford. She was the principal's wife. From those brochures I decided to which colleges I would apply—two women's colleges, Bennett and Radcliffe. At Mrs. Binford's urging, I also applied to Virginia State College.

Michael Clarke Duncan, who won the Oscar nomination for supporting actor in *The Green Mile*, credits his mother for his success. She was determined that he would become an actor and not a football player. He would probably have been one of the greatest linebackers or tacklers who ever played football, but his mother knew he had a rare talent when he showed his acting ability in his rendition of the reading of *Dick and Jane*.

According to a recent *Washington Post* article, March 9, 2003, there is a disparity between black Americans and blacks who immigrate to the United States from the Caribbean and sub-Saharan Africa. Many of these immigrants live in the Washington area. On an average they stay in school longer than American blacks, Asians, and whites. Not only do they surpass black Americans when it comes to education, but also in their median income. It must also be noted that these achievements are actually higher, because of the small number of black people admitted to the United States because of the country's racist policies. Oakton's Thierry Kamuanga from the troubled Congo speaks perfect French, but puts forth an extraordinary effort to learn English in Lin Booth's class—*English and Speakers of other Languages* (ESOL). Thierry's country, The Democratic Republic of the Congo, has vast copper reserves. It has one third of the world's industrial diamonds. Since its independence from Belgium it has been plagued by numerous political problems.

Data having to do with success also applies to Haitian immigrants who manage to reach the shores of the United States in their rickety and leaking boats, and who are not turned around by the U.S. Coast Guard. Those of us who have been in America for more than two hundred years can learn from the newly arrived Africans who come to this country. Warring factions have displaced some of those who come to the United States. They lick their wounds and manage to take advantage of the American system of free enterprise. The Lost Boys of the Sudan are the best example of those who come to the United States to take advantage of our educational system. Some immigrants were even slaves in their own country. They come to America believing that our country is "the land of the free," and they make it so.

There was another study done to determine if the white establishment chooses to discriminate against blacks by using the names parents chose to give their children. A number of applications were sent to companies from supposed applicants bearing such first names as Lakeisha, Latisha, Ebony, D'Andre, Tamika, Mo'nique, Aisha, and Kareem. They were systematically rejected or received no responses. If you are a Kareem Abdul Jabaar, Shaquille O'Neil, or LeBron James—it doesn't matter what your first or last name happens to be. Names identifiably black began appearing in the 1960s. What's in a name? A great deal! Black females are usually easier to identify by race than any other group. Hispanics and Asians are usually in the first and second category with African Americans coming in third as a group. Even before the study was done I have been able to look at my student roll at the beginning of the school year and determine which students were black. While reading the *Washington Post*, I can often identify by their first names the blacks that appear in negative news articles, especially those articles depicting blacks as being on welfare, committing a crime, or being in jail. There are actually more white people and other races on welfare than blacks, but the stereotype always has the blacks on welfare in the majority.

Parents have every right to choose a name for their son or daughter. The fact is that certain names put our kids at a disadvantage. Black-sounding names cause stereotyping. We live in a racist society, and it is profitable as well as to our advantage to have a white-sounding name. We are doing a dis-service to our children if we make up odd names for them, such as D'Andre, which really does not make sense. I have also seen other names with an apos-trophe thrown in at the beginning. An apostrophe stands for a letter that is left out, or it shows possession or ownership. In French this punctuation mark has several different meanings.

Prince George's County in Maryland is one of the wealthiest majority-black-counties in the United States, according to several *Washington Post* arti-cles in recent years. It is also the county in the Washington area with the most problematic schools. Likewise, it has the greatest number of people who give the most charitable contributions to religious institutions. Blacks give 25 percent more of their earnings to religious institutions than whites. These parents would fare better if they kept more of their earnings for the education of their children.

Prince George's is the county with the greater number of mega-church-es with such names as "Jericho City of Praise." There are also mega-salaries for the ministers. These churches and ministers claim to offer programs such as drug ministry, after-school care, and massive food services, all worthwhile programs. However, it is usually the less affluent who give a greater part of their income to the church while receiving little in return. It is the minister who lives in a big house and demands a Lincoln Town Car or a Cadillac.

Sociologists coined the term "mega-church" in the 1980s, and they are most often Protestant. There are two thousand to three thousand Catholic parishes, but in a Catholic mass, the sacrament of Holy Communion is the primary focus rather than the priest. Catholic schools have long proven that black students succeed in their strict environment where they fail in other schools. However, these students only succeed if both parents and school demand acceptable behavior of these students.

The majority of the mega-churches is located in the South and West and has a weekly attendance of two thousand to three thousand. Most have sports and physical fitness programs, but no organized academic programs or schools associated with the church. Fairfax County and other counties like it have a public educational system that works. We just have to make sure that all students and parents take advantage of all that is offered. France, England, Italy, and other countries in Europe built magnificent cathedrals and churches, and they served a purpose. But that was then, and this is now.

Predominantly black colleges served a great purpose then, and they should serve an even greater purpose now. They are competing with the white institutions for the small pool of black or minority students, and in many cases black colleges and universities are losing the battle. We should not give up on our historically black institutions. They are the institutions that produced my generation of lawyers, doctors, and teachers.

Our white institutions are producing a cadre of basketball and football players more interested in tattoos and decorative and exotic hairdos. White institutions discovered in the 1960's that these athletes, particularly basketball players, bring millions of dollars to their schools. An exception is Duke University that monitors the academic records of its athletes, black and white. The professional teams in their quest for the almighty dollar are now taking talented student athletes directly out of high school. The end result is that we have black children thinking of these athletes as their role models and basketball as their key to fame and fortune.

I became keenly aware of the role of black institutions during orientation week at Bennett when we sang:

The Preference Song
There are many, many schools in the East
*   And in the West.*
Sometimes you may question as to which one
*   Is the best.*
If you really want to know
*   There is one that will stand out,*
It's dear old Bennett College,
That's the school you hear about.

CHORUS
Some prefer to go to Spelman;
*   Others A & T,*
Some say here's to Talladega;

21

> *Others Johnson C.*
> *But Bennett College is the best, girls,*
>   *Lift high your colors bright,*
> *Raise your voices in a cheer, girls,*
> *For the dear old BLUE and WHITE*
>   *Rah-rah-rah!*

During the 1928 presidential campaign, Herbert Hoover spoke of America's bright future; "We in America are nearer to the final triumph over poverty than ever before in the history of the land." Most Americans agreed. However, suddenly, in 1929 the United States found itself in the worst economic depression in its history—the Great Depression. Most of America's citizens' attention was focused on Washington, D. C., on inauguration day in 1933. Millions of Americans began to lose faith in the American dream. After that day came "Black Tuesday." Stock prices declined rapidly.

Like most blacks, my parents did not have the means to invest. Though this was the 1920s view of triumphing over poverty they had not used their savings to invest in stock. They had none. So in 1929, when the United States found itself in the grip of the worst economic depression in history, my family survived. Farmers lost everything in many parts of the country and joined countless others looking for work. The farmers in Southwest Virginia fared better. My father was able to hold on to his ten-acre farm and Uncle Flood his one hundred and twenty-five acres. I suppose there were sharecroppers in Charlotte County, but I never knew any. People I knew worked their own land.

President Franklin D. Roosevelt promised that he would lead the nation out of the depression. He favored relief programs that gave jobs to the unemployed. One of those programs was the Civilian Conservation Corp (CCC). The purpose was to help young men from poor families. The CCC set up camps in rural areas where young men lived and worked. Their job was to protect and restore America's natural resources.

My brother Willoughby was a part of this government program that was one of many programs established by President Roosevelt. Americans could feel good about themselves if they were doing a job, rather than taking a handout from the government. How proud my brother was of his khaki CCC uniform that resembled a military one. During the depression years, my father left the farm and his family for Baltimore, Maryland.

World War II began in 1939. He planned to work at the Bethlehem Steel Company until the war ended. Mama and George Robert continued to work the farm, but they planted only small vegetable gardens.

My father died when I was very young. I was only five years old, so my memories are those of a child. In my world of grown-ups and tall furniture, grown-up voices spoken above me, cups and plates were on counters too high for me to reach. But now I saw my father in my world on the floor, motionless, and very, very still. But that is all I remember. In my child's mind I could not take in the immensity of what had happened. There he was on the floor, crashing into my world from on high. To this day I can't grapple with it; I can't get my child's mind in this grown-up body around this sudden loss of my father. It stalks my memory. I overlay it with grown-up insights and experiences.

My father would come home on some weekends, and it was on one of those weekends that he dropped dead in front of Mama and me. People had a habit of diagnosing their own diseases back then. Members of the family described his death as an asthma attack. It didn't matter to me how and why he died. I only saw that my mother was thrashing about, and asking the repetitive question *"why?"* A five-year-old has no understanding of a death in the family, even her father's. I see in my child's mind my father lying on the floor and Mama screaming for her other children; and Mama wearing black for months, and on the day of my father's funeral the undertaker bringing to the house a beautiful spray of red roses that was to go on my father's casket.

Children didn't go to funerals, not even to their father's. My father died of a heart attack. Mama often told me of the conversation they were having just before he dropped to the floor. He was speaking of the future, my future. His words were, "No one knows whence his bread comes, and especially Fannie Lillian." (Me!) His last words still puzzle me. One might get the impression that he was not a religious man. Most adults of his day believed that "the Lord would always provide." My father just did not have time to finish his conversation.

I wonder if he came home to die. He only came home once a month, so he could have easily died in Baltimore, away from his wife and children. He must have had a premonition that he was going to die, and that was why he came home that particular weekend. Mama always said he had a sixth sense.

I was with my father when he died at the age of forty-seven, and I was with Mama when she died at the age of ninety-four. Well I was almost there. Paul and I were called to Mama's nursing home around five in the morning during the blizzard of January 11, 1996. When my husband and I arrived at her bedside she was lucid but writhing with pain. Dr. Tibor Ham, Jr. had begun prescribing morphine. It was Mama's diseased kidney that had begun acting up again.

We were not that concerned, because Mama had recovered from her kidney problem many times before. On two occasions Dr. Ham had told me that Mama would die if she did not have surgery. Her first operation had been for a bleeding stomach ulcer. When I went to see her, she was bleeding from every cavity, but she was still alive. She was eighty-five at the time, and had never been inside a hospital. The first operation was a success; the bleeding stopped. She was never to walk again.

She was confined to Fairfax Commonwealth Nursing Home, which now serves as an INOVA facility. While doctors were prepping her for the kidney surgery, she had a massive stoke. Needless to say, they did not remove her kidney. Instead she was placed in the Hospice area of the hospital to die.

After a couple of weeks, I was told that she would be going back to the nursing home, and Hospice would continue to monitor her. After a month, there was no need for Hospice. Through all of her stays in the hospitals while dealing with the kidney problems and a host of other illnesses, she was like a brave soldier going into battle. To me, knowing my mother so well, it was a battle with the Angel of Death. I believed Mama's fortitude would keep her with us. I really expected her to at least reach her one hundredth birthday. She died five years shy of that goal on January 11, 1996, on my son's birthday. That date has an ironic twist to it. Perhaps Paul III might someday tell his side of this story.

Paul and I stayed with her during the early morning hours, and then returned home. Paul went to work. I went back to the nursing home. The nurse continued to give her the prescribed doses of morphine for pain, and Mama slept peacefully most of the day. About two-thirty in the afternoon, I went home. I decided that I had better call my sister, Eliza Etta.

As soon as I hung up, I received the call that I should return immediately. I rushed back to the nursing home, but Mama was gone. I sat with her until they came to take her away. It was fate, or God's will, that I did not see her take her last breath. Seeing the undertaker zip Mama up in the body bag will stick in my mind forever.

Mama had not joined a church when she came to live with my family, so we had no church service. I wished she had become a Catholic like the rest of us. The priest would have been able to give her the beautiful "going home" service she deserved. She would have hated having people who did not know her saying things about her or about themselves. The Catholic Mass is all about the dead as well as the living. There is something mythical about the priest saying ten "Hail Marys" for the dead.

We brought Mama home for an overnight stay. Friends and family were able to spend the evening hours with her. As she lay in the coffin in our living room surrounded by relatives, neighbors, and friends, the expression on her face told me that she was now in a peaceful place. I looked at my mother's face. It was a good face, timeworn and imprinted with a thousand worries and joys. My mother had seen the best and the worst life could offer. She had conducted herself with grace. Simple acts, too. Like watching me read and smiling with encouragement. A good mother. A good woman.

We had a small service the next day at the cemetery with family members and a few friends attending. We buried her fittingly under a giant oak tree, at the National Memorial Park in Falls Church, Virginia, just like the one in our back yard in Drakes. There was heavy snow on the ground during that blizzard of 1996. Mama loved this beautiful winter setting. She is now spending winter, spring, summer, and fall in her very own back yard. Most of all, I can visit with her whenever I want to, and I can say as many "Hail Marys" as my heart desires.

The death of both my parents stalks my memory. I overlay it with grown-up insights and experiences, but always they lie just beyond. Very still! A great and abiding presence through all my day! And how fortunate I am. I am advancing in years myself. I have known the good and bad that life has to offer. But my fortune has been grounded in a loving home where we had little by way of material things, but oh, how rich in love and support, how warm were my mother's arms, how much strength I could draw from her strength, and so many memories of little things that make up the meaning of my childhood and youth. I can summon my mother's touch, I can see her in the garden or working in the kitchen, I can hear her tread as she moves through those days, taking care of all of us.

And my father. A much loved mystery of a man whose last words were for me, his concern for me. Yes, I puzzle over those words, but they were my champions! I continue to go forth in my life with my father's words and my mother's touch.

Mama thought asthma had something to do with my father's death. I don't think so. The way he died was often described as "asthma of the heart." He suffered from asthma, but since he was carrying on a conversation, an asthma attack seems unlikely. He simply had a heart attack. today the old term "cardiac asthma" is known as "congestive heart failure."

When I was little, I thought that I, too, would one day drop dead of an asthma attack. Mama treated my asthma by sewing a piece of wool fabric inside my undershirt. She saturated the cloth with Vicks Vapor Rub each night. I wore this concoction all the winter months. No one in school ever teased me about smelling like Vicks. I suppose it was not a bad smell. Luck was with me and my asthma changed to hay fever when I was twelve—before I entered high school.

There is a new theory as to why so many children today, especially boys, are afflicted with asthma. It is believed they live in such a sterile environment that their bodies do not build up antibodies against bacteria. These children are in contrast to children who are born on farms, or in other rural areas, where they are around farm animal waste and a much less sterile environment in general. Having a pet, such as a dog, is also thought to be a deterrent to this chronic condition. This theory would not hold true for children in the area where I grew up. My father was a farmer most of his life. My cousin Octavia had a severe case of asthma, and many a night Uncle Flood would have to go and fetch Dr. Watkins. Octavia grew up on her father's farm. She married a farmer. However, none of Octavia's thirteen children had asthma, so perhaps it is true that those children who grow up around dirt in rural areas and farms are less vulnerable to asthma. My case of asthma in our family may have been just a fluke, and the present day theory has merit.

The closest hospital was more than two hours away, and even if my father had lived long enough to reach Richmond, there would still have been the problem of finding a hospital that would take him. Dr. Watkins, who made house calls, was also quite a distance away. By the time my older brother walked to Dr. Watkins's house and brought him to our house, there was nothing that could be done for my father. None of the people in Drakes ever went to the hospital. I remember both black and white people just got old and died. I knew no one who died young, except my father.

I know almost nothing about my father's family. Many years later I met a cousin, Algie Davis, through my adopted brother, Gilbert Miles. Algie died a few years after we met. Gilbert was really my first cousin, whom my father never legally adopted. The fact is there were no legal adoptions in Drakes. He later took the name of his stepfather, so his legal name was John Gilbert Pollard, but everyone around Drakes and thereabouts knew him as Gilbert Miles. To Gilbert we were sister and brother.

Gilbert's father was a white man, and Gilbert could pass for white, and he often did when he went north. His father, Robert Dickinson, claimed Gilbert and his mother as his family years later in New Jersey. They lived as a family until his father's death in 1955. Gilbert never took his biological father's name. Until the 1960s, miscegenation was a crime in the state of Virginia. Gilbert died of cancer in 1999. He wrote his own obituary that included the following:

> *I, John Pollard was born March 1, 1923 to Mary Pollard and Robert Dickinson. I am married to Elizabeth B. Pollard.*
>
> *God was good to me for seventy-six years. These years weren't easy, but trusting in God I made it.*
>
> *In 1992, I moved back to Virginia and joined Mossingford Baptist Church.*
>
> *I served in the United States Army during World War II and served the city of Newark, New Jersey, Police Department for twenty-seven years.*
>
> *I leave my wife Elizabeth and sister Fannie Lillian Miles, cousin Algie Davis, brother-in-law Paul L. Bellamy and John Henry and a host of other relatives and friends.*
>
> *I have always said, "Where you are I once was and where I am you must surely come. Live right and trust in God and you won't have trouble coming where I am."*

I regret not have spent more time with Gilbert after his move to Virginia. I regret not always having this man in my life. He was in my life such a short time, this man who was my first cousin, but considered me his sister.

As a result of the contact I had with Gilbert in recent years, I have learned a little more about our father's family. One of his sisters, Josephine Miles, married Allen Davis. From this union Algie was born. Algie, my first cousin, married Alice Wilborne. Algie, Jr., Herbert, Roy, Myrtle, and Ester are my cousins. I now attend the Davis Family Reunions, which are held every two years in Clover, Virginia, not far from my little town of Drakes Branch.

Dr. Watkins was the only doctor I ever knew when I was growing up in Drakes. He was a white man without one ounce of racial prejudice. He would make house calls at any time, day or night. He didn't care if you were black or white, rich or poor. His waiting room was once integrated, but he was forced to divide his big waiting room into two small ones when the whites complained vehemently about having to sit with sick colored people. I am sure Dr. Watkins had a car, but I always saw him walking up to our house after a brother or neighbor had gone to tell him he was needed.

Dr. Watkins was the kindest man I knew with impeccable bedside manners. When I was about nine or ten I was bitten by Miss Annie's dog. Dr. Watkins treated the wounds while assuring me that it wasn't as bad as it looked. I don't remember if he gave me a tetanus shot, but the penny-like scar on my right arm is a reminder that he gave me the only shot that was required at the time, smallpox. There were no vaccines available in the 1930s and 1940s for most childhood diseases.

Dr. Watkins cared for me when I contracted measles, chickenpox, mumps, whooping cough, and my many bouts with asthma. Mama dearly loved Dr. Watkins. She turned to her Dr. Watkins for whatever ailed her. While I was in college Dr. Watkins was shot and killed during a robbery as he walked home from his office. How is it possible that such a kind and gentle man would meet with such a violent death? His killer, a black man who grew up in the area, was found as a result of the story being written in a magazine dealing with *The Ten Most Wanted*. There were almost no murders in my hometown. The only one I remember is that of the good Doctor Watkins.

How does one grapple with an event like that? Here was a warm and gracious man who exemplified how the races could get along together, if they would but try. He, too, is part of my reflections on when I was young. He is part of the hope for what could be in our country, and in the world for that matter. And I say that advisedly after my travels to Africa. I think my mother would agree with this: that simple lives lived well and with caring others are the ultimate refutation of the evils in the world.

I was the youngest of Mama's four children. From her marriage to George Lee Ridley, there were three children. Willoughby Lee, who was born at 9:00 P.M. January 9, 1923, Eliza Etta was born 2:00 A.M., September 17, 1924, and George Robert at 11:45 A.M. February 8, 1928. Mama returned to Drakes Branch for the birth of each of her children, so her mother could have the pleasure of delivering each of her daughter's children. My grandmother listed George's race as Colored, and Willoughby's, Eliza's, and my race as Black. My siblings' father's occupation is different on each birth certificate—an elevator boy in a law building on one, and a laborer at the docks on another. My father's occupation is listed as a farmer.

Mama met George Ridley while working in Richmond. They later moved to Philadelphia. It is in that city that he worked on the docks. My mother's first husband supposedly died of jaundice, a disease that discolors the skin and whites of the eyes with a yellow pigment.

Several years later Mama met and married a widower, William James Miles, Sr., who was twelve years her senior. Mama showed a rare respect that I have seen no other wife show toward her husband. She called my father Mr. Miles in life and death.

Mama's children by George Ridley and I never referred to each other as half-sister or half-brother. We had two different last names, but we were always just brothers and sisters. In this part of the south, people often used the first and middle names, or a merging of the two names. Eliza Etta became Lizetta, George Robert was known as George Robert, and I was Fannie Lillian that sounded something like "Fanleen." My son jokingly refers to me by that name. I have never learned to pronounce my strange sounding nickname. Willoughby's name was too long, so his middle name Lee was never used.

After my father's death, we left the farm and moved into my grandmother's house, much closer to town. We were now living a few yards from a brick elementary school with running water, electricity, and central heating. I wasn't allowed to go to this school. When I started school at Organ Hill Elementary School, George Robert was in seventh grade.

I began first grade in a small clapboard building that was always in need of a paint job. This elementary school was located about three miles outside town. There was a sidewalk until we reached the town limits. Then it was necessary to walk a two-lane road, always being mindful of the danger of cars and especially trucks.

The school was so named because it was located on a high hill shaped like an organ. First and second grades were in one room, third and fourth grades in a second room, and fifth, sixth, and seventh in the third and largest room. There were three teachers, no aides, and no principal. Each teacher was the master of his or her classroom. There was a county supervisor who was to oversee the school, but I don't recall her ever visiting my classroom. The teacher was responsible for making the fire during winter months and once in a while, for a treat, Miss Mosley or Miss Hall would cook a pot of beans or soup on the potbelly stove.

The children in my neighborhood would walk to school together. One of the boys was the neighborhood hooligan who would terrorize a six-year-old, me. One day he began by calling me a name, "gapped-dog teeth," because I was losing my baby teeth. My brother George Robert hit Curtis over the head with my tin lunch box. For that he was suspended from school for a few days. Mama was really upset about his denting my lunch box.

Later, when George returned to school, he was expelled for taking our ice pick to school. He was always doing something really crazy. He was an exception to the playground-fighting rule. Back then, school fights were settled by the fist and not by lethal weapons. He could have returned to school the following year, but by then he had decided to work in a cousin's restaurant in Richmond.

Mama was always threatening to send him to reform school. I never knew where this reform school was, and George Robert never went there. He never went to jail either. He turned out to be a productive citizen. In fact, George worked until he was seventy-three years old without drawing Social Security. However, his refusal to take advantage of the Social Security to which he was entitled, had more to do with his desire to appear younger rather than his love of work. When he finally decided to draw Social Security, he called me to get his Virginia birth certificate. He had so many different ages on his work records he needed proof to show that he was now seventy-three years old. Other than the ice-pick incident, I don't believe he ever broke the law except for smoking reefers during the 1940s.

The cousin with whom George lived owned a restaurant in the black area of Richmond known as Church Hill. It was a vibrant area filled with beautiful homes, black-owned businesses, and churches. Mama and I loved to visit George and our Cousin Lucille. Cousin Lucille lived above her restaurant. Mama enjoyed talking with the restaurant's clientele and helping Cousin Lucille with the cooking. I spent the days taking advantage of the good food and watching television.

It was in the restaurant that I saw my first television program. The screen was about six by ten inches or smaller, and was displayed at the top of a large console. I suppose the height of this piece of furniture was to permit all of the patrons to see the screen. Mama was able to see one of her favorite singers and piano players, Fats Domino. She would often sing and play his signature song, *On Blueberry Hill.*

The only downside to visiting our cousin was the bed bugs. I learned the true meaning of the expression when one is parting company for bed. "Don't let the bedbugs bite!" Cousin Lucille never sprayed for the bedbugs like Mama did.

We often took the train to Richmond to visit another of Mama's relatives from her first marriage. She lived in Dinwiddie, Virginia. Dinwiddie was her first husband's hometown. There was a car just for black folk, so Mama and I met many good friends traveling back and forth from Drakes to Dinwiddie,

Richmond, Washington, and New York on this southern line.

For most of my life, I thought my brother George Robert was gay. Perhaps I was wrong. When I was growing up parents believed in the maxim, "Children should be seen and not heard." Parents also believed we were deaf. We could actually hear adults talking to one another! There were clues that George might be gay. There was a type of grass that grew in bunches around our house. It grew in long strings like human hair. George Robert enjoyed plaiting and styling bunches of grass. I did too.

As a teenager he must have enjoyed girls. I heard Mama yelling and chasing a girl out of the house. Mama had caught them in bed together. The girl lived in the last house on the lane. I wasn't supposed to know about this incident. Mama discussed it with my older brother, Willoughby.

During the war, George met the love of his life—beautiful Anne. He met Anne after he left Richmond and moved to Brooklyn, New York with our sister Eliza. I never knew what happened to this relationship.

George Robert should have been eligible for the draft by the time the Korean War (1950-1953) began. Recently, when I asked him about the draft, he gave me a song and dance about segregation in the armed forces. George Robert could not have refused to serve in the military because of segregation. When I continued to press the subject, he said he was not going to tell me.

By the late 1950s and early 1960s it was known that George Robert was probably homosexual; however, the word was never used. When I was in college George Robert set up housekeeping with a man named Ray. Ray appeared to be his love partner. The family would visit often with George and Ray. The visit would be like visiting any married couple. It was as though Mama and everyone else was in denial, and Ray was just another member of the family.

George and Ray separated one summer after his niece, a college student, came up from North Carolina. She worked in Brooklyn during the summer. She and George Robert fell in love and later moved in together. The relationship did not last more than a couple of years.

By the early 1980s when the AIDS epidemic among gays was rampant, George Robert was out of the gay scene altogether—that is, if he were ever a part of that scene.

He never goes to the doctor or dentist, and thinks of himself as being younger than I. George Robert has never known the happiness that fatherhood brings, and he would have made such a good father. He told me that he knew he had a child in Detroit, a child that he has never known.

Being gay is not a normal situation. No one seems to have an explanation as to why one chooses to love a person of the same sex. Today George Robert appears to be neither gay nor bisexual. He may never have been either one. I only know if all human beings were gay then the human race would soon disappear. I would not have had my father and there would have been no Mama. Additionally, Noah would not be able to save us when the floods come again.

While substituting in Janice Taylor's Spanish class, I learned that the Mayans predicted the destruction of the earth as Sunday, December 23, 2012. Maybe somehow human cloning will save us. That is if the nations of the world do not destroy the earth with their weapons of mass destruction before 2012.

Nevertheless, George Robert should not be ashamed if he were gay. Today, it is even fashionable to be gay, or to go through an experimental period. I have always loved him because he's my brother, George Robert, gay or straight. I have friends who are gay. I would even substitute at the New York high school for gays, if I had the chance.

The summer of 2001, Nikki and I spent several days in Paris, in the Marais (the Marsh) section. In Roman times the north of the Seine River was known as the swamp. Later it was drained and made habitable for humans. The famous, or infamous, Bastille Prison was located in this area. The beautiful square, La Place de la Bastille, is now where the prison once stood. Like New York's Soho district, the Marais is now a neighborhood of beautifully restored houses and the Royal Palace constructed by Henri IV, and later changed to the Place de Vosges. Several museums are also in the area. Today it is also known as the gay section of Paris.

We stayed in the Tulip Inn Little Palace, which was also near the Beaubourg area. It has an English name, but it is a typically French three-star hotel. The receptionist once tried to give me directions to a restaurant in English. Not understanding much of what he was saying, I said, *"Parlez français, s'il vous plaît."* The restaurant recommended by our friend Frederic called Le Colimaçon is owned and run by gays. The food was excellent and is reasonably priced. Nikki and I had three meals there. Nikki remarked that everyone probably thought we were gay.

I think, too, that having George Robert in my life has equipped me to better understand the changes in our society, the social forces at work on all of us. Life does not stand still, the velocity of change appears to be increasing. George Robert's life has helped me deal with this. What I have learned can also be transferred to other social issues in terms of inquiry, acceptance, and understanding.

Eliza Etta had three children, Frank, Jr. and two daughters, Jacqueline and Johnnie. Frank, Jr. died in 2003. Willoughby has five children—Willoughby Jr., known as Butch, Aaron, and Paul, and the girls, Jonah and Rita. My nieces and nephews all grew up in the Bedford-Stuyvesant section of Brooklyn, New York. It became crime-infested after World War II. When I lived in Bedford-Stuyvesant, Blacks had not taken over the neighborhoods around Albany Avenue where we lived. Jews owned the neighborhood supermarket and smaller stores. A black man owned the candy store around the corner. If Blacks were willing to work together they could have taken over the neighborhood stores and other businesses when the Jews left Bedford-

Stuyvesant and moved out to Long Island.

Back in the 1940's and 1950's the streets in my sister's neighborhood were safe. There were parks and playgrounds that were the favorite hangouts for the neighborhood kids. During the summer months, my friends and I would stay out long after dark "jumping double Dutch," until our parents yelled out of the window, calling us in. Mama and I would take little Frank to the park almost every day.

We lived in six-story apartment buildings with an elevator operated by a young man. The elevator ceased running at midnight, so there was always a mad rush to be back. The Apollo Theater where Eliza Etta worked part time was a block away. She worked behind the refreshment counter. Her three children and I were able to get in free. We could also have one serving of popcorn or a candy bar. We must have seen every film of the 1950's.

When I was in college Eliza Etta would often call on me to fill in for her if she could not make her evening shift. This extra bit of money came in handy, especially when I was between factory jobs. I usually had at least two factory jobs each summer. Getting another was no problem as there was a high-rise building in New York City that must have housed two or three hundred employment offices that catered to blue collar work.

All of my nieces and nephews were still in the Bedford-Stuyvesant section of Brooklyn when it was a haven for drug dealers and gangs. All of these children and their children are relatively successful and productive citizens. Most have a college education and advanced degrees.

When Paul and I were in Egypt in 1995, we visited a mosque. The guide listed and explained the ten basic teachings of Islam. At the top of the list was, *Family comes first.* My family and I have tried always to follow this tenet. If a member of the family needed help, I made every effort to provide that help, especially if it was a worthwhile cause such as education, just as my family always gave me help when I needed it. No one in my family is waiting for the "Reparation for Slavery" legislation that some of our black leaders say we are entitled to. We could really use the money, but life is too short! Too short to wait around for reparations that will never come.

Mama usually wrote to me every week while I was in college, teaching in South Carolina, and later when I moved back to Virginia. I still have the letters she wrote me while I was in college or whenever we were not together. Rereading these letters brings me closer to her. She always used a day of the week rather than the date. The dates are clear on the envelopes. Stamps are now five cents instead of three. Her envelopes are addressed—*Bennett College, Box 325, Greensboro, N. C.* and when Paul and I lived in an apartment on *Route 2, Box 94, Vienna, Virginia*:

Monday morning
April 20, 1958

Dear Darling Baby,
I hope you are fine. I am still having trouble with my back. Hope it will soon be all right. The rest of the family is doing OK. I called you Sunday, but you were out, so I know you are all right. I guess I will receive a letter from you today. I hope and trust that no news is good news. I am sending you money, and I hope you receive it OK.

It is real cold up here. How is it in North Carolina? Did you have to wait long in Washington? How was your stay in upstate New York? Hope you had a nice trip. Did you go to church yesterday? I put it off again. I was late getting to Eliza. I missed the train. Johnnie and I went to the movies today, but I went to sleep as usual.

I am putting your card where I can see it. I am going to bed in Little Frank's bedroom. Take care of yourself and good night.
Bye, Bye Sweetheart,
Your Mama

•   •   •

Tuesday, February 23, 1965
1020 108th Street
Forest Hills, New York
C/o Mrs. Stanley Morse

Dear Fannie Lillian,
How are you this cold morning? Fine, I trust. As for me, I am thankful to say to the Lord, I am happy and well. I find that he is the only one to thank. Wasn't it awful about that Malcolm X's death on Sunday? My pastor is also active in the civil rights movement, so I am not going to church until things calm down. He is keeping children from going to school. There are always lots of cops around him.

So much for that. I am looking for a new apartment, so now I am staying where I am working. Write me at Eliza's. I have not seen Willoughby in weeks, but I know he will come to see about me if I need him.

Write soon,
Mama

Mama also kept many of my letters. She brought them with her when

33

she came to live with us. In this one I am writing to her after Paul and I are married. Stamps are now ten cents. I too often use days rather than dates:

Sunday

Dear Mama,
I am glad your cold is much better. I went to Ashville, North Carolina last weekend. I stayed from Thursday until Sunday. I flew down with members of my sorority to a convention. It was quite an enjoyable weekend – just what I needed to make it until school closes. I didn't tell you about it ahead of time because I did not want you to worry about my flying.
Ralph is much better and is supposed to go back to work. We hope and pray that the surgery was a success and all of the cancer was removed.

Love to all,
F. Lillian

• • •

Sunday
August 5, 1979

Dear Mama,
I hope you are feeling well. Everyone here is doing fine. I heard from Nikki this evening. They started home today from her soccer match in Canada. They are now in Rochester, New York. She will be arriving home tomorrow.
We'll be back at school very soon.
Nikki will be going to eighth grade in the fall. We are giving her and Pauly a chance at public education at Luther Jackson. We will switch them later to a Catholic high school.
I hope you get a chance to see Aunt Luella from time to time.
Love to all,
F. Lillian

Mama would walk to town, about a ten-minute walk, each Sunday morning to buy a batch of salted herring for our breakfast treat and the *Richmond Times Dispatch*. When Mama came to live with my family years later, it was necessary to buy two Sunday subscriptions to the *Washington Post*. Mama was the first one up, so she would claim the newspaper. It would be afternoon before we would get to read the paper. Later we dropped the subscriptions because Nikki and Pauly were newspaper carriers. The children would remember to save an extra copy just for grandmama.

It's worth noting that Mama was reading the *Washington Post* and tackling the news with a modest third grade education. As a teacher I ponder that. Today we have so many reading improvement programs, remediation programs to help our students read. But back in those days when my mother was eagerly awaiting the *Washington Post*, there was a genuine thirst for reading, for knowledge. Perhaps with the advent of television, and computers, we are losing the art—joy—of reading.

The first set of encyclopedias that I owned was a set of *Funk and Wagnall's* that Mama ordered on a volume-a-month plan. Schoolbooks were not rented or given free to students as they are today. If books are too big to fit in backpacks, students in Fairfax County are given an extra book to keep at home. It was necessary for Mama to find someone who had a car to take her to the Charlotte County Book Depository located in the county seat ten or fifteen miles away. She had to buy my set of books each school year. However, there was never a year that I did not have all of my books on the first day of class.

Each day I carried my book bag filled with books in one hand and my lunch box in the other. I never misplaced or lost a textbook. When I was teaching in South Carolina, I enrolled in the International Collectors Library Book Club. I received the classics bound with an antique cover. I loved books because Mama did. The first set of books I bought when I moved to Fairfax County was a set of the *World Book Encyclopedia*. I realized in high school the limitations of *Funk and Wagnall's*. Nikki and Pauly used my set of *World Book* throughout elementary and high school.

Mama, in her desire to provide us with the best, insisted that my sister and I take piano lessons. She had Uncle Flood take her to Lynchburg, Virginia, to buy a piano. Like the other furniture in the little room, she brought the large upright piano back on Uncle Flood's pickup truck. Eliza Etta took piano lessons from Mrs. Dusenburg, and I took lessons from Mrs. Binford during my lunch period. I don't know what Mrs. Dusenburg charged. I paid my piano teacher twenty-five cents per lesson. Neither of us were very good piano students. My daughter Nikki tried both piano and harp. She wasn't musically inclined either. I also insisted that Pauly be exposed to a musical instrument as well. He tried piano and trumpet. He failed at both. The piano and the harp are still on display in our living room. The money spent on music lessons was not wasted. Both children have some idea how these musical instruments work, and they developed an appreciation for different kinds of music. Pauly plays a lot of rap music when I am around just to irritate me.

Mama went to work soon after my father's death. Her salary as a domestic was, on average, three dollars per week. Another job that Mama held was as cook in the only restaurant in town, owned by Clifford and Dorothy

Tharpe. Blacks were not allowed to eat in the regular dining room, but they were permitted to buy food through a side window. I would help Mama with her chores in the kitchen. We would eat our meals in the restaurant kitchen. When I was little I would accompany her to all her jobs.

When she served fancy dinners, it was a real treat for me, especially the savory dishes that she could not afford to prepare at home. Most of all there were the delicious pies and desserts she made.

Mama and her friends would tell of the jokes they played on white folk. They were not malicious jokes, but those that made life a little easier. A friend told the story of the meringue pies. She baked a couple of pies for her mistress's dinner party that had to be cooled right away. She placed the pies to cool on the outdoor windowsill. When she went to check on them, she discovered that the cat had walked across the pies. She repaired the pies with whipped cream.

This story reminds me of an incident at a wedding shower that Nikki was giving for Daphne Jackson. Everyone at the potluck shower was out on the patio. The food was left on the kitchen table. While we were outside, Dumpling, the Lhasa Apsa, was left alone in the house. Dumpling was known to first jump on a chair and then onto the table. The young lady who brought the spinach casserole asked, "What happened to the cheese?" Nikki and I looked at each other in disbelief; Dumpling, who was usually in the midst of any activity in the kitchen, was nowhere to be found.

However, there were sometimes cruel jokes that were played on the white people. Cooks would sometimes spit in the food before it was served, or if food dropped on the floor, it was put back on the plate and served. Mama never did these awful things, but she told stories told to her by her grandmother. During slavery, often the white mistresses did not want to nurse their children. They would have a slave wet nurse their babies. I could never understand this practice. Drakes had no public water fountain, but when I worked in South Carolina, Belk's Department Stores had water fountains labeled *white* and *colored*. How stupid is it to let your baby take milk from the breast of someone you abhor, yet refuse to share a water fountain?

The fact that we made such a small amount of money did not mean we were poor. I received a small Social Security check from my father's account because of his work at Bethlehem Steel in Baltimore. The checks stopped when I was eighteen. No one told Mama that I could have continued to receive the check until I was twenty-one if I were still in school. Back then, an ice cream cone and a soda were five cents, a stamp three cents, a post card one cent. If we needed extra money for an emergency, my brothers and sister would send it to us.

When I was in the sixth or seventh grade, I began working for Miss Lucy. She lived in an apartment on the second floor of her parents' home. She had the whole upstairs, which had been divided into a small kitchen, a sitting room, and two bedrooms. I used to iron every Saturday for Miss Lucy, down-stairs in her mother's kitchen area. She paid me a whopping twenty-five cents per hour. I would iron very slowly, so that I would make at least fifty cents.

Miss Lucy had three children—Carol, her daughter, and the twin boys, Nip and Tuck. Her husband was Jite. He published Drakes' weekly newspa-per, *The Charlotte Gazette*, with Miss Lucy's brother, Sam Tucker. Mama worked for her mother, Mrs. Tucker. She did the cleaning, washing and iron-ing. Mrs. Tucker had one of the old washing machines with a wringer above the lid. Miss Lucy must have washed her clothes by hand, because they were never very clean. I would iron them anyway.

When Miss Lucy and her family moved into their new home, it was clos-er to where we lived, so both Mama and I worked for her. We would baby-sit the children on the weekend when Miss Lucy and her husband wanted to go out on the town. I also earned extra money as a playmate for Carol, Nip, and Tuck. For this job I was also paid twenty-five cents an hour. There was no set number of hours that I would spend with the children. When the chil-dren got tired of playing, I would go home.

Miss Lucy would fix lunch for the four of us. It reminded me of the tea parties I used to have with my dolls and my dog Toby. Miss Lucy's food was real, not like the food I made out of water and mud. She had no qualms about serving me while I sat at the same table with her three children. Miss Lucy had a Dalmatian she called Sarah. She gave me Lucky from one of Sarah's litters. Miss Lucy was beautiful and kind, and she had a head full of bright red hair.

My second job was also ironing. Mrs. Wingo took in roomers when the Drakes Plant of Burlington Domestics was being built. It became one of the county's largest employers. Mama cooked dinner for a dining room full of hungry construction workers. It's funny how I remember some things. They appear to have no connection to anything else and carry no significance. One day for some odd reason I was ironing clothes in Mrs. Wingo's bathroom. Her daughter, who must have been around thirty years old, came in to use the bathroom. She didn't ask me to leave, so I continued my ironing. While she was using the toilet, she passed gas. She said, "Excuse me!" I replied, "You are welcome!" I guess Mama hadn't prepared me for that situation. I just couldn't think of any other polite response.

There was no television in our home. In fact no one in Drakes had a tel-evision, not even the white folk. There was no public library in my town. We blacks were not allowed to use the small library in Charlotte Court House, the nearest town. There weren't even any places where I could buy a book. I wondered what the people in Drakes read. I would use the money I earned to buy comic books at Mr. Crouch's Drug Store. He was better known as the Grouch. Mr. Crouch would be rude to even a three-year-old child. When Eliza Etta's children would come down for the summer, each evening we would get dressed up and walk to town to meet the six o'clock train.

Afterward, we would go to the drugstore for an ice cream cone. While Mr. Crouch was making the cones, Jackie sat on one of the counter stools. Mr. Crouch yelled, "Get down!" without even saying "please."

Every Saturday I bought two comic books with my earnings—*Wonder Woman*, *Hopalong Cassidy*, and the *Classics*. I won a year's subscription to *Wonder Woman* by writing about a woman I admired and considered to be a hero, or heroine in my case. I wrote about Florence Nightingale. I don't remember why I didn't write about a black person. It may have been because I thought I would not win, or because there were not many books I had read about black people.

My name was listed in an issue of *Wonder Woman* as a second place winner. The congratulations I received boosted my self-esteem. The congratulations also made me realize I was not the only one in Drakes reading comic books.

Nevertheless, Florence Nightingale's life is one that merits the admiration of every child. "The lady with the lamp" cared for the sick no matter what danger she encountered, without regard for the patient's status in life. She fought for women to have the freedom to choose their work.

When we had our children, my husband and I made sure that they were exposed to famous black people, to the black cultures of Africa and the Caribbean, and of course to France and her people. They knew about our culture not just from what they learned during Black History Month. They have seen first hand the contributions blacks have made to civilization in the distant past as well as the present.

When I left home for college I had stacks upon stacks of comic books. I never threw any of them away, and because I was the only one who read them, they were in mint condition. I have no idea what happened to the collection.

Several years ago, I began a much more expensive hobby. When I began working at Woodward & Lothrop department store, better known as Woodies, I fell in love with the store's large collection of Lladró porcelain. For Christmas 1985, I told Paul that all I wanted for Christmas was a small statue called a Lladró, and that he could find it at Woodies. Even with my employee's discount, he could not understand how a tiny statue could cost so much money. He bought it for me anyway.

Since 1985, my collection has grown to approximately thirty pieces, mostly black figures. They are bought for sentimental reasons because they represent a place I have visited. There is a soccer player, a baseball player, and a golfer that represent the sports that Paul, Nikki, and Pauly love. I have a Geisha from Japan, a jazz player from Harrods's in London, a gondolier from the QE2, a cocker spaniel from Barcelona, and the graduates from St. Martin, the French side. There is also a nun kneeling in prayer. The title is *Meditation*. She represents my conversion to Catholicism. Coincidentally, *Meditations* is the title of René Descartes' philosophical work concerning his proof of the existence of God.

I bought several expensive pieces in Madrid. I have two Martin Luther King Lladrós. One I bought when the piece was first issued, and the second at Woodies "Going out of Business Sale." While traveling with a group of my students in Madrid, I found many bargains in a large shop that sold only Lladrós. Pauly had substituted for a couple of my students whose parents would not permit them to travel to Europe in 1991 because of the first Gulf War.

Pauly had to return early for a college dance. He promised his girlfriend Jackie he would take her. I sent him home with his duffle bag full of Lladrós. Later, I learned he had been chosen by customs to open his bags on arriving at Dulles Airport. "How did you explain a bag full of porcelain?" He said he told the custom officers, "Those aren't my statues. They belong to my mother, and she is still in Spain. I'm just taking them home for her. What would I want with a bunch of glass statues?"

Saddam Hussein's son Uday also had many boxes of Lladrós in his palace in Iraq. One figurine was priced at thirty-five thousand dollars. I hope Uday admired its beauty as well as the price tag. He is no longer on earth to admire his collection. He and his brother Qusay were both killed in the second Gulf War, and their bullet-riddled bodies displayed for the world to see.

According to David Letterman, one of my favorite comedians, the Hussein brothers are on their way to Hell—even though they were embalmed and accorded a Christian burial. I wonder what happened to Uday's vast collection of Lladrós?

I like Dave Letterman. I usually stay up at least for the beginning of his program where he cracks jokes. His jokes usually have something to do with what is happening in the news, especially things having to do with our leaders. A few months ago Dave had as a guest, General Tommy Franks, who had recently resigned as commander of the armed forces in Iraq. Of course the general expounded on how well the war was going, and why we invaded Iraq. The general is sure that we will find the dictator's stash of chemical and biological weapons of mass destruction.

Dave asked many of the pointed questions I and other Americans have been asking. If we knew that Saddam had nuclear weapons that could reach the United States in a matter of minutes, did we not think he would use them if we attacked his country? Those weapons weren't even used on our fighting forces within Saddam's country.

Secretary Colin Powell was even more adamant about how great things are now in Iraq. That's a good thing! But wasn't President Bush a little fearful that the weapons would be used? I was!

I also bought interesting pieces of Lladró not only because they were beautiful, but also because they were much cheaper in France, England, and Switzerland, and of course in Spain. They are also cheaper in the Caribbean, especially in St. Martin and Barbados. I have been to Valencia, Spain, where the Lladró brothers first produced their porcelain pieces in 1941. Unfortunately Charletta, my friend and traveling companion, and I had to leave early to meet Nikki in Provence; so I did not get a chance to visit the Lladró factory.

Today there are close to four thousand different figurines. Those that have been retired are the most valuable. At the present time I have only one retired figure, "The School Boy," retired in 1995. I am not sure why I began collecting these figurines, other than the fact that they are beautiful works of art, and so far removed from my childhood comic books and marbles. I also have smaller collections of *Byer's Choice Caroler* dolls. I began the collection with characters from one of my favorite Christmas stories, *A Christmas Carol* by Charles Dickens. Most of the original story characters are now retired.

Since then I have bought other characters from Dickens's London— "The School Teacher," "The Chestnut Seller," and the "Salvation Army Bell Ringer." There is "The Golfer," representing Paul, and the "Lavender Sellers," representing Provence and displayed as a table centerpiece at Nikki and Dave's wedding. The *Carolers* are displayed at Christmas time along with my collection of the porcelain houses and shops representing Dickens's London, and villages in England.

On my first trip to France I bought a doll in the traditional dress of each of the provinces I visited. While in Provence, I bought a few pieces of Santons. These are small clay figurines that were originally created to represent the Nativity. The scene consists of village people bringing gifts to Jesus. They are dressed in provincial dress. Unfortunately, most of the dolls I bought in 1962 were lost when our crawl space flooded a few years back. Only the doll I bought in Paris survived. Nikki and I now have a small collection of dolls together. I still regret having lost my marble collection and my comic books from the 1940s and 1950s.

There were only a few recreational activities sponsored by the town. The Southern Railway ran from Richmond to Danville. Meeting the six o'clock train, was a pastime. It was a way of learning who came to town and who was leaving. Thus, the grown-ups had ample topics for a happy, lively, and newsworthy gossip.

"Eliza Etta is in town. Miss Jannie has her grandchildren for the summer."

"Cousin Alex left on the six o'clock train, bound for Baltimore."

A carnival came to town once a year—in the Spring. The most thrilling activity for everyone was the high dive that took place at eleven each evening. A handsome man with a perfect physique would ascend a fifty-foot platform and dive head first into a small tank of water. I would hold my breath until the diver hit the water and came up for air.

The entertainment also included sideshows, a merry-go-round, the fortuneteller, and other attractions. The Haunted House, the Hall of Mirrors, the Leopard Lady, and Tom Thumb were my favorites. I could be scared to death in the Haunted House, and see myself as fat instead of skinny in the Hall of Mirrors. The Leopard Lady was really a black lady with an illness, vitiligo. Tom Thumb was a small, even-proportioned man we used to refer to as a midget. In 1962, I saw a presentation in wax of the real Tom Thumb in Madame Tussaud's Wax Museum in London. However, Madame Tussaud first established herself in Paris. Today, her museum contains life-size models of the famous and the infamous people such as Luciano Pavarotti, Oprah Winfrey, Michael Jackson, and of course the Royal Family.

When I was a little girl, I didn't know that there was another Tom Thumb, whose real name was Charles Sherwood. He was born in Bridgeport, Connecticut, in 1838. His small, doll-like body was perfectly formed. He was so bright by the age of six that Phineas T. Barnum thought he was an adult. Barnum persuaded his parents to let him be exhibited as Tom Thumb in his New York Museum. He later took him to Europe where he entertained the Royal Family.

Today, I still enjoy the carnivals that come to Vienna, and the Barnum and Bailey Circus when it comes to Washington. Several years ago, my grandchildren and I visited with another Tom Thumb, one of the little people, when the circus came to town. Some day, my grandchildren will see the real Tom Thumb—in wax. The yearly carnival was the only place where whites and blacks mingled freely with one another for a fun activity.

When I was about eleven or twelve years old a movie theater opened in town. The news, cartoon, and a full-length film were shown every Saturday evening beginning at seven o'clock. Blacks sat in the balcony and whites downstairs. On most Saturday evenings, one would find Mama and me watching a western starring Roy Rogers and Dale Evans, Hopalong Cassidy, Tex Ritter, Red Ryder, and films based on Zane Grey's novels. There were also superstars like Rin Tin Tin, a dog named after the French story *Tin Tin*. There was also *Our Gang*, a series of short comedy sketches about a group of mischievous white kids, one black kid, and a gentle pit terrier named Pete.

The best known and my favorite animal performer was Lassie, who starred in several movies and later a television series of the 1950s. Actually, there were several Lassies. When they grew old they were retired. I went to the movies often during the war when Mama and I were living in Brooklyn. We saw such stars as Joan Crawford, Gary Cooper, Barbara Stanwyck, Cary Grant, Clark Gable, Judy Garland, Humphrey Bogart, Loretta Young, and Marlene Dietrich. I enjoyed all of the films of the 1940s and 1950s. My favorite film was *Leave Her To Heaven*, the story of a possessive wife who would used any means to keep her husband all to herself. The films I saw back then are now shown on Turner Classic Movie channel. For some reason the owner of the theater in Drakes Branch leaned toward the Westerns. I remember seeing only a few films on Saturday evenings that were not Westerns.

Although the films Mama and I watched on Saturday evenings during the 1940s and 1950s appealed to the white audience, we found them enjoyable and a learning experience beyond our own. Films like *Our Gang* and *Amos and Andy* were funny, but today are considered demeaning. Great actresses like Hattie McDaniel and Butterfly McQueen were criticized for their roles in one of the greatest film of all times, *Gone With the Wind.*

Nevertheless, the black actors who played their roles were earning a living. That is the exact reasoning black actors give today for taking the roles that are handed to them, "There just aren't as many varied roles for us as there are for white actors and actresses." The roles Hollywood forced them to accept, until recently, usually showed negative character portrayals: blacks as thieves, killers, drug dealers, prostitutes, and every other self-destructive, race hater.

Going to the movies on Saturday evening was an innocent way for Mama and me to pass the time and enjoy each other's company. I never thought about it back then, but we were the only mother-daughter combination attending these Saturday evening "flicks."

The films of the 1940s and 1950s were much more uplifting than the films today's children watch. There were no R-rated films. I am glad I didn't see scene after scene of black people killing each other, or being just plain mean. There were no scenes that Mama had to be wary of—no sex or violence except for the violence that was a part of the whites, so-called, "Settling the West." *Amos and Andy* were not cruel to one another, and neither were members of *Our Gang.*

The movie theaters in Fairfax County were also segregated when I came to the area in 1959. My friends Blakely and Dee Weaver would take me to the movies in Washington, D. C. We would also go to the black Howard Theater. It was at the Howard Theater that I saw the *Ike and Tina Turner Revue*, "Moms" Mabley and other black stars. Later, when I learned to drive, I would get in my Corvair and go into the District day or night whenever I wanted to. I saw many of the movies of the early sixties at the movie theaters in the District. When Mama came to live with me, we would also attend shows at the National Theater and the Kennedy Center. Carjacking was unheard of.

Children now see films consisting of an all black cast with mega-stars. There are few films that tell a good story without sex, violence, and dialogue where every other word is a curse word. I have always admired Denzel Washington as a leading man, and I placed him in the same category with Sidney Poitier and Harry Belafonte, that is, until he portrayed the abominable character in *Training Day* for which the, mostly white, Academy of Motion Pictures, Arts, and Science selected him best actor of 2002. His performance in such films *as Malcolm* X and *Philadelphia* were much more deserving for advancing the art of motion pictures.

I tuned in to Cinemax to see how deserving Halle Berry was of the Oscar for her performance in *Monsters Ball*. Not wanting to miss any of her performance I switched early to the appropriate channel, only to catch about twenty-five minutes of the pornographic acts and foul language of the all black cast of *Booty Call*.

For some reason that escapes me, certain roles for black actors are limited. However, Sidney Poitier, Harry Belafonte, Lena Horn, and Dorothy Dandridge apparently found roles that were uplifting. Self-respect should not be for sale at any price.

Was it just a coincidence that these wonderful actors won the Oscar for their excellent portrayal of characters that no parents should want their children to emulate? Some of my friends tell me that the acting of Denzel and Halle shows their talent for playing diverse roles. I wonder about the rightness of white executives handing out roles to talented black actors. It reminds me of slavery's overseers. What we need are more black executives.

I never go to the movies nowadays anyway. If I were to go, I would like to see well-produced films such as *The Pianist*, and *Chicago*, which I saw on stage and *Antwone Fisher* directed by Denzel Washington. But I'll just wait until they are on videotape.

I haven't learned to work the DVD player Pauly and Lela gave me for Christmas. It holds five DVDs at a time. I have been able to get one to come up on my small television screen, but it is usually the one I don't want to watch. Technology and I have an ongoing relationship of bewilderment and discovery.

Our most enjoyable entertainment was visiting friends and neighbors. We would take a shortcut through the woods to visit Mrs. Cousins and Ethel, Miss Daisy, and Miss Alpine. Or we would take a shortcut in the opposite direction and visit Miss Gracie. This path took us through endless rows of corn and vegetable gardens, but it was the fastest way to reach Miss Gracie's house.

We probably spent more free time with Miss Gracie than any other of Mama's friends. I don't remember Miss Gracie ever coming to visit us. We were always going to her house. I guess it was just easier for Mama and me to visit her than to have all of her children and grandchildren come over to our place. Her youngest daughter was one year older than I. We were friends as long as I can remember. All of her older children had gone north; however, they sent their children home to live with their grandmother, Miss Gracie. She usually had a total of six or seven grandchildren plus her teenage daughters Gracella, Frances, Myrtle, and Elaine who was my age.

All of us would play games like hopscotch and marbles and at dusk, then in total darkness, we'd play hide and seek. Miss Gracie's house sat on stilts, which lifted it about fifteen inches off the ground. The house was one of the best hiding places because the seeker looking under the house could not call out a person and then race him home. So if you were a good runner it was difficult to be called out of the game because the whole house was a hiding place.

Later, as teenagers, we would listen to 78 rpm records on Miss Gracie's Victrola, a trademark for phonograph. Our favorite recording stars were The

Ink Spots, Johnny Mathis, Nat King Cole, The Platters, and of course Mama's favorite, Fats Domino. If we dropped one of the records it would break into a dozen pieces. Miss Gracie would have something to say that would then end our evening of fun.

During the winter months my friends and I spent a lot of time playing inside and outside each other's houses. Though we did not get blizzards in southwest Virginia, we did get our share of snowfall. It was at Miss Gracie's house that Elaine and I learned from her older siblings to roll balls of snow to make a snowman. Once the snowman was complete there was no shortage of hats, scarves, and mittens to dress *le bonhomme de neige*. Just one or two inches of snow were also plenty to make bowls of snow ice cream for all of us kids.

I don't remember ever missing a day of school because of snow. In fact, most years I didn't miss any days at all. However, after coming to northern Virginia in 1959, children and teachers often got their wish granted for at least two or three snowstorms during the school year. I can remember several blizzards during the 1960s, 1970s, and 1980s. In the 1970s we were out of school for a week or more.

At the time I was rooming and boarding with Mrs. Mae Hall. There was a power outage for five or six days, but we were lucky because Mrs. Hall still had her wood-burning stove in the kitchen, so we had a way to cook and to keep warm. She also had an ample supply of oil lamps.

Since moving to Vienna, there have been several blizzards, most of which I have enjoyed. In the late 1980s, there was a February thaw that caused our crawl space to flood. Paul was out of town, so I called the fire department. I was asked, "How much water are we talking about." I responded, "About one or two feet." The fireman's answer was, "That's nothing. We are dealing with people who have five or six feet of water." Lucky for me the water didn't get any higher in the crawl space.

Since the blizzard of 1996, I have been wishing for a winter like the good old days, cold and lots of snow. I got my wish during the winter months of 2002 and 2003. Snow was on the ground from November through mid-March. For the most part, temperatures also remained below or near freezing during this same time. While there were still five or six inches of snow on the ground, we got a warm rain. Once more our crawl space was flooded. This time we used our wet vacuum to suck the water out. We worked the vacuum so hard, the motor burned out. When Paul went to buy another, they were all sold out. We then used a bucket to dip the water out of the crawl space. Later in the evening, the rain froze, causing an inch thick frozen glaze on top of the snow that didn't melt. We then got a second five or six inch snow on top of the ice. I should be careful what I wish for!

The winter of 2002 and 2003 brought many beautiful snows. But the most beautiful snow I have seen has been in France. It is the snow seen on France's highest mountain, which is also the highest mountain in Europe.

The French call her "La Dame Blanche," "The White Lady." The first time I saw Mont Blanc was in 1962 from the beautiful city of Lucerne, Switzerland. The snow-clad Alps and the Jura mountains cover about three-fourths of Swiss land. Crossing the Swiss Alps into France, I was able to see Mont Blanc even more clearly from the city of Grenoble.

In August 1995, Nikki and I, along with our friends Yanni and Thierry Delahousse, took the world's highest aerial tramway car from Chamonix to the Aiguille du Midi, one of the lower peaks of Mont Blanc. To me it seemed like the highest peak. When the cable car would shake violently as we ascended, Nikki and I would hang on to Thierry. He was right when he told us to be sure to bring our jackets. It was freezing up there, even though it was eighty degrees down in Chamonix. When we reached the top, those who left their jackets behind wished they had not.

Mont Blanc is about thirty miles long and ten miles wide. There is always a thick blanket of snow, and from the viewing area we could see several skiers and climbers who were attempting to reach the summit. I became very sad when I saw the melting glaciers. Even though it was extremely cold, the warming of our planet Earth was evident. The sun softening the snow during the day also increases concern about the notorious Mont Blanc avalanches.

When we were leaving the summit, I was the only one of the four whom the guard asked to present a passport. When I asked, *"Pourquoi?"* He said that I could be trying to enter France from Switzerland. The Swiss also visit Mont Blanc from the Swiss side of the Alps. I then asked, *"Qu'ce que ce passe, si je n' ai pas de passport?"* (What would happen if I did not have a passport?) *"C'est simple!"* He would turn me over to French immigration. Thierry, our French friend, looked much more *Suisse* than I do, and he didn't have to show his passport. I found my passport that I had hidden underneath my blouse—away from the pickpockets.

Nikki refused to take a suggestion from her mother. "Always wear your valuables under your clothes like your underwear." A couple of years ago I thought a young Frenchman was getting "fresh" with me when he kept pushing up against me in the crowded Métro car. He wasn't! He was pushing up against me to reach Nikki's latest style purse hanging from her shoulder.

The next morning, Nikki discovered that my encounter with this Frenchman had resulted in her losing her Visa Check-card and the Frenchman spending fifteen hundred dollars in a couple of hours, less than the time we had just spent in the Rodin Museum. His shopping expenditures for that one afternoon included: several antique pieces, enough gallons of gasoline to fill his car, and several telephone calls to countries on the continent.

The thief could not see where his hand was roaming, so he took Nikki's museum pass and her telephone card as well. She was really alarmed that he had taken the phone card she used to call Dave each evening. He carefully left the Euros, hoping that Nikki would not have immediate use for her check card. But "All's well that ends well." Her bank quickly stopped payment on her card, and replaced all her money (except fifty dollars) when she returned to the States.

William Watkins, Miss Gracie's youngest son, served in the Korean War. Everyone knew him as "Dick." Dick was my brother George's age. He finished Central High School on the GI Bill, along with one of his sisters. He went on to get a college degree in tailoring at St. Paul's College. He was a role model for all of Miss Gracie's children, grandchildren, and me. Dick was always correcting our grammar and bad behavior.

Like me, Elaine didn't remember much about her father. He also died when she was very young. The Watkins lived in a three-room house very similar to ours. On the first floor were the combination sitting room and bedroom, the dining room, and the kitchen. Miss Gracie didn't have electricity either.

Elaine and I would practice curling each other's hair. We would heat the straightening comb and curlers by putting them down the chimney of an oil lamp. Upstairs was one big room that was the bedroom for all the children.

The one staple that Miss Gracie always seemed to have on hand was a big pot of navy beans containing several pieces of fat-back meat—all fat and no lean—and a pan of hot biscuits. Mama and I were always welcome at Miss Gracie's table.

Communications were accomplished by a note, or speaking directly to a neighbor, the local store, or the doctor. The people Mama worked for had telephones with a party line. Two or even three families, or more, would use the same telephone line. After lifting the receiver you would need to listen to see if someone was already using the phone. There was a crank on the side of the telephone that would connect you to an operator, who in turn would connect you to the party you wished to reach. (Listening in on your neighbor's conversation was an ideal way to learn what was happening in the neighborhood and the whole town.)

When I first came to Fairfax County, Mrs. Mae Hall had a party line with her neighbors, the Gaskins. Evidently these two families did not listen in on one another. When I came to Luther Jackson School as a single teacher, just about every male teacher made a pass at me. One even had the nerve to call me at Mrs. Hall's to ask for a date. My immediate response was, "Is your wife coming along?"

In South Carolina, my roommate and I did not have a telephone. The band teacher was continually harassing me. He even sent a note toward the end of the school year asking for my summer telephone number and address. The note was just a folded piece of paper, and the student who delivered it didn't even read it. At least, I don't think he did.

One administrator, "Mr. Smith," had a reputation for making both wanted and unwanted advances toward married or unmarried teachers. Mr.

Smith picked me up at the bus station when I arrived for my interview, and when I arrived later to begin the school year. He also took me to and from the train station when I returned to Brooklyn for the Christmas holidays. He never tried to get "fresh" with me. In fact, he was overly polite. "Fresh" was the term Mama always used. It meant, "to hit on" in today's vernacular. I guess I just wasn't his type.

There were no black doctors, lawyers, or dentists that might have served as role models when I was growing up. There were no sports figures or movie stars that I chose to emulate. But there were ordinary people like Miss Grace, Miss Alpine, Miss Daisy, Mrs. Cousins, and Mrs. Dusenburg. They were my teachers. And then there was *Mama*.

Lucky children have parents as role models. Luckier children also have role models around them, in a society that offers them as the norm. What I had were the stories about my father's strength and hard work, the only memories of him, when I lost him; when he had a heart attack and came crashing down to the floor in my child's world, but filling the enormous space was Mama.

I could not have had a finer role model. She filled my world with quiet wisdom and unstinting support for my dreams and hopes. She was a warm maternal presence, an abiding kindness, always there for me. Thinking back, I wonder what her true thoughts were about my going off to college. She had supported me wholeheartedly, she was proud of me I know. But did she have private thoughts that she kept to herself? What if Mama had had a chance to go to college? In a sense she did go; I took with me all that she taught me, all that she advised me, all that she held up as to what was right and good. Together, we did well in our studies.

Uncle Flood, John, Cousin Leory, Anna Belle and daughter Dorothy, Aunt Luella
- circa 1937

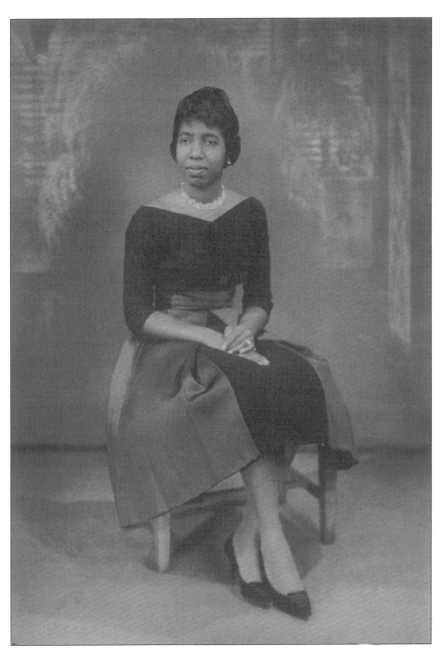

Brooklyn, 1951

1964

1964

Chapter 2

All happy families resemble one another;
Every unhappy family is unhappy in its own way.

Tolstoy, *Anna Karenina*

Mama had a vegetable garden. Her brother Flood had a farm of more than a hundred acres about fifteen miles out of town. Uncle Flood's farmhouse sat smack in the middle of his land. As far as one could see in all directions was his land. There were beautiful rolling hills, meadows, streams, and forests. Uncle Flood raised everything on his farm—chickens, ducks, geese, guineas, hogs, cows, horses, and mules, and once in a while I would see a beautiful peacock. He had every fruit tree that would grow in southwest Virginia, and gardens with an abundance of vegetables; many I could not name. His money crop was acres of tobacco.

Southwestern Virginia is a place of beauty, like the south of France. Uncle Flood's farm was covered with trees like those found in many parts of France: oak, pine, ash, beech, and poplar. Most of the trees in southern France stay green year round, and so did many of the trees on Uncle Flood's farm. There were many places for the boys to explore on the farm, but the one thing that was lacking was a genuine cave. Perhaps a cave would have satisfied my cousin Ulysses Morton's quest for adventure, and he would not have attempted to test the power of dynamite that caused the loss of two fingers.

As I journey from Pau to the Lascaux Cave near the Vézère River Valley of southwestern France, I am reminded of the tree-lined road that led to Uncle Flood's farm house. The Dordogne region contains the most beautiful and most famous cave paintings in the world. I was fortunate enough to see the actual cave paintings in 1962.

To reach the area of the prehistoric paintings one had to enter through a series of iron doors. Soon after my visit the caves had to be closed because of deterioration. This, despite the French Government's best effort to preserve them. They are no longer open to the general public and visits to Lascaux are by invitation to people in certain professions, including those who are involved with museums and the sciences.

Near the cave there is a reproduction of about one hundred of the original drawings that have been placed in a man-made cave above ground. Four boys looking for a dog that disappeared into a hole discovered these caves in 1940. I was lucky in another way; our guide was one of the boys who discovered the caves.

Paleoanthropologists believe that paintings depicting humans, like those found in Lascaux, can be compared to the fossils that indicate modern humans appeared in Africa one hundred thousand years ago. They did not leave the continent for fifty millennia, but when they did, they settled in Eurasia and replaced the Neanderthals. Before the caves closed down, to reach the grotto of Lascaux, it was necessary to navigate a narrow dirt road through woodland for about a half mile. A similar path led to Uncle Flood's farm.

In spite of all that Uncle Flood had, he still wanted the interest he held in Grandmother's house and land within the town limits of Drakes Branch. My father had been paying the taxes on my grandmother's land for years, so Mama thought her brother should deed the land and house over to her. "Flood has so much land, why would he want this measly piece?" For several years, Uncle flood would not budge. He insisted he had the rights to our property as well.

When Willoughby returned from the war, he moved to Washington, D.C., a few hours away. He would come down often to try settling the dispute between the two of them. After both Mama and Willoughby's pleading with Uncle Flood, he reluctantly changed his mind. He signed the house and land over to Mama. Today, I still own that parcel of land. Even though Paul tries to convince me to sell. I can't. It would be like giving away a part of me.

I wonder how a mother could give a little baby a name like Flood. Perhaps he was a flood of joy when he was born. Three girls were older than he, and my grandfather was longing for a son. Mama was the youngest. Uncle Flood could hardly read or write, but he was a pure genius when it came to making and counting money. He was born on February 29, 1894 in Charlotte Court House, Virginia. He boasted that his birthday only came every four years. He married Aunt Luella in 1915.

Uncle Flood was a kind man except for his occasional avarice. He was an avid hunter. He always had a pack of hound dogs that he trained to hunt squirrels, rabbits, raccoon, fox, deer, and everything on four legs. My uncle would have loved living in France, especially Provence. There he could also hunt and eat everything running around on four legs, even foxes and ferrets.

Mama sold our cow soon after moving to grandmother's house. She had tried to teach me how to milk a cow, but I wanted no part of this chore, especially since I would never drink milk that was not pasteurized. We continued to have our vegetable garden. Mama canned the surplus of string beans, tomatoes, and greens for use during the winter months. Uncle Flood would bring us additional vegetables and fruits from his farm and parts of the slaughtered hogs and cows. Mama and I always had an ample supply of food.

I now realize that we lived on a very healthy diet. For breakfast every morning Mama always cooked a large pot of oatmeal or cream of wheat, along with a hearty pan of biscuits. But as a child, even though we did not have an abundance of food according to today's standard, I was a picky eater. I never liked the so-called soul food. Once I put a little piece of chitterling in my mouth, at Mama's urging. Having it in my mouth conjured up in me the awful smell of the boiling chitterlings. I spit it out, and it went flying across the table. Mama gave me a good scolding, but she never again tried to force me to eat anything I didn't want.

I did have to eat all that I put on my plate. If I left a crumb, she would remind me that I had to scrape my plate clean because of all the starving children in the world. I wondered, *How could my full belly help all the hungry children the world over?* Neither would I eat what I thought were odd or unsavory parts of the hog, cow, or chicken. I would not eat chicken liver, gizzard, feet or pig feet, hog jowls, pig knuckles, jaw bones, pig's or cow's tongues. I would also stay away from the rabbit, squirrel, deer, pheasants, and wild turkeys that Uncle Flood brought us from time to time.

Uncle Flood's cows provided a lot of milk. I was never able to drink milk straight from the cow, even after it had been cooled in Uncle Flood's spring at the bottom of a steep hill. I did like the butter and buttermilk that Aunt Luella made. She placed the milk or cream in an earthenware or wooden churn, and with a wooden dasher, or wooden stick with a round blunt end like a potato masher, she would plunge up and down in the churn until butter formed. Butter is the fat that is separated from the milk. Buttermilk is the liquid that is left after churning the cream to make the butter.

Margarine, a mixture of water, salt, and vegetable fats, was used to replace butter which was rationed during the 1940's. It was sold with a little packet of yellow powder that required Mama do the coloring in a large mixing bowl. When we ran out of Aunt Luella's butter, Mama mixed a batch of margarine.

Like Mama, Aunt Luella did lots of canning during the summer months. She also made jams and jellies from the fruits that grew abundantly around the farm. She made a delicious sweet pickle from the rind of watermelon. For lunch, Aunt Luella would always serve us kids hot biscuits that we would dip in butter and molasses.

Mama's canning was on a much smaller scale. She used a large canning pot, and never graduated to the pressure cooker of the 1940s. The pressure cooker was designed to give home canners a less expensive way to process food. There was always a possibility that the pressure cooker could build up too much steam and explode. Aunt Luella escaped serious injury when it happened to her. Mama never got a pressure cooker.

We couldn't have a freezer. We never did get electricity because of Mean Miss Mable. All the meat and vegetables that Uncle Flood brought us had to be eaten fresh, except those that were smoked, salted down, or canned. Some of the food could be kept longer if we put it into the well bucket and let it go down into the well.

Our original icebox opened like a flat top freezer. The whole area where the ice was placed was galvanized. Food could be preserved for most of the week by being placed around the ice. Later Mama bought a more modern icebox. It had a door that opened on the left for the block of ice.

Every Saturday morning during the summer months the iceman came. Mama would always buy a fifty-pound block of ice. To the right was the storage area for food similar to our present-day refrigerator. There was no place for storing frozen foods like ice cream.

When we made our ice cream, it had to be eaten within a few hours. The gadget for making ice cream was called a churn, and it consisted of a three gallon wooden bucket for packing the ice and salt. A galvanized can containing the custard, made from milk, sugar, eggs, and flavoring, would be placed in the middle. Turning the handle attached to a dasher inside the bucket caused the custard to freeze. After thirty minutes or so of vigorous churning we would have ice cream in flavors of vanilla, strawberry, or peach. A real treat for me was licking the ice cream dasher. Whenever a family made ice cream on Sunday, there was an obligation to share it with others in the neighborhood. Even Miss Mable would share!

Aunt Luella was more of a sister than a sister-in-law to Mama. She was half white, but looked like a full-blooded white woman. Her mother was the daughter of slaves. Her father had been the master or overseer on the farm where her grandparents had remained after the emancipation. Aunt Luella could easily pass for white, but there was no use trying in Drakes. Uncle Flood was black as coal, and they were always together. They had three children, Octavia, Fitzhugh Lee, and Geneva.

Octavia and her husband, Ulysses, had a child every year. By the time they finished they had thirteen children including twins. Uncle Flood and Aunt Luella arranged the marriage between Fitzhugh Lee and Lucille. It was what we used to call a shotgun wedding. Several months later William Lee was born.

After the war, Fitzhugh Lee moved to Washington, D. C. with my brother Willoughby. Lucille stayed on with her in-laws. Fitzhugh Lee visited with his wife only once. On that occasion he fathered a second son, James. There was also a rumor that he had fathered two children by one of Miss Gracie's daughters. These two children were also my friends. They were a couple of years younger than I.

While living in Washington, Fitzhugh Lee met Mary. He had five or six children by her. I knew their kids when we were children, but have since lost contact with them.

My cousins Geneva and Estelle moved to Brooklyn, New York during the Great Migration, the moving of thousands of Blacks from the South to the North. Estelle was the daughter of Mama's sister, Gay Nell. Eliza Etta followed her cousins a few years later. They all met their future husbands in the Savoy Dance Hall or the Cotton Club in Harlem during the war. There was a black cultural flowering in Harlem during the 1920s and it continued into the 1930s and 1940s. This movement became known as the *Harlem Renaissance*. Everyone seemed to be producing shows on Broadway. Writers like Richard Wright, Langston Hughes, Claude McKay, Countee Cullen, and Zora Neale Hurston worked alongside musicians and artists like Bessie Smith, William Johnson, "Duke" Ellington, Louis Armstrong, Aaron Douglas, and Meta Warrick Fuller.

When I was in Paris in 1997, with a group of students and their parents, Karen Nicole Williams, a young teacher (whom I often substitute for) who had done her study/travel assignment before leaving the States, directed us to a Hayward Gallery Exhibition in Paris. When we arrived at the gallery, we found an extraordinary exhibition on the Harlem Renaissance. Karen and her sister, Kristen, who was still in high school, picked up a number of books about this important period in black history. I bought an informative book entitled, *Harlem Renaissance: Art of Black Americans* in English. In the 1920s Harlem, "the cultural capital of Black America," was host to some of America's best writers, actors, musicians, and artists. They were writing, producing shows on Broadway, and some were leaving for Paris to paint and sculpt. My sister and cousins knew where to go to meet a man of distinction. John was in the Navy and Leroy and Frank were in the Army. They were all on leave and were spending an evening in Harlem. Harlem—the place to be.

I thought it was a twist of fate that Geneva had no children and Octavia had thirteen. Geneva later adopted two children, Arthur and Joyce. I had no siblings at home after the age of six. My cousins who lived on the farm were like brothers and sisters. Aunt Luella sometimes had a mean streak. If we got into simple spats, Aunt Luella would take the side of her grandchildren. She once forced Uncle Flood to take us home immediately when I got into a fight with her oldest grandchild, Joyce. Her anger only lasted a couple of months though.

Uncle Flood would come and get Mama and me, and we would spend several days on the farm. The month of August was often spent there. It was great fun to watch the whole Wilkes and Jennings families at work, pulling, handing, and stringing tobacco. There were lots of different conversations going on. The children too young to participate in the work played nearby, eavesdropping on the adults' conversation.

I was always curious as to how the elders in my family chose names for their children. At some point in school they must have studied Greek and Roman mythology and history. How else could they come up with such lofty and beautiful names? Octavia is from the Latin name, Octavia Augustus. Coincidentally, Octavia married a man who had the latin name Ulysses. Miss Mable's daughter was Augustus. George Robert had a girl friend called Lucretia. Ulysses always reminded me of his Greek counterpart Odysseus. He was a great provider for his wife and children. He first built a house on Uncle Flood's land, but later opted for his own farm, with almost as many acres as his father-in-law.

He was like the Greek and Roman heroes in another way. Three or four times a year, Ulysses would go on a binge, a drinking spree that would last for weeks. He would return completely sober and very ashamed. Octavia would be waiting for him with open arms. Years later he was found dead in the woods not far from where he lived. He had lost his beloved Octavia a few years back, and his children were now all adults, except for his youngest daughter.

I reflect on him sometimes. What deep loneliness was in him? Was it all due to the loss of Octavia? What would account for the binge drinking? What drove him to do that, to leave and spend blacked-out days somewhere, until his mind cleared and he remembered what he had, and headed for home, head down. There is also the manner of his death: to wander off into the woods, another and final loneliness.

Aunt Luella outlived her husband and her three children. She died at the age of one hundred in the early 1990s. In 1984, at the funeral of her youngest daughter, Geneva, she had said, "The saddest time in a mother's life is to witness a child dying before you." She had witnessed the death of all three of her children. Octavia, Fitzhugh Lee, and Geneva died years before Aunt Luella.

There were no families in town who were described as rich. Mrs. Elvira Payne, who lived in a big brick house that resembled a small castle, was the richest person I knew. She was also the meanest white woman I knew. Her last name was most appropriate. She was a real PAIN! She had been married four or five times.

I now understand why Mama worked for her for quite a long time. She could take me to work with her. During that time she was on a series of boyfriends, and Mama would have to prepare breakfast as well as dinner. One evening, after Mama had prepared a big dinner party and we were clearing up afterward, she accused me of taking an extra piece of cake. We hadn't even eaten dinner yet. I would never eat dessert before dinner, and Mama told her so.

Mrs. Payne wasn't all bad. When Mama took Little Frank home for a few months, Mrs. Payne would let Mama bring both Little Frank and me to work. It was really hard getting his baby carriage up the back stairs though. They were really steep. Mrs. Payne never suggested that we used the front door that had only one step.

Other than Mrs. Payne, the other white people were referred to as either "well-off" or "poor white trash." Mama never used those terms, so of course I wasn't allowed to. There were no millionaires in my town. All of the blacks were poor according to today's standards. No one had even heard of welfare and government handouts. Yet, I knew very few people who were without food and clothing.

When I was in first grade there was a group of children that the upper classmen called "Wheel of Cheese." Their father had broken into the deli shop and stolen a wheel of cheese. Back then we bought our cheese by having a wedge cut from a single wheel. The father was caught, and like Victors Hugo's character, Jean Valjean, he was put in jail for stealing to feed his hungry children. The name-calling was one of many cruel jokes that children often played.

Christmas of 1941, Mama and I went to spend the Christmas holiday with Eliza Etta in Brooklyn, New York. Her apartment was directly in front of Our Lady of Victory Catholic School. We stayed in Brooklyn for about a month. I didn't mind at all missing almost a month of school. My pastime was watching the coming and going of the students after they returned from their Christmas vacation.

In the morning, I would sit in front of the window and watch the children as they arrived. The girls would spend most of their time chatting in small groups. The boy would play kick-ball, wrestle each other, or some other game that boys like to play. At exactly nine o'clock a nun would come out and ring a bell. The students would scramble to their assigned places in line—the girls in front of the line and boys in the back. I saw the exact same scene played over and over again when Nikki and Pauly attended Our Lady of Good Counsel in Vienna. Most of the students at Our Lady of Victory were white, but there were a few blacks. All of the nuns were white. However, at OLGC most of the teachers were lay teachers, not nuns.

How I longed to go to a school just like Our Lady of Victory! When the Bedford-Stuyvesant section of Brooklyn became mostly black, Our Lady of Victory became Martin de Porres Catholic School. Saint Martin dePorres was born in Lima, Peru, in 1579, of a Spanish father and a Negro mother. He grew up in poverty and developed a deep understanding and love of the poor. When he was very young he went to work as an apprentice to a surgeon-barber where he learned medicine and the care of the sick and wounded. He had the gift of healing and is credited with curing the Archbishop of Mexico who was fatally ill. St. Martin died of a fever in 1639, and was beatified in 1873.

My brother Willoughby married Dorothy Theresa Brown in 1945, a year after he returned from the war. She was born December 31, 1923 in Prince William County, Virginia. Dorothy was Catholic, and after moving to Brooklyn both Dorothy and Willoughby became member of Our Lady of Victory in 1958. Their children Willoughby Jr., Aaron, Paul, Jonah, and Rita all attended Martin de Porres Roman Catholic School, formerly Our Lady of Victory. Willoughby died of prostate cancer in February 1991, and Dorothy died in September 1998.

Frank, Jr. was born on December 20, 1941, so he was a little more than two months old when Mama brought him back to Drakes. Mama thought she could do a better job of taking care of the baby while Frank was in the army and while Eliza worked. I got milk for the baby by walking each day to the other side of town to buy a quart from Miss Annie. I wished Mama had not sold old Bessie.

The Great Depression ended when the United States began supplying goods to nations at war. Blacks in the South moved to the North to fill jobs created by the war effort. George Robert left Richmond for New York. The summer of 1942, Mama and I moved to Brooklyn, so that Eliza would have her son with her. Mama baby-sat Little Frank, as Frank, Jr. was called. I enrolled in Our Lady of Victory Catholic School, whose students I had envied almost a year before, as they had gone to and from this beautiful school building.

America experienced rationing for the first time during World War II. American families were issued a book of coupons each month. Products that were rationed included sugar, coffee, fuel oil, gasoline, rubber, and leather products. These necessities limited public consumption and provided resources for American servicemen. Coupons for products that Mama and I had no use for were shared with family members and neighbors.

World War II had begun when the Germans invaded Poland in September 1939, and the British and French had declared war on Germany. Demands for weapons and war material created an economic boom in America. Life in America was normal when the war began raging in Europe. But I had lost my father. Mama and I could hear the distinctive voice of Edward R. Murrow as he delivered his eyewitness account of the war. In the background we could hear bombs exploding and the air raid sirens. All of it came into our kitchen and sitting room.

The United States had begun to build up its military before the attack on Pearl Harbor. In 1940, the threat of war led Congress to pass the first peacetime draft in American history. Americans from all ethnic groups and backgrounds made up the millions who served in the armed forces. My older brother Willoughby quickly enlisted in the navy, because he thought he would be drafted into the army. Mama told him that he really should not volunteer for the navy because he couldn't swim. Evidently swimming was not a prerequisite, because he had already enlisted when he told Mama about his joining up.

The military, at that time, followed strict segregation practice. Black Americans were limited to certain jobs and kept out of advanced training. As the war progressed, however, segregation was eased. While in the navy,

Willoughby became an excellent cook. Blacks were allowed to work in the mess hall and to perform other menial tasks. The Mess Man branch was the only branch officially open to black sailors. When a battle was raging, they took part in the fighting and excelled in their assigned tasks in battle, often in spite of the racist attitudes of their superiors.

Dorie Miller, a Mess attendant, was serving on board the *USS West Virginia* when the Japanese attacked Pearl Harbor on December 7, 1941. He was first assigned to carry the wounded sailors to safety, including the wounded captain of the ship. Later, he manned an anti-aircraft machine gun. Before the sailors were forced to abandon ship, Dorie manned an anti-aircraft machine gun. It is not clear how many Japanese planes he shot down, but for his heroism, he received the Navy Cross.

The United States Victory in World War II included the efforts of the Tuskegee Airmen, who rose above the prejudice and forged a distinguished record of valor. They had gone through a training course in 1942 at the Tuskegee Army Airfield in Alabama. The Secretary of the Army approved the establishment of an all black 99th Fighter Squadron. Hundreds of black men were trained to fly in combat, exhibiting great skill. It is an historical fact that no American bomber was lost when escorted by black pilots of the 99th Fighter Squadron. They achieved success in spite of the odds against them, and their success paved the way for President Truman to eliminate discrimination in the military.

Willoughby did not speak of his time spent in the Pacific. Sometimes, just in passing, he would speak of the Japanese attacking his ship and the planes coming so close that he could actually see the pilots as they dove at them. When the Japanese attacked Pearl Harbor, the United States suffered heavy losses. Many American ships were either lost or damaged. Mama knew only that Willoughby was on a destroyer somewhere in the Pacific. It was months before she knew he was all right.

During the war Mama and I used to go to a Pentecostal or Holiness Church every Sunday evening just to pass the time. As an eight or nine-year-old, I found amusing the lively singing, shouting, and other antics, such as falling flat on the floor in a trance-like state and talking in a strange tongue (Glossolalia). To me at the time, shouting or feeling the Holy Ghost seemed like just an animated dance. I especially enjoyed the young man who played the piano. He played the same rock and roll-like rhythm to whatever hymn was being sung. There was a constant rapid movement of hands and feet by the members of the congregation. They could be sitting, standing, or going up and down the aisles. No one could doubt their spontaneous joy and fellowship, which was referred to as being "happy."

One evening after Willoughby had returned safely from the war, we went to service at the Holiness Church as usual. Mama suddenly felt the spirit of God, jumped from her seat, and began shouting and screaming in the name of the Lord. She was "happy" because my brother had returned to the mainland from his tour of duty in the Pacific. After this episode, I never again went to the Holiness Church with Mama. I don't know why I was so embarrassed, since the whole congregation became happy at every church service. Mama becoming happy was accepted as part of the service. Additionally, there was no one else there who even knew us. Back then I could sometimes be a real brat.

Mama was not usually an outwardly religious person. She did not feel she was committing a mortal sin if she missed a church service now and again. Mama lived the life the way I think a Christian should live. She taught me the child's prayer, and made me say it each night:

> *Now I lay me down to sleep.*
> *I pray the Lord my soul to keep*
> *If I should die before I wake,*
> *I pray the Lord,*
> *My soul to take.*

She would continue by telling me to ask the Lord to bless family, friends, and everyone else in the world. She never was full of "Praise the Lord," though she would occasionally utter a "Lord, have mercy!" Mama did not believe that every facet of her life rested in the Hands of the Lord. Her favorite expression for bouts of good luck was, "Let me knock on wood." Every time I hear my young next-door neighbor, Pegah (Peggy), who is Iranian, say, "Let me knock on wood," I see my mother knocking on the nearest wooden table or chair.

I was surprised when I heard Peggy use this old expression. Today's children don't know old or bright sayings like, A stitch in time saves nine, or, A penny saved is a penny earned. Evidently expressions like those I committed to memory are found in many languages, including Farsi. I know they are found in the French language for I learned to say them in French and taught them to my French students. I don't remember being taught these expressions in school, but committed them to memory from hearing Mama and her friends repeat them to guide us toward a useful and worthwhile life.

Mama lived by the adage, The Lord will help those who help themselves. She had every reason to play the victim because all her life she was truly a victim of racial prejudice and Jim Crow laws. Mama made the best of living in a harsh segregated society. She had to endure all sorts of demeaning words and deeds. Nevertheless, she fought back in her own way. There were two tasks she would not do for white people—wash windows and sweep yards. On one occasion Mrs. Scoggins, a woman for whom she often worked, asked her to sweep the back yard. Most people did not have grassy lawns but yards of sandy clay, especially the area in the back of the house.

"I don't sweep anybody's yard," responded Mama.

"You must think you are just as good as I am," Mrs. Scoggins retorted.

"I sure do." Mama answered.

Mama wasn't fired. I also believed that I was inferior to no one when I was growing up because Mama told me so, and she always treated me as if I were really special.

"You have to believe in yourself, and you have to believe that most people in the world are good. Even if you have doubts sometimes."

Mama registered to vote in spite of the fact that the poll tax took almost a week's salary. During elections the town sheriff, Mr. Tharpe, would come around and tell Mama for whom she should vote. The sheriff was the husband of the woman who owned the restaurant where she worked. Mama would readily agree with the sheriff's candidates of choice, but when she went to mark her ballot she would vote just the opposite of what she had been told.

Voting meant going to the polls, checking in, taking a ballot, and marking your choice with the pencil provided, and then sticking it into a big box with all of the other ballots. There were no complicated methods such as punching holes, or touching a dot, like those used in the 2000 presidential election.

This fiasco in Florida caused George W. Bush to be elected president. Coincidentally, his brother Jeb was governor of the state. Al Gore, who won the nation's popular vote, lost the election. Our nation has made much progress in race relations, well, sort of. Back then, if a black girl had been carrying a sign reading, "Hail to the Thief!" while attending a presidential inauguration, she would have been arrested and thrown in jail—if not worse.

Mama was a member of the Presbyterian Church, as was my father and all of us children. Presbyterians, like Catholics, do not take the Bible literally. Mama was remiss in reading the Bible. The Bible was never at the top of her reading list. When I was a child in Drakes, it was required that I memorize a Bible verse each week for Sunday school. Roscoe Eubanks, a classmate who was also in my Sunday school class, recited the same verse each Sunday—the shortest verse in the Bible, *"Jesus wept."* I never resorted to reciting this particular verse, but with Mama's help I learned a new verse each Sunday.

Other than helping me with the Bible verses, Mama rarely picked up the Bible. Uncle Flood and Aunt Luella gave me my very own Bible when I graduated from high school. I have carried it with me always. Today, it is right beside my computer. I look at my Bible each day, and think, *I am going to read at least one verse each day. I'll start tomorrow!*

Back then the church was the center of all cultural and social activities. I really didn't walk the mile to church every Sunday purely for the religious instruction. I went for the companionship. I would go to Sunday school even when Mama did not attend the church service. There I would meet my friends—Theodora Dusenburg and Mable and Edwina Eubanks. Both

Mama and I would attend evening services when a quartet or any group of gospel singers appeared on the program. The church would be packed when the singing groups appeared. My two other friends, Clara and Dorothy Brown, who were Baptists, would also attend these musical programs. There were also special programs and talent shows for the children. At one talent show I played a piano solo, and at another I directed the children's choir. I wasn't very good at the piano, and I definitely cannot sing. I inherited neither of Mama's musical talents

We also went to programs at St. Michael's Baptist Church, especially the yearly revival. Each year the Baptists would have what they called a revival. A revival consisted of a week of services, often with guest ministers. The week would end with young people and some old people "getting religion." This meant that they had received a calling from God to join the church and accept God as their Savior. Their entrance into the church would culminate in a baptism in the creek down the hill from the church.

The preacher would stand in the middle of water in his clerical robe. There would be several people waiting to be baptized, and one by one they would step into the water and walk to the middle of creek where the minister would be standing. After a short official ceremony for each person, the preacher would say something like: "I baptize thee in the name of the Father, the Son, and the Holy Ghost." The preacher would hold one hand behind the neck and the other behind the shoulder or back and dunk them head first into the muddy water. The young people were our friends and acquaintances. For my Presbyterian friends and me, this was a sight to behold. We were thankful that we believed in just the holy water.

I never felt on any given Sunday that God was calling me to join the church. The Catholic Church with all of its strict rules accepted the sprinkling I received as a legitimate form of baptism. I could never manage being immersed in a pool of water. We had Bible School every summer. A college student appointed by the state governing body of the Presbyterian Church usually taught classes. In addition to learning the Bible stories and religious songs, there were also arts and crafts. The Bible School teacher often roomed and boarded with Mama and me.

I always wanted to become a Catholic. First of all, during the war I attended Our Lady of Victory Catholic School in second and third grade. It was the same school where I had watched the students go in and out almost a year before. Even back then, Mama thought I would get a better education in a parochial school than in the public school. I am not sure why, perhaps because I had come from a school like Organ Hill, she thought I would fare better in a structured environment. Actually, the New York Public Schools were excellent back then. I would have learned much more, in a public or a Catholic school, than I could have ever learned in the segregated and inferior schools in the South.

Mama sacrificed and paid the small fee for my not being Catholic. All of the teachers were nuns, who dressed in the traditional habits of the time that revealed only their face and hands. Each wore a wedding ring to show that she was wed to God.

There were no classes for "special needs" students. All students were placed according to age and grade levels. If you failed the grade you were kept back until you passed that level. If you broke a disciplinary rule you were punished. I received five licks on my hand for switching shoes with a classmate when we were supposed to be working quietly. We merely wanted to see how we would look in each other's shoes.

Mama showed the same concern in Brooklyn as she did in Drakes. If I did not return for lunch or after school at the set time, she would come looking for me. I would find her knocking on my classroom door. This upset me as well as the nun. Mama had usually looked at the clock wrong.

Another time she had a reason to be upset. I had watched a fight after school near the convent. A nun herded the boys who were fighting and the girls and boys who were watching into the church's courtyard. By the time she had finished lecturing us, fifteen or twenty minutes had passed. I met Mama halfway home.

I loved the religious teachings I received in the Catholic school. I was also required to attend mass every Sunday, even though I was not Catholic. If I did not go to mass, I would be in big trouble on Monday. Mama did not require me to go to the Presbyterian Church she attended. She could have forced me to go to two religious services—Catholic and Presbyterian—but she didn't. There was more than one mass on Sunday, and mass only lasted an hour. I would walk the three blocks alone each Sunday, rain or shine. I actually enjoyed the formality of the church service, but I was sad that I could not take communion.

One of the highlights and fun times of attending our Lady of Victory was the school bazaar, held before the Christmas break. A bazaar was like our present-day Fun Fair. There were a lot of activities, and booths that sold extraordinary Christmas ornaments and decorations and lots of gift items. One gift that I longed for but never got was a doll dressed like the nuns who taught me so well. I have only the kneeling nun in my Lladró collection called "Meditation."

When my brother-in-law returned from the war, Mama and I moved back to our home on the branch, and another chapter in my life began.

There was a second reason I continued to be drawn to Catholicism. I went to a Methodist college. There we had to take religion and philosophy. Imagine my actually enjoying a religion and philosophy class taught by Dr. Armstrong. He talked very loudly, and he could be intimidating. I remember speaking to him after class about an assignment. When I left I said, "Goodbye." He responded with a very formal, "Good morning, Miss Miles!" He made me feel as if I had broken an important rule of etiquette. Nevertheless, I enjoyed the course in religion and philosophy, but I was sometimes totally confused as to the part God should play in my life.

In one of my French classes at Bennett we discussed René Descartes' *Meditations on First Philosophy.* His most widely known philosophical ideas are those having to do with hyperbolic doubt. *Cogito, ergo sum,* or *Je pense, donc je suis.* The argument is that though he may doubt, he cannot doubt that he (himself) exists.

My professor, Madame Raidford, explained that though Descartes was skeptical concerning the philosophical and theological position in the Church, he still maintained his Catholic faith. Madame called it *"Le Pari."* Descartes says that if there were a wager being taken as to whether or not there is a God, he would always take the side that says, *"There is a God!"* *"Pensé être."* "I think therefore I am." When I have doubts about the presence of God, I remember the great French mathematician and thinker Descartes, and I remember Mama.

Mama was a great piano player though she played by ear. She could hear a song just once and pick it out on the piano. With a little practice she could sing and play any song perfectly. Her most happy tune was a song called *Railroad Bill* that we would all dance to. I never heard Mama sing the words and do not know if it consists of only the music. She would sing and play hymns like *Onward Christian Soldier, Rock of Ages, Nearer My God to Thee,* and *What a Friend We Have in Jesus.* Her favorite hymn was *The Old Rugged Cross* by Rev. George Bernard. The first verse and chorus went like this:

On a hill far away stood an old rugged cross,
The emblem of suffering and shame;
I love that old cross where the dearest and best
For a world of lost sinners were slain.

So I'll cherish the old rugged cross…
Till my trophies at last I lay down;
I will cling to the old rugged cross.
And exchange it some day for a crown.

Another favorite hymn of Mama's contained the lines: *I'm going to put on my golden shoes and dance all over God's heaven!*

I can see Mama dancing all over God's heaven. I know she now has her crown and golden slippers.

I have come to believe that an only child is always a dreamer. I had an extraordinary imagination. My brothers and sisters were all several years older than I. My childhood was essentially like that of an only child. It was just Mama, Toby, and me. Toby was a tiny brown and white mixed-breed dog. Mama got him from Mr. George Brown, the town's only veterinarian. Actually, Mr. Brown lived in my second favorite town, Keysville. Mr. Brown was also the father of Dorothy and Clara. I recently asked Clara how her father learned to be a vet. Mr. Brown didn't have a doctor's degree in veterinary medicine.

"He learned the trade from his father, just as his father learned the trade from his father."

When Mama wanted a puppy to be neutered or spayed, she would get word to Mr. Brown and he would come and pick up our puppy. It is simply amazing how we managed to communicate with one another back then without telephones. After Mr. Brown performed the surgery and the dog recovered, he would bring it back to us.

Mama and I were not big on holiday celebrations except for Christmas. In fact, I never had a birthday party. No one I knew ever had a birthday party. Anyway, I didn't need birthday parties to have a celebration. My friends and I were always in and out of each other houses. Teachers didn't recognize birthdays either. It would have been somewhat difficult with three grades in a room, and it would have made for an awful big party. Nevertheless, in my imagination I was always having a party. I had my own little playhouse underneath the big oak tree. There were old pieces of furniture that Mama no longer used. The food I prepared were gourmet dishes made from mud, known to grown-ups as "mud pies." The dishes I prepared were those I saw in magazines at the white folks' houses where Mama worked. My little dog Toby, my two little white dolls, were my guests at all occasions—the Fourth of July, Mama's birthday, and of course my birthday.

I should have taken my dolls with me when I left home. They were dolls with tin heads. There was a slit in the scalp for tying a ribbon. I have no idea where Mama got them. My dolls would be collectible items today, so would the pieces of old furniture I used in my playhouse. I would dress Toby up in my dolls' clothes, and sit him at the table along with my dolls. I would place breadcrumbs on top of the mud, and Toby would eat his serving as well as the dolls' portions.

Mama tolerated my party antics with Toby. It was difficult for her to provide celebrations because of problems with baking cakes in a wood-burning or oil-burning oven. Her cakes would rise and then fall. Mama did make lots of apple and blackberry turnovers. There were many blackberry bushes on our property and the property around us. I never knew who owned those plots of land. Anyway, I would pick blackberries on our property and on the surrounding areas which were not snake-infested. Mama's turnovers were the best!

Back then, gourmet food was never on our kitchen table. Mama liked pig feet, chicken feet soup, cow's tongue, chitterlings, and every part of the cow or pig. She would joke that her favorite part of the chicken was the last part to go in the hen house. We ate lots of hot dogs and Spam. Mama never cooked chitterlings. The awful smell made me sick to my stomach.

Many of the dishes Mama would make and eat are considered delicacies in France. Marie-Josée, my friend, served my students and me cow's tongue when we visited her in 1976. My students ate every bite. I don't know if they knew what it was, or if they were just being polite. I knew what it was, so I was just being polite when I cleaned my plate.

When Nikki, Charletta, and I were having dinner in a restaurant in Aix en Provence, we ordered something from the menu that indicated we were getting "pork and cabbage" for three. When the waiter brought our main dish, it was a platter of cabbage topped with pig's feet. I ate the cabbage but not the feet, but looking at the pig's feet lying on this bed of cabbage reminded me of Mama and her love of both pig's feet and cabbage. She also loved the juice that came from the boiled cabbage. She called this juice "liquor."

Every time my friend, Charletta, goes to France she must have at least one serving of "des escargots." Lots of folk in Drakes ate snails, frog legs, and turtle for dinner. There were a variety of mushrooms to be gathered by foraging in the woods. Mama never picked wild mushrooms. She didn't know the difference between the good ones and the poisonous ones. I am glad she didn't try to figure out the difference.

With the number of dogs and pigs on Uncle Flood's farm, maybe there was a possibility that they could have been trained to hunt for truffles on his exclusive land holdings. If I had been visiting the South of France back then, I probably could have sneaked in a couple of truffles for Uncle Flood. He could have tried growing them.

There was also souse, deli-type meat that Mama would buy at the general store. She would fry it, and that would be a special treat for her but not for me. Aunt Luella would also make it from several parts of the hog during hog-killing season. I stuck with fish and chicken, and now and then we would have beef or pork chops. I hated the fish Mama prepared. It was always full of bones, and I was forever getting a tiny bone stuck in my throat.

Having chicken every weekend also presented a problem. Every Saturday when Mama and I went to town we would come back with a live chicken. Mr. Paulette kept crates full of chickens on the front porch of his store. Saturday afternoon, there was the usual ritual of Mama holding the chicken by its head, wringing and wringing the neck until no breath was left in the chicken. She would throw it to the ground, and the chicken would flutter around until it was dead. Mama would then pick up the chicken, put it into a dishpan, pour boiling water over it, and pluck out all its feathers. As I sat on the backsteps watching Mama kill the chicken, I should have felt sorry for it, but I didn't. Everyone in Drakes killed chickens the same way. This is the way we prepared for Sunday dinner. Meat was always bought fresh. Sometimes we had to kill it to eat it.

Mama and I would never visit Uncle Flood during the hog-killing sea-son. The only reminders of the hog-killing season were the big black iron pots used to scald the hogs, and the meats that Uncle Flood brought Mama and me. Slaughtering hogs was too violent a scene.

Back then no one knew about the health advantages of having a diet of only fish, chicken, and fresh vegetables. There were no fast food restaurants. We didn't have the weight problems so prevalent today. I rarely saw anyone who was overweight. Like the French, people walked everywhere. I now fol-low the diet of my youth—fish, chicken, vegetables, fruit, and low-fat vanil-la ice cream.

It was many years later that I began eating so-called gourmet foods. I never learned to cook very well. I don't really like to cook so I haven't put forth much effort to learn. After Paul and I were married I prepared meals that he liked by using some of Mama's old recipes and his mother's. I also did well by following the recipes in a cookbook, *Joy of Cooking* by Irma S. Rombauer and Marion S. Rombauer Becker.

Marie Josée René-Gabriele was an exchange student from the University of Paris who lived with us for a year and a half during the 1970s. She gave me the Rombauer cookbook. I wondered if she gave me that cookbook because she did not like my cooking. My favorite dessert recipe was from a cookbook published by the Vienna Presbyterian Church in the 1960s. It's called a *7-Up Pound Cake* by Joanne Cook, and preparation is as follows:

1/2 lb. butter or margarine	*1/2 c. vegetable shortening*
3 c. sugar	*5 eggs, unbeaten*
3 c. sifted flour	*1 tsp. Vanilla*
1 tsp. Lemon flavoring (optional)	*1 7-oz. Bottle 7-up*

Cream shortening and sugar, add eggs and continue beating until fluffy. Add flour gradually. Add flavorings, mix well. Add 7-up, mix well. Pour into large tube pan and bake at 325 degrees for 1 hour and 10 minutes.

When Mama and I first came to Vienna, we used to go to the black Presbyterian Church in Alexandria. I decided that was too long a drive every Sunday morning, so Mama and I integrated the Vienna Presbyterian Church without incident. Mama was reluctant to join this all-white congregation, but she was soon won over. Reverend Horace Lukens welcomed us with open arms. The congregation followed suit. I participated in the Women's Circles for several years and taught Bible School for a couple of summers when Nikki and Pauly were small.

Reverend Lukens married Paul and me. Paul switched from Episcopalian to Presbyterian after we were married. Pauly and Nikki were baptized in the Presbyterian Church. I don't believe I participated in the

68

cookbook publication. I like good food; I just don't like cooking it. Nevertheless, Nikki and I once took a cooking class at one of Paris's world-acclaimed cooking schools. A famous French chef, Françoise Meunier, gave a few hour lessons to a small group in her studio. Nikki and I joined in this participatory session, which featured a sampling of traditional French specialties. Our menu consisted of:

> *Soufflé au Bleu (soufflé with blue cheese)*
> *Pointe de Cabillaud, Concassee de Tomates Fraiches et*
> *Beurre de Tomates (Cod with freshly crushed tomatoes,*
> *Rosemary and Tomato butter)*
> *Crème Brulee á la Vanille de Bourbon*

Françoise is a Cordon Bleu graduate. The world's most famous school had relocated to a new and more modern building in Paris in 1988. At the end of the school year, students are faced with a difficult exam. They have to prepare a dish named by the chef minutes before. If they are successful and the chef approves, they will receive their first diploma. They can continue by enrolling in more advanced courses and go on to earn the most coveted prize, Le Grand Diplôme de Cordon Bleu.

The Cordon Bleu Cooking School is almost as old as the Eiffel Tower. This institution dates back to 1895, when a woman named Marthe Distel began publication of a magazine called La Cuisiniére-bleu. The magazine contained articles written by famous chefs in which they shared recipes and gave advice concerning all the pleasures of elegant dining. The title comes from a sixteenth century French knight's order called Ordre du Saint Esprit whose members included royalty and were called Cordon Bleus because they wore a blue ribbon. A magnificent dinner followed each meeting. By the eighteenth century Cordon Bleu referred to anyone who excelled in a particular field. Later the term was associated with great cooks.

It is also said that students at the famous military school Saint Cyr, once attended by Napoleon, wore a blue sash. Their skills included a mastery of cooking. Finally, there is another story that tells of Louis XV bragging to his mistress that only men made great chefs. His mistress, Madame Berry, invited the king to a dinner. The king asked, "Où est l'homme qui a préparé ce repas?" "C'est une cuisinière. I think you should honor her with nothing less than the Cordon Bleu," replied the lady.

The Cordon Bleu class Nikki and I attended at Françoise Meunier's cooking school was mostly observation. There were three teenagers in the class, so Françoise involved them in many of the preparations, so they would not feel left out. Françoise also showed us the correct way to open a bottle of wine and to slice cheese. Cheese must always be sliced in the form of a wedge. The best part of this course was eating the food we prepared.

Those who pass their examination at the Cordon Bleu School in Paris are members of a special group. Nikki and I did not qualify for membership even after several hours of being taught by a graduate of Le Cordon Bleu. However, now that Nikki is married, she tries her best to use what she learned in Françoise's cooking class.

The only other classes or seminars having to do with dining were the lectures I attended while crossing the Atlantic, New York to Southampton, on the QE2 in 2000. Paul Burrell, Princess Diana's butler, gave a series of lectures on fine dining—mostly table setting and etiquette. He refused to take questions having to do with personal issues involving the Royal Family. Since the QE2 crossing, Paul Burrel has written a book in which he tells all the juicy secrets of the Royal Family. His book on fine dining and etiquette was all sold out on the crossing from Southampton to New York.

I should have at least gotten his autograph, as a couple of months later he was arrested and accused of stealing some of the Princess's treasures. He was later acquitted after Queen Elizabeth remembered that he had told her about objects he had taken for safekeeping.

There was another tragedy connected with this voyage. One of the chefs disappeared in the middle of the Atlantic. Either he jumped overboard or he was pushed. And the theme for this crossing was "Families!" When the search was announced, Charletta thought it was a child who had strayed from its parents.

Charletta doesn't like to cook either, so she didn't attend any of Paul Burrell's lectures. I would relate to her some of the things I learned in these sessions. "I am not interested in learning about setting a formal table with a finger bowl and all. I never give fancy dinner parties. All of my guests would probably be like the story of one of the Queen's guests. They would think the finger bowl was a glass of water and, like the Queen, I too would have to be polite and drink from my finger bowl. So much for formal dinner parties!"

Paul and I were among a select group of Queen Mary 2 "patrons," Cunard past guests, who pre-qualified for advance notice of the 2004 maiden voyage of the largest, longest, tallest, widest, and grandest ocean liner in the world. We chose not to take the maiden voyage from historic Southampton across the Atlantic. First of all, it was sold out before we received our invitation. I suppose we were near the end of the list of Cunard past guests having traveled only three times on the Queen Elizabeth 2. Secondly, there was a tragedy connected to the twenty-one story liner before it set sail. While docked in St. Nazaire, France, a gangway collapsed killing thirteen people and injuring thirty, mostly workers and their families on a special tour of the nearly completed ship. However, this tragedy would not have deterred us, for no one chooses when or where he or she will die.

Nevertheless, we chose to be closer to home and visit from the Queen Mary 2 the beaches of St. Thomas; the most fantastic party on earth, the Rio Carnival, and Salvador de Bahi, Brazil's most African-influenced city.

The general stores in Drakes and the towns around were not filled with Halloween costumes, elaborate Halloween decoration, or row upon row of candy. Children made their own costumes out of potato sacks and old clothes. I never went "trick or treating," so I never had a Halloween costume. Mama and I went to bed unusually early on Halloween. We hoped and prayed that none of the teenage boys in the neighborhood would come and trick us. Back then Halloween was more tricks than treats. The pranksters would spend the evening putting firecrackers in rural mailboxes, overturning sheds and outhouses, breaking windows, and chalk-marking store windows in town. If treats were given out, they were apples, pears, or other fruits, but no candy. Penny candy was too expensive to give away in quantity.

When Nikki and Pauly were little, I would make them costumes and buy a mask if they wanted me to. Often they would just mark and paint their faces into a mask. Paul and I would go "trick or treating" with them. When they were teenagers, they would put together their own costumes. We used to get lots of neighborhood kids, and often we would run out of candy and use replacements such as apples and oranges. Our community was nervous at this time because of the razor blades in the apples scare.

Going to pumpkin patches and finding the perfect ones for jack-o-lanterns was also an annual ritual. We would walk to Vienna to see the traditional Halloween parade. It was a long cold walk, and even colder when standing on the sidelines watching the high school bands, clowns, floats, the Shriners in their tiny cars, and the many Halloween costumes. The Vienna parade, like so many activities, was cancelled during the fall of 2002. When I was teaching, I dreaded going to school the day after Halloween. I would have to waste time being on the lookout for students who were munching on candy and then leaving the wrappings in the desk.

Paul's birthday is October 31. We used to celebrate his birthday at home. Now Nikki and I (and Pauly if he is home) take him out for his birthday. I usually send out cards for every holiday, even Halloween. In 2002, I inadvertently picked out a pack of cards with this message, which was especially apropos for this particular Halloween.

And a
Good scare
Was had
By all…

HAPPY HALLOWEEN!

A few weeks before Halloween the whole metropolitan area of Washington was held hostage by a serial sniper. During this period innocent people were randomly killed, and three others were critically wounded. Law enforcement spent weeks trying to figure out the reasons for the killings. The prevailing theory is that Mohammed's intended ultimate victim was his ex-wife, who lives in Maryland. She has sole custody of his children. Everyone in the nation, and especially in the Washington area, were affected by the shootings. I was afraid of going into the kitchen in the evening and turning on the light for fear of being shot. Our large picture window made me feel terribly exposed. No one was safe anywhere at any time.

Chief Moose, who was heading the investigation, had stated that we were safe in our homes, but he had also said that children were safe in their schools. Tragically, the sniper promptly shot middle school student Iran Brown, as he entered his schoolhouse door.

Finally the nightmare ended. Officials from two counties in Maryland, three counties in Virginia, and the District of Columbia joined forces to apprehend the killers. The snipers' own stupidity caused their downfall. They boasted of a crime they had committed in the Deep South. A fingerprint had been left behind. The faded blue 1990 Chevrolet Caprice with New Jersey tags driven by John Williams, also known as John Mohammed, and his accomplice, Lee Malvo, was spotted at a rest stop in Maryland. The police or law enforcement agencies had stopped them at least ten times during the same three-week period of terror. An eyewitness had even mentioned that an old beat-up car had been seen near a couple of the shootings. The officials had been looking for "a white man in a white truck."

Only a black person can understand the shock felt by the black community and each black person individually when it was discovered that the men who caused such fear for so many were black. Every law-abiding black person feels guilt and shame when another black person commits such a horrific crime, and this was the cruelest. Their mad rampage stretched from Montgomery County in Maryland to the city of Richmond, two and a half hours away. It was later learned that other shootings had been carried out in other parts of the United States.

Racism and stereotyping cause the guilt and shame that we feel. The experts profiled the killer as being an intelligent or cunning white man because it is widely held that most serial killers are white males with above average intelligence. It never occurred to either white or black people that the Washington sniper could possibly be black, let alone two people who were black. I, like millions of others, was shocked when the picture of John Mohammed was flashed across the television screen. Serial killers are supposed to be white! Would I or other members of my family be looked upon as possible serial killers?

Why or how a whole race of people can share in the guilt of one of its members is difficult to understand. Whenever a horrific crime is committed, I pray, " Please God, don't let him or her be black!" I should only be thinking of the victim.

Do all Germans share the burden of guilt because of the devastation caused by Hitler? What about the Japanese and the atrocities they caused as they sought to control the Pacific and Asia? What about the French who have relatives that collaborated with the German invaders? Then there is a whole list of white serial killers such as Bundy, Yates, Dahmer, and Berkowitz, and the most famous of all, Jack the Ripper and the Boston Strangler. Are all white people viewed as potential serial killers?

Then there is the case of Jayson Blair, the newspaper reporter at the *New York Times*, who lied his way almost to the top of his profession. He is an intelligent young black man who chose to be arrogant, lazy, and dishonest. He is also an accomplished liar, an alcoholic, and a drug addict. He is now an appalling negative example who undermines the benefits of Affirmative Action. Then, there is Montgomery County Police Chief Charles Moose who wanted to write a book about the Washington Sniper. He was forced to resign because of the county's Ethics Committee ruling. He wanted to write his book before someone else did. Why should he not be able to write the book and make millions? What about all the others who write books while in office—congressmen, senators, first ladies?

John Mohammed was tried and sentenced to death in a Virginia court. Lee Malvo was sentenced to life in prison. However, their journey has not ended, there are other jurisdictions who wish to try the pair. It's a waste of taxpayers' money to try Mohammed again. He can die only once. As for Lee Malvo, I believe his life should be spared, as he was a child under the evil influence of an amoral man.

Black folk should celebrate their families. If we all did this then we would learn to celebrate each other. When I became a wife and mother, we celebrated birthdays to bring us closer and to affirm each other. Nikki and Pauly had birthday parties with neighborhood children and schoolmates. If there was no birthday party, I would bake a cake just for the family. Paul and the children would buy a cake for me.

The biggest birthday present Mama ever got was a trip to Quebec and Montreal. In July, 1972, Paul, the children, and I picked her up in Brooklyn for a two-week vacation. Leaving early on Sunday morning we started our journey north. We stopped first in Boston for a brief tour of the city and the ferry ride to Martha's Vineyard. In Quebec and Montreal we took guided tours of both cities. We returned to Brooklyn by coming through the Catskills and the New York capital, Albany.

Upon her return to Brooklyn, Mama boasted to her friends that she had done three things she thought she would never do. She had stayed in several hotels and motels, taken a trip on a boat, and she had been to a foreign country. She remembered this trip with Paul, Nikki, Pauly, and me as being her very best birthday present long after she had lost her short-term memory.

Today, Paul and the children take me out to dinner and I do the same for them. But my birthday present to them is more elaborate—a long trip to a foreign country of my choice. I usually combine Paul's Father's Day present with his birthday present. He has only been to France three times. He doesn't like the French way of life, especially their preoccupation with eating.

His birthday present in 1999 was the Newport Jazz cruise on the *Queen Elizabeth II*. I knew he would enjoy this cruise because jazz is his favorite music. The ship sailed from New York to Nova Scotia, stopping for sightseeing and tours of ports along the North Atlantic and an extended tour of Nova Scotia. While in Nova Scotia, we took a tour of the black section where runaway slaves had settled after their escape from the United States. On the return journey we anchored for three days and nights just off the coast of Newport, Rhode Island. The jazz festival could be heard from the decks of the QE2, or we could go ashore using small but sturdy boats that were at our service to and from the port.

Another big birthday/Father's Day present was a fifteen-day Renaissance cruise on the Mediterranean. At the time Renaissance Cruises had seven ships named according to the order in which they were launched. On any given day, Renaissance Cruise ships were sailing in different parts of the world. We were on *R6*.

Each day we visited a different port and by the end of the fifteen days we had visited fifteen ports on the Mediterranean. When I presented Paul with a father's day card in which I had enclosed the itinerary, I began talking about all the ports along the Mediterranean where I had not been. Nikki remarked, "Mommy, is this trip a present for Daddy or for you?"

"It's for Daddy, but I'm sure I will enjoy it as much as he will. I can't wait for our adventure to begin."

We began our journey by driving to JFK Airport, where we boarded one of two chartered planes to Barcelona, Spain's second largest city and principal port. We were scheduled to leave on the second of the two chartered planes. The passengers on the first plane never left the runway at JFK. The plane had mechanical troubles and was replaced by planes from several other airlines. Some of our fellow travelers missed Barcelona and caught up with the rest of us a couple of ports later.

Nevertheless, in addition to enjoying the comfort and luxury of a beautiful cruise ship, we visited many magnificent and quite different ports. In Barcelona we spent a lot of time walking and exploring Las Ramblas, one of the world's most exciting promenades. A statue of Christopher Columbus stands high on a lofty column and overlooks the port. It was our aerial landmark back to the port area and *the R6*.

From Las Ramblas we attempted to find Picasso's Museum. The Picasso Museum contains many drawings, paintings, and engravings by Spain's most famous artist. I had visited this museum a couple of times with students, so I explained to Paul what he had missed—the Picasso that most people do not know. This museum contains the early work of Picasso, which is in sharp contrast to his later paintings. "At first glance you will be able to recognize the subject Picasso is depicting."

After asking for directions from several Barcelona natives, we arrived at the museum only to find it closed.

This reminds me of an incident that happened to Charletta and me in Marseilles. We asked a Provençal the directions to the Museum of Mediterranean Archaeology. He spent several minutes giving me the directions, and then he said *"Il est fermé aujourd'hui."* Meanwhile, Charletta had walked away. When I caught up to Charletta she asked if I had gotten the directions. I said I had, "But the museum is closed today. We must begin our visit to the museum tomorrow from this very spot!"

Paul and I then took a cab to the Church of the Holy Family (La Sagrada Familia) the masterpiece of Antonio Gaudi. The architect began the construction of this most unique edifice in 1884. He was unable to complete the structure, because he was run over by a tram in 1926. His work was restarted in 1940, but continues to be hampered because Gaudi left no plans or notes.

From the church we took a cab to Montjuic, a mountain park on the south side of the city, and then a cab back to Placa de Catalunya, Barcelona's largest and busiest square. We took a leisurely walk back to the ship for lunch. We were late leaving the next morning because we were waiting for the passengers who were left behind in New York. Our next stop was a shorter stay at Palla de Mallorca, Spain, where we visited the famous Mallorca Pearl Factory.

Our ports in France were Marseille and Nice. Paul and I had been to Marseille a couple of times before, so we just hung around the old port, *le Vieux Port*. In Nice we met Victoria Chasse, an American from Seattle, Washington. Victoria took us to the fishing village of Villefranche in her rented car. Victoria had become "French," leaving all her American ways in America. Only the French would take two complete strangers they encountered in a foreign restaurant and a foreign city for a ride in a rental car. And it would only be in France that we would go for such a ride!

I sat up front with Victoria, and I was needed. I had to remind her when were coming up on a red light on the Promenade des Anglais. Victoria was spending several months in Nice in hopes of buying a condominium along the French Rivièra. According to legend, Hercules opened his arms and Villefranche was born. It sits on a big geological bowl filled with blue Mediterranean water. "You just have to visit Villefranche!"

Victoria dropped us off by the old port. There we encountered a man who was stoning to death a couple of giant octopuses he had caught. He said he was killing his dinner, and asked me if I would like one for our dinner. I responded, *"Non, merci, nous allons au restaurant ce soir."* I was also thinking that I could no longer eat my dinner after seeing it being killed. His action conjured up a picture of Mama killing our Sunday dinner.

In reflection, I find it both odd and comforting that I can travel the world and experience memories of Mama and my life as a child. Mama is always with me in spirit and in my heart; yet here I was in Villefranche, and I found echoes of my life. What do other lands and cultures have in store for me that will bring back remembrances of Mama? It is as if the world is this common mosaic of life's experiences. We have but to travel to distant shores to find these common experiences, to find in them a celebration of our past, and to be reminded again of those who love us.

After our encounter with the fisherman, we continued along the port to reach the narrow alleyways for the climb to the hillside restaurants. The Rue Obscure is one of the strangest streets in France. People live in tiny houses on this street, totally protected from the elements. During World War II, these houses were hiding places for some of the French Resistance fighters. We took a cab back to the *R6*.

Our next port was Ajaccio, Corsica, and the birthplace of Napoleon Bonaparte. Napoleon's home is now a museum, but it remains as it was when he was a little boy. Can anyone imagine Napoleon being a little boy? It was difficult to locate the house where he was born. It was well hidden among the narrow streets and passageways. After asking several times and getting the usual French directions, *C'est tout droit! Etc.*, we found La Maison de Napoléon.

Seeing his birthplace was well worth our time and effort. A large plaque showing Napoleon's family tree intrigued me. France's greatest military leader, and perhaps the world's greatest statistician, was born on the island of Corsica on August 15, 1769. He was the fourth of thirteen children of Buonaparte and Letizia Romolino. The spelling of his last name was later changed to Bonaparte. His father was a member of nobility and when France annexed Corsica in 1769, his family received nobility status.

He was educated in French military academies where his height of only five foot two earned him the name of "Little Corporal." Napoleon fought in the French Revolution and is the most popular dictator that France has ever known. My friend Jean Claude is a member of a Napoleonic order or fraternity. As Paul and I made our way back to the ship, we were able to give more detailed direction to other tourists who were looking for the museum.

A friend had told me about Lucca, one of Tuscany's most beautiful cities. San Martino's cathedral in Lucca dates back to the eleventh century. A brick wall surrounds the medieval city itself. Within the wall is the ancient city where people live and work—with all modern conveniences. The new city of Lucca is outside the wall.

Then we docked at the port city of Livorno. It is a city overwhelmed by the large liners awaiting passengers who had departed for other destinations such as Pisa and Florence, or with passengers aboard who do not wish to stray far from the ships. Bombing during World War II destroyed most of the city. One can only explore the town's few remaining monuments or its newly built shopping mall.

I checked my map of Italy and realized Lucca was not even two hours away. I asked Paul if he wanted to see this ancient city. He said, "No," but I decided to go anyway. He then changed his mind, not wanting me to take off by myself.

After breakfast the next morning, we set out for the railroad station a couple of blocks away. We bought round-trip tickets and immediately boarded a train that would get us back to the ship in the early afternoon, each time changing in Pisa. We arrived around nine at the station in the new city of Lucca, and took the short walk to its ancient beginnings. The train back was supposed to leave at three, getting us back in time for departure.

We visited the sights of Lucca, stopping only for lunch at an outdoor café. We left Lucca around three to make the connection in Pisa at three-thirty. The station monitor listed the train to Livorno as being on schedule and the track listed was number four.

We waited and waited on the platform, but no train. I kept running back to the monitor and to the ticket agent. Both indicated that the train would be arriving on schedule. There were a few Italians on the platform but none spoke English. They were watching the monitor as well. They didn't know what had happened to the train either.

Thirty minutes past the time we were supposed to leave Pisa, we realized we had no choice but to take a taxi. We ran to the front of the train station and told the first driver in line that we had to get back to the ship as it was departing at five. It was now four thirty. Luckily, the driver spoke English.

Driving at more than one hundred kilometers per hour, the driver got us to the area where we could see the *R6* towering above the warehouses. However, getting through the traffic maze to the ship was a feat in itself. We kept running into dead ends. The driver finally got us within walking distance of the ship. I gave the driver a bunch of lira, way too many, but there was no time to count. Anyway, I am terrible at counting foreign currency especially, when there are thousands of units to the dollar. I am sorry that the European currencies are now a part of history, but euros are much easier to count because one euro corresponds more closely to our American dollar.

After handing the cabbie a handful of lira, I took off running. I reached the ship just as the crew were about to take in the fake palm trees and pull up the gangplank. Paul was still a short distance away. I had difficulty finding my ID card among all the pockets in my vest. I had to find it, so it could be swiped. Otherwise, they were not going to let me on the ship. By this time Paul had arrived with his card in hand. We were not the only couples who were late. There were two other couples missing. The ship sailed without them. They did what we would have done; they took a train or taxi and met the ship at the next port, Civitavecchia.

After the previous day's experience, we did not stray too far from the ship while docked in Civitavecchia. During breakfast we engaged in conversation with a lady who was all alone because her friends had taken one of the tours to Pisa or Florence organized by the cruise director. She asked what we were doing. We said that we were not venturing too far from the ship, and asked if she would like to accompany us.

We did a lot of window-shopping, as there wasn't too much of interest in the city. I bought Pauly an Italian-made sweater that cost a fortune. I gave it to him for his Christmas present. A few months later, I asked why I had not seen him wearing it. He said he had given it to his cousin, Brian, because it was too small. I was really upset with him. The sweater cost one hundred fifty dollars. He could have given the sweater to his father, who is much smaller than he is. I hope Cousin Brian appreciated the sweater, but I don't think he did. I never saw him wearing it.

We learned from our walking companion that she was retired and living in Florida. There was another passenger in his forties whom we heard talking very loudly to all who would listen on the flight over. We met him while boarding the ship in Barcelona. His goal was to get to know everyone on board the *R6*. Paul thought that he was a CIA agent, though I don't know why he would be interested in us.

The night before, he had shared a table with our walking companion and her friends. She was now upset with this fellow because of a remark he had made. Learning that they all lived in Florida, he had said that he wasn't interested in ever going back to Florida, because it was now the state belonging to a lot of Jews who had completely changed the resorts to places where Gentiles no longer wanted to go. Paul and I could not understand why this man didn't realize that he was sitting among a group of Jews.

Her story reminded me of an incident in Greece when we were traveling with "Go Ahead Vacations." We were having dinner with a group of fellow Americans. A middle aged lady asked Nikki what school she attended. Nikki said she had finished undergraduate and graduate school, and was now working for a private company aptly named "Sparta." She went on to explain that "Sparta" received large grants from the Department of Housing and Urban Development. The purpose of the grants was to solve problems associated with federal housing development.

The lady began her story. She said she also had a job working with the residents of a public housing apartment building. This job often took her to the development. Each day a very rude black parking attendant would greet her. One day she got up the nerve to ask him why he seemed to dislike her so much. He replied, "I hate all deadbeats who are on welfare." "Imagine that! He thought I lived in this public housing complex."

Our fellow traveler continued, "I don't understand why this man didn't know that the only people who are on welfare are black." Nikki did not answer her but she was thinking, *Well, actually, most people on welfare are not black. They are white. I should know.*

She was looking into the face of a white woman, and she did not want be rude. The lady was looking into Nikki's face as well, but she saw no connection between Nikki and the people who lived in public housing. But "No man is an island…" With our strange cultural ambivalences, she did not think Nikki would find her remark offensive, even if it had been true.

When Paul and I returned to the ship we found a large ugly ship called the *Napoléon* docked beside our ship. It wasn't like any cruise ship Paul or I had ever seen. We were in a rush to get back for lunch, so we didn't eavesdrop on the conversation between fellow passengers and the *Napoléon's* crew. We ate lunch on the side of the *R6* facing this strange vessel. Below we could still see various passengers talking to members of the crew including an officer. There was a lot of head shaking on the part of the crew.

After lunch, I decided to inquire about the *Napoléon*. I approached the officer.

"*Qu'est-ce que c'est, le* Napoléon?"

M. le capitaine répond, "*C'est un bac.*"

The Napoléon wasn't a cruise ship. It was a ferryboat, but not any ferry that we had ever seen. The captain then said he would show us around. He took us over every inch of the vessel, showing us the captain's quarters, the dining hall, the dance floor, the empty car park, the brig, and the computers that controlled all aspects of the ferry, including directing the ferryboat to back up, go sideways or just about in any direction. He said he could not show us a cabin as they were all occupied.

His ferry, with Corsica as its home port, would dock at ports along the Mediterranean on weekends. The passengers would use their cars to visit the town and cities. When we had finished the tour I asked for his name and address. He was Louis Lamoureux from La Garde, France, near Toulon. After he wrote his name and address in my book, he said, "*Regardez le nom de famille.* (Notice my name.) His last name means, "the lover."

I haven't quite figured out why he thought it was necessary to point this out to me, especially since Paul was with me. He also told us that he had a wife and three children. We still exchange Christmas cards each year.

The French are the most lovable people in the world. Paul recently met a young Frenchman and his American wife. He encountered them on the orange line that runs from Washington to Vienna. Paul said, "We must invite them over. They are in the same situation as Dave and Nikki." So we did!

Denis is originally from Pau, the capital of the French Basque Country. His wife, Victoria, is from Front Royal. They met when she was a student in Paris. I am the only American Denis has ever met, outside of France, who had heard of Pau, much less been there. He invited me to come over to the French Embassy where he worked and have lunch—all for a mere eight dollars. He also offered to buy euros at the embassy before we left on our next trip to France. He is able to get a much better rate there than at our bank or even in France. The French *joie de vivre* is rubbing off on Paul. Only the French would become friends with strangers they met on the Métro.

Our next destination was Messina, Sicily. I had always wanted to visit the home of the Mafia. Medina is one of the island's most beautiful cities even after misfortune after misfortune, including invasions, earthquakes, and bombardments during World War II. We could see the cathedral of Messina looming above the city. There were no taxi stands, but after a wait on the main street, we saw a taxi in the distance. The driver stopped, and we asked if he could take us to the cathedral. He spoke English rather well and French very well. He wanted to practice his English on us, so we conversed in English. He gave us some of the history of the city, and when he dropped us off back in town he gave us his well-used guidebook called *One Day in Messina*. I didn't see even one person I thought was a member of the Mafia. The taxi driver's last advice was, "Come again to Sicily, stay longer, and perhaps you'll see or even meet a member of the Mafia."

Malta is thirty-five miles south of Sicily. It is an independent state but remains a part of the British Commonwealth. Valletta is the capital and chief port. Most of the people speak Maltese, but parents may choose whether their children are taught in Maltese or English. Paul and I had no language problem there. Shopping was great, especially for leather goods. We finished our Christmas shopping there. Paul, who does not like to shop, bought three pairs of shoes for himself made of the finest leather. Three Christmases later, he is still retrieving Christmas presents from his Malta shopping bag.

We docked within the old city, which was a short distance from the ship. Nearly all of the people of Malta are Catholic. We found a beautiful Catholic Church a short distance down from the main thoroughfare of the old city. After attending a part of the mass, we returned to the ship loaded down with our purchases of the day.

Later that evening, a number of our fellow travelers asked about the mink coat Paul had bought for me. There were only a few black couples on board the *R6*. The couple they were confusing us with appeared to be on their honeymoon as they always sat at a table for two. They were also much younger, especially the woman. But all blacks look alike!

Paul would never buy me a mink coat, and I would never wear one. I have this thing about animal fur. Pauly says I shouldn't wear leather shoes either, if I am so concerned about the animals.

Our next stop was Corfu, the most popular of all the Ionian Islands. We encountered our first rainy day while in Corfu. We docked within walking distance of the area called "Old Town." On the south edge of Old Town is the sixteenth century church of Agios Spiridon, the Bishop of Cyprus in A.D. 319 and Corfu's patron saint ever since his remains were smuggled into the island from Constantinople in the fifteenth century. His remains are kept in a silver coffin beside the altar. They are objects of great veneration for the healing power attributed to them. I wish I had been diagnosed with acid reflux disease then, in 2000. Perhaps I could have been cured!

Corfiote mothers invariably name at least one of their sons "Spiros." When Nikki and I were in Corfu a few years before, every male we met was Spiros. After seeing the church and the coffin of St. Spiridon, Paul went back to the ship and I continued to shop in Old Town. *R6* was within my sight at all times.

This time I met no one of interest in Corfu. The last time, Nikki and I met a very kind English woman, Sheila Gregoriadis from Woodford Halse, England. She invited us to her hotel for a drink. She asked how we knew that she wasn't Greek when we spoke to her in Old Town. She had been speaking Greek with a couple of ladies on the square. I said without thinking, "The ladies weren't understanding your Greek very well." Each year she takes her vacation alone on the island. We invited her to come visit us in the U. S. She said she had no interest in ever coming to America.

Our next stop was Dubrovnik, Croatia, a medieval walled city on the Dalmatian Coast that is more than a thousand years old and remains untouched by the modern world. It is one of the most famous cities on the Adriatic. It won its independence from Yugoslavia in 1991. We spent the morning walking along its narrow, cobbled lanes that took us back into centuries of history. There were no neon signs or noisy traffic to mar our view from the top of the city wall. We could see clearly one of our destinations, the coast of Italy.

While docked in Naples, we decided we would hail a cab to take us to Pompeii, the ancient city that was destroyed by the eruption of Mount Vesuvius in A.D. 79. For hundreds of years the city lay buried under cinders, ashes, and stone until excavation began in the 1500s. About half the city has now been uncovered. I had been to Pompeii before, but Paul had not. We did not take a formal tour but used our hand-held maps.

We had an agreement with our driver that we would meet him at the taxi stand at 1 P.M. for our return to Naples. We found his fare reasonable, after asking several drivers and comparing their fares at the suggestion of the cruise director. However, we suspected he made other runs while we were touring the city.

Anyway, he was waiting patiently when we returned to the appointed meeting place. I have always found that European taxi drivers keep their word. In Greece Nikki and I would often leave the *Go Ahead Group* and take off on our own. In Corfu we had a driver named Spiros take us to the little beach of Agios. We pointed out the spot where he should meet us at five.

After spending a few hours at the beach, we went to our meeting place. Spiros was waiting patiently. On our ride to and from the beach, we asked Spiros about his going through numerous traffic lights and signs. He said it didn't matter; no one obeyed traffic signals and signs. He also told us that Greece has the highest number of traffic fatalities in the world. We believed him, for all along the highways and roads were flowers and personal mementoes dedicated to those who had lost their lives in traffic accidents. Spiros may not have been paying attention to the traffic signals and signs, but Nikki and I were.

In Naples, Paul and I feasted on genuine pizza, the only one cooked in a wood-fired brick oven with the traditional toppings of tomatoes, mozzarella, and fresh basil, in the colors of the Italian flag and devised in honor of Queen Margherita. Our waiter boasted that it was the best in the world. It was!

After lunch, we took a walking tour of the city of Naples, taking care not to stray too far from the ship. We ended our walk in front of a towering structure that had the look of both a cathedral and a palace. On entering the building, we sat down on the café terrace, marveling at the architecture.

While Paul was getting a snack from the bar, I walked over to a couple sitting a short distance away. I asked them if they spoke Italian. They both shook their head, "No!" I then asked if they spoke French. The husband said he spoke a little bit of French. We carried on a short conversation in French.

Our main subject was the history of the big plaza where we were now standing. The husband explained that this was really a big shopping mall and there were many malls like this one all over Europe. His explanation was given in his halting French. I remarked that I had never seen such a magnificent shopping mall. I then said to Paul in English, "We had better get back to the ship."

We exchanged names and addresses with Mr. and Mrs. S. W. Jarvis from Surrey, England. We now correspond at Christmas time.

On the way back to the ship, I stopped to ask a group of Italian policemen why they always travel in groups. An English-speaking policeman said there was a lot of crime in Naples. There must be lots of crime in many parts of Italy. One often sees three or four policemen riding in one tiny patrol car, or groups of four or six standing around. We never saw a policeman patrolling alone. The criminals he was referring to were pickpockets, purse-snatchers, and muggers. Just as we arrived at the *R6*, two policemen were breaking up a fight between an elderly man and a younger one. They gave the younger man a long lecture and let both of them go. In the United States, both of them would have been arrested for disorderly conduct. I love the policemen in other countries, particularly France and Italy. They are way friendlier and always very handsome!

When we arrived in Venice (Venezia), we found that our ship was some distance from San Marco Square. We tried to note the direction we were walking, but our plan did not work. After going in and out a series of narrow streets and crossing a number of bridges over the many canals along pedestrian passages, we came across a diminutive black Frenchman from Marseille. French usually works for me in both Italy and Spain..

"*Nous sommes perdus!*"

"*Je vous emmène.*"

He led us to San Marco Square. After we visited the Cathedral of Saint Mark and the Doge's Palace, we spent the rest of the day on the Piazza of Saint Mark and in and out of the shops and cafés that surround the square. Getting back to the ship was our greatest challenge of the day. We took a water taxi that appeared to be way over its limit of passengers. We were pushed onto this boat like sardines, and I feared both being crushed and drowned. I think drowning is a horrible way to die.

The taxi's last stop put us close to the sea. The *R6* was nowhere in sight. We asked a number of people who pointed us in the direction of the port for cruise ships, so we kept walking, taking care to stay close to the sea. After a very long walk, we came upon a taxicab whose driver was trying to make a U-turn on the narrow pier. We yelled, and he stopped. He agreed to take us to the ship.

The early evening was spent getting directions for disembarking the next day. We were scheduled to leave on the second chartered flight the following evening. This meant that something had to be done with us passengers the next day. No one ever explained why the two planes could not take off at the same time. The cruise director had a plan. After checking our bags at the airport we were loaded onto two buses for a two-hour drive from Venice to Padova.

According to legend Antenore, a Trojan prince, founded Padova, or Padua. It became one of the Roman Empire's richest cities. Today it is a busy city, much of it being rebuilt after the bombing during World War II. We were dropped off near the center of town, near the largest square in the world.

Paul and I visited the Cathedral of St. Anthony whose tomb is in the treasury chapel. His skull is displayed on top of his casket. I also went to confession. When I entered the first booth, the priest recognized me as an American. He said, "Father Michael in the next booth speaks English." I confessed my sins to Father Michael, which were basically the evil thoughts and words I had had for the despicable characters in a nonfiction book I was writing at the time, *Defaming Teddy*. I had thought that I could speak to the priest in English, and he could ask God to forgive me in Italian because God understand all languages. The first priest must not have thought this strategy would work. Anyway, Father Michael said I was forgiven. I left church with a light heart and less guilt. We attended the noon mass performed in Italian.

It was our second day of drizzling rain, so the rest of the day was spent in a café having a leisurely lunch. Around four we returned to the bus for the trip back to the Venice Airport. We boarded our charted flight to New York and home. I should have asked Father Michael to pray for our safe return.

Both Renaissance Cruises and the chartered airline are now out of business. We had a wonderful Mediterranean vacation, though.

Paul never spent a cent. He was always looking for an ATM machine, but when he found one he could never remember his PIN number. I was always lending him money. He has never paid me back. I was supposed to pay for his ticket! His spending money was his responsibility. Paul really took advantage of my generosity! This was his best birthday ever! On our next vacation, I must remember to bring my ATM card for our joint account.

It was always a family tradition for Paul and me to have the children's birthday party at home, even if we four were the only ones in attendance. Today, it is a common practice for parents to have parties at Chuck E. Cheese or some other recreational center. I dislike these parties. There are too many families and too many children we don't know in attendance.

A few summers ago, I was visiting with one of Pauly's friends who had recently moved into a beautiful new home. My grandchildren, Pearis and Paul IV were later invited to their daughter, Cheyenne's, third birthday party. When I noticed Pauly was going a different direction than before, I asked, "Aren't you going the wrong way?" He replied, "Oh, the party isn't at their house." I was disappointed. They had such a beautiful place for a birthday party. Pauly now has his children's parties at his house, or we celebrate their birthday in Vienna.

Thanksgiving marks the beginning of my favorite time of the year. For several years, Yvonne and her family have shared Thanksgiving dinner with my family. One year she bakes the turkey and the trimmings and I make the vegetables and dessert. Each year we alternate the tasks.

When I was little, Thanksgiving meant we were to thank God for all our blessings, no matter how small. Mama and I never had a big Thanksgiving dinner. We usually had chicken or just a regular meal unless we were in Brooklyn with Eliza and her family. Eliza is a great cook, so she would prepare a typical American Thanksgiving dinner. On some occasions, Uncle Flood would come and pick up Mama and me. Since he was an avid hunter we would dine on wild turkey and ham. I would eat only the ham that was taken from his smokehouse. Since killing season had not been over long, there were lots of parts from the hogs Uncle Flood had recently slaughtered.

The time between Thanksgiving and Christmas was the time to prepare for the biggest holiday of the year. I would take the axe, go to a field in back of the house, and cut the most beautiful little tree I could find. Mama and I would decorate it together. During the war years Eliza Etta, Cousins Geneva and Estelle, George Robert, Mama, and I were all living together at 15 Albany Avenue in Brooklyn. Christmas was really a big celebration, especially when the families from other apartments were in and out of our apartment.

After we moved back to Drakes, we often returned to Brooklyn for the holidays. Eliza Etta took over the apartment she and her cousin had shared during the war. Estelle moved down to the second floor with her husband John and their children. Geneva and Leroy bought a house out on Long Island.

Every Christmas Eve, Eliza Etta and Little Frank would go in search of a Christmas tree. They would return with a tree that reached the ceiling of her apartment. The tree would be gotten at less than half price, but it wasn't the bargain that Eliza Etta was thinking of. She thought of Christmas Eve as a holiday in itself—a holiday for preparing for Christmas day.

We would spend the evening decorating the tree with the many and varied ornaments she had collected over the years. Eliza Etta would then spend the rest of the evening baking cakes and cookies and homemade rolls. Mama would crack the walnuts for the cookies, and Eliza Etta would spend a lot of time chiding her for eating more nuts than she was putting in the bowl. Christmas in my sister's home began with Christmas Eve. I, on the other hand, like to savor the season, so Christmas for me begins the day after Thanksgiving.

When Mama and I went to live in Brooklyn, we left Toby with Uncle Flood. Uncle Flood hunted for food as well as sport. He kept his hound dogs penned up when they were not hunting and chasing prey; however, there were many times when they would all escape from the enclosure and go off foraging on their own. It was on one of these occasions that Toby ran off with the hounds. He did not return. I had lost my playmate forever. I never said, "Goodbye."

I always had a pet. A few years after Mama and I returned to Drakes, Miss Lucy gave Mama a Dalmatian from one of her dog's litter. We named her Lucky. She forgot me when I went off to college. She passed away without my knowing when and how she died.

Children need a pet. I need a pet. People with pets live longer. After Lucky, my third pet was also a Dalmatian, but a lot different from Lucky. Paul had seen a "Dalmatians for Sale" sign on his way from work. Nikki and Paul were about two and three years old at the time. They were excited about the prospect of having a dog. Paul named the puppy Janice after a girlfriend he knew. I never could figure out why he would name a dog after a girlfriend.

Janice was the typical puppy, lovable and playful. However, when she was older, the children were afraid of her. When she was in the house we would tie her to the oil tank in the basement. Janice would often break loose and run through the house like a cyclone. Nikki and Pauly would have a fit.

By the time Janice was five, she wasn't a pet at all. She was now a vicious guard dog. She would permit no one to enter her fence or our home. Once when Pauly took her food downstairs to her, I yelled to him to bring Janice's dish back to the kitchen. I had some scraps from the table to add to her meal. Pauly reached down to pick up the bowl and Janice bit him in the chest. Pauly had on a couple of layers of clothes, so Janice's teeth did not pierce his skin.

Brandy, the poodle, was given to us while we still had Janice. Janice never physically attacked Brandy, but she often showed her dislike for him. Brandy would not go near Janice. One evening while playing with a toy, he accidentally let it fall within Janice's reach. I tried to take the toy from Janice. She grabbed my hand between teeth and would not let go. Only after my screaming with pain and the rest of the family's interference, did Janice let go of my hand.

Paul took me to the emergency center. My hand could not be stitched up, but I was given a tetanus shot. Janice's rabies shots were always up to date. Our neighbors, the Fortunes, told us that we should get rid of such a vicious dog. Reluctantly, we took Janice to the animal shelter, and asked to be called if Janice were not adopted in a couple of days. Someone who wanted a beautiful but vicious dog got his or her wish. For a while, I had two dogs, Janice and Brandy.

When our neighbors' daughter Lenata moved away, she gave us Brandy, the miniature poodle. Christine and Ridgeway Fortune already had Susie, a standard poodle. Brandy was now our only dog, unless you counted Susie. Susie would always come over for visits. When the Fortunes were on vacation, we kept Susie for weeks at a time. Paul would not allow Brandy in our bedroom, so he would sit at the door until Paul went to sleep. He would then sneak in and sleep under my side of the bed.

Brandy would go wherever the family would go. Once we took him to Binghamton, New York, for one of Nikki's soccer tournaments. We left Brandy in the motel room while we attended the games. When we returned, the front desk clerk told us that when the maid opened the door to clean, Brandy had run out. Nikki, Pauly, and I covered several blocks around the motel, but to no avail. Before returning to the motel we stopped at a police station nearby and reported the missing Brandy. He was wearing a nametag with our home address. The police would call the motel or home if anyone turned him in.

As we walked back to the motel, we heard whining coming from a big used car lot not too far from the hotel. We walked in the direction of the whining, and whom should we come upon? Brandy was standing near a brown station wagon almost identical to ours. Aren't dogs supposed to be colorblind? We told the hotel not to clean our room for the rest of the weekend. Brandy loved to go for rides. Whenever he heard the rattle of my car keys, he would jump for joy, and scratch the door until it was opened for him. We had to put a plate on the door to protect the paint.

When the Fortunes left for the weekend, or for longer vacations, we would keep Susie. It was like having another child. Susie was a member of our family. Nikki and Pauly would fight over whose room Susie would sleep in. Each of them would conveniently forget whose room Susie had slept during her last sleepover. Brandy did not care where Susie slept, as he knew that he would be sneaking into my bedroom. Susie lived to be about fourteen or fifteen years old. Both Nikki and Pauly were in college when Susie was put to sleep.

Brandy was not neutered, so if he was not watched closely, he would sometime run off. When we were packing to take Pauly to college, Brandy sneaked out of the house without our realizing he had left. When I discovered that he was missing, we frantically called the animal shelter. No luck, but I left my telephone number. The next morning I received a call from a lady who said that she had found a poodle. I went to check, but it was not Brandy.

Later in the day, I got a call from a veterinarian in Chantilly who had an injured poodle. It was Brandy, but he was beyond recognition. One of his legs was crushed and would have to be put in a cast. His whole body was covered with scrapes and bruises. A car had hit him. The driver had brought him in. The vet said that he would try to save Brandy but it would be very expensive. I said, "Save him."

He stayed in the hospital for more than a week, at a cost of more than fifteen hundred dollars. He came home with a cast. He learned to walk by leaning against the wall.

I was told if I should smell any kind of odor around the cast, that Brandy should be brought in immediately. Late one evening I had to take him in. The doctor cut his cast off, treated his legs with antibiotics and replaced the cast. Brandy learned to walk with the cast, and after a few weeks it was removed, but he still had a crippled leg. He lived for two years after the accident, but he never fully recovered.

The first Christmas after Brandy's accident, Nikki and Pauly gave me a present, a Cocker Spaniel. On Christmas Day, I opened a beautifully wrapped package. It contained a lot of newspaper. I was told to keep digging. To my surprise I found a book called *Caring for a Cocker Spaniel*. Nikki and Pauly explained that they had picked out a puppy for me, but it was not yet ready to leave his mother.

Two months later, we picked up Demetrius, a name Pauly picked out. He just liked the sound of the name. I was in love with Demetrius from the moment I saw him. Demetrius was already trained to a cage, so we bought a cage from the breeder. Whoever got home first would let Demetrius outside. Demetrius would then have the run of the house.

Demetrius was always the perfect dog, except when we had guests. When a stranger would pet him he would pee. He never broke this habit. For a while I had both Brandy and Demetrius. They got along well with each other. When Demetrius was about ten years old, he lost his hearing. He learned sign language though. When I made a motion with my hand to go into his cage or to go outside, he understood. Demetrius also learned to read my lips. I could have a conversation with him. He particularly liked when the grandchildren came to visit. Pearis and Paul, IV were about his height, so Demetrius could easily pinch a cookie or whatever food they had in their little hands.

Pauly's college girlfriend, and later his wife, loves dogs as much as I do. When she was at Hampton, she got a Lhasa Apso named Dumpling from the animal shelter. When Jackie went home during college breaks and summer vacations, she would leave Dumpling with me. The first year, while she and Pauly were in graduate school, I kept Dumpling. Demetrius and Dumpling were like brothers. When Pauly and Jackie were married, they got a second dog, a Beagle, that they named Douglas. The "Three D's" they were called.

I have bites on my kitchen chairs and a bite out of my dining room rug from Douglas' puppy days. Most of the time they were "The Three Musketeers," one for all and all for one. When they did get in a fight, Demetrius and Dumpling would team up against Douglas. They never actually fought. The two of them would chase Douglas around the house or the fenced-in area. When they were let in the back door, they would race for the snack dish in the kitchen. Dumpling, the smallest of the three, would always win. Demetrius would follow me up and down the stairs, no matter how often I went up and down. Dumpling and Douglas were smarter than Demetrius in one sense. When I was having a busy day going up and down the stairs for one reason or another, they learned to wait at the top of the stairs until they were sure I was going to remain downstairs for a while.

Even after Pauly and Jackie were divorced, I still kept Dumpling and Douglas. And later when Jackie and her husband Sam were out of town. Dumpling and Douglas were my dogs. According to Jackie, when they came up to the house, they were always delighted that they were coming to visit us.

Demetrius caused a problem if he stayed in any home except his own. He whined the whole night, so neither Jackie, Sam, or our foster son Chanty would keep Demetrius in their townhouses. Once was enough! There were too many complaints from the neighbors. When Chanty volunteered to baby-sit him at home, his whining would result in a sleepless night for the sitter. Demetrius always missed his mommy.

When we went to visit Paul's parents we always had to take Demetrius' cage. Demetrius hated visiting Suffolk. He hated being in his cage all weekend. I think Paul's father disliked dogs because he had never had the pleasure of having a pet of any kind.

Paul, when we were first married, did not seem to have any problems with our having a dog. It was he who first came up with the idea of getting Janice the Dalmatian. He didn't seem to resent Susie, Dumpling, or Douglas who spent a lot of time with us.

At some point, he decided that Demetrius would be the last dog that I would have. I think the older he gets, the more he is like his father. A few weeks after we returned from our Mediterranean cruise, Demetrius became very ill. I first noticed that he had difficulty walking up the five stairs leading from the den to the foyer. He no longer attempted to come upstairs to the bedroom. The kitchen was no longer his favorite place.

The veterinarian described his illness as something like a stroke in a human. He improved, but at times he would develop other symptoms that were at times less serious and other times more serious. When he was outside, he didn't look through the sliding glass door to signal that he wanted to come in. He no longer raced upstairs to check his snack dish. He was now walking like an old dog. He didn't follow me up and down the stairs a hundred times a day. Cockers are prone to ear infections. His years of having problems with his ears and his age caused him to have all of the symptoms of a very old dog. For a couple of years, antibiotics strengthened his walk and freed him from pain.

In March of 2002, I spent a week in New Jersey helping Paul and Lela move into their new home. When I returned I sensed something was wrong. I did not go in search of Demetrius as I usually did when returning from a trip, nor was there any sign that Demetrius knew I was home. After an hour or so, Paul said, "I had to put Demetrius to sleep." I refused to listen to Paul's explanation of what had happened to Demetrius, my constant companion for fifteen years. For months there were feelings of resentment, before I realized that I would never have been ready to let Demetrius go.

I am a dog lover. Toby, Lucky, Brandy, Janice, Demetrius, Dumpling, and Douglas knew that I loved them. Well, I am not really sure about Janice. Paul was never really cruel to any of the dogs, but they knew that he really wasn't fond of them. Nikki and Pauly are dog-lovers, like me. When Pauly was a little boy, he would share his chicken noodle soup with Brandy. Paul IV likes dogs also. He would give Demetrius a kiss along with everyone else before he went to bed. Mama always knew that I, as a child growing up alone, needed a companion. Mama loved dogs as much as I do. I am getting me a dog!

I can probably hold off buying a puppy for a while. When Nikki, Dave, and I were in Paris a couple of years ago, they bought Chanel, a Yorkshire terrier. Though Chanel is with her parents most of the time I often have the pleasure of babysitting my "grand dog." This suits Paul fine! He even tolerates Chanel sleeping in our bed. However, he objects to her sleeping between the two of us.

Chanel responds to both French and English. I can't live without a dog!

As of October 2004, I don't have to! Nikki and Dave bought me my own two and a half months old Yorkshire terrier—in Paris no less. Nikki suggested I name him Jacques in honor of my French professor Jacques Houdaille. At the time we were having dinner with M. Houdaille and his granddaughter Jasmine Kripalani at a very chic Chinese restaurant that welcomed dogs. Jacques Houdaille is delighted with his namesake. The *patronne* cupped tiny Jacques in her hands and remarked that he would make an excellent cup of soup. We kept a close eye on little Jacques especially when the waiter showed us how well he fit into his pocket.

Chapter 3

Still sits the school-house by the road,
A ragged beggar sleeping;
Around it still the sumachs grow;
And blackberry-vines are creeping.

Whittier, *In School-Days*

Organ Hill was the same three-room schoolhouse I had attended in first grade. There was no electricity or running water. There were the same old wooden desks built for two with the hole for a bottle of ink. Ink cartridges and ballpoint pens had not been invented. The battered teacher's desk showed years of use as well. The blackboard with white chalk dominated the front and the right walls of the room as one entered from the outside.

My going to school in Brooklyn meant that I would skip the second of the three classrooms, reserved for the third and fourth grades taught by Miss Dora Hall. George Robert had her as a teacher. She was one tough character. When I returned to Drakes for Theodora Dusenburg's funeral in 1994, I saw Miss Dora getting out of her car. "I thought she was dead." I said to Clara. She was then in her late nineties. She looked much the same as I remembered her almost fifty years before. Sadly, Miss Dora Hall passed away in January 2004 at the age of one hundred and four.

My teacher in fifth, sixth and seventh grades was Reverend Venable. He drove a Model T. Mama asked Rev. Venable if he would give me a ride to and from school each day, as he passed through town each morning and afternoon. Through fifth and sixth grades I waited for my teacher in front of Mr. Foster's store. I no longer had to take the long walk to school with the rest of the children from my neighborhood. Of course, my classmates teased me unmercifully, as I was considered the teacher's pet. So each day I could look forward to some girl looking at me and mouthing before recess, "I am going to beat you up." I usually managed to avoid a fight, and most of the girls did not carry out the threat. But I could never avoid the bully, Ella, otherwise known as "Beady."

We once got in a big fight that resulted in her hitting me so hard that I ended up with a knot on my forehead. It took a very long time for me to live down this fight. In addition to that humiliation, both Beady and I got a whipping with a hefty tree branch from the Reverend. He left all the leaves on the branch though.

The few times I got a whipping from Mama, she would make me break my own switch—meaning I would go to a nearby tree, break off a branch, and bring it back to her. She would then slide her hands down the branch to remove all the leaves. I can't remember what I had done wrong.

On one occasion, while she prepared the switch, I took off running. I played around for an hour or so on the swings in back of the white school. I thought, after such a long time, Mama would think I had run away from home and she would forget about the whipping. No such luck! I sauntered back to the house. Mama went about whatever she was doing, ignoring me in the process. After a few minutes, she grabbed me and gave me the whipping I deserved. That is the one and only real whipping Mama ever gave me. Corporal punishment was not outlawed in Virginia schools until the 1960s.

One would think that after that episode with Beady, Mama would have let me walk to school with the other children. Instead, she told Beady's mother that Beady had better not touch me again.

"Are you crazy? Why would you want to walk three miles to school when you can ride?"

One would also think that Rev. Venable would not want to be chauffeur to this angry fifth or sixth grader. I refused to utter a single word to him when I wasn't in the classroom. We traveled the three miles in complete silence.

The summer before I entered seventh grade, a number of students who lived to the west of Drakes Branch were transferred from the Keysville Elementary School to Organ Hill Elementary. It was too far for these students to walk ten to fifteen miles to school. A hand-me-down bus from the white school was found to transport these students. The bus had to pass through Drakes Branch in order to reach Organ Hill on the other side of town.

The other children and I who lived within the town limits were now provided with bus service. The bus had two long seats on either side and one long seat in the middle. If the bus made a sudden turn, we would all lean into the turn. The child sitting at the end of the middle seat would slip to the floor. Of course, the mischievous boys found this extremely funny, and would exaggerate the sharpness of the turns. The bus driver was a veteran of World War II who was completing high school on the GI Bill. He wasn't the safest driver around.

Three of the new girls who transferred to Organ Hill became my best friends for life. They were the sisters, Dorothy and Clara Brown, and

Theodora Dusenburg. Sadly, there are only two of us left. Theodora passed away in 1994, and Dorothy in 2000. Now that I am *"une dame d'un certain âge,"* I find myself reminiscing about past experiences, especially with people who have influenced my life—students, teachers, friends, neighbors, and famous, and sometimes infamous, people. I feel very sad that over the years I have made no effort to make contact with some of these people. I was the only one of the four friends who did not have a father in the home, but their fathers gave me much support and encouragement.

There was also Cousin Alex, my grandmother's first cousin. He would come around at least once a week, usually just before dinnertime on Sundays. My favorite joke to play on Mama was to look out the window and say, "Here comes Cousin Alex!" —even when he wasn't coming. Mama would look anyway.

I would also play jokes on Cousin Alex. He expected to be fed when he came to visit. If Mama wasn't home, I was expected to fix him a snack. I would secretly open a can of Lucky's dog food. Just before he put the spoon in his mouth. I would yell, "That's not beef! It's Lucky's food!" I played many tricks on Cousin Alex. He took them all in his stride. He used to tell me about the thriving brick-making business he had had, and the beautiful home he had once owned. He would point out to me where his brickyard had been located. It was down by the railroad tracks and I could see old bricks and rusted kilns. He had lost everything he had during the Great Depression.

I enjoyed his stories of prosperity, and felt sad about the tragic loss of his livelihood. He had been married twice, and had several children by his first wife. Cousin Alex was now a widower in his seventies and eighties. All of his children lived in Baltimore. He would visit them from time to time, and when he returned to Drakes, he had plenty of stories to tell of his visit to the big city. He was a man about town, and when he came calling, Mama and I learned what was happening around town. Cousin Alex moved to Baltimore when I was in college. He died a few years later, so I was told.

To remember Cousin Alex is to remember the good times in Drakes. The bearer of stories around town, and with me, the teller of stories from his younger years. Today I have friends who have suffered hard times of unemployment, and illness, and other setbacks in their lives. But I think of Cousin Alex and all he lost in the Depression. Yet he lived a long life, he contributed, he overcame, and lived, I believe, a successful life. He let me play jokes on him. I think that says a lot for the human spirit.

In addition to my fifth grade classes at Organ Hill, there were also the sixth and seventh grades that shared the same room. There were few disciplinary problems. Two classes were given seatwork, while the teacher worked with the third class. Our good behavior may also have been due to the fact that Reverend Venable was an extremely stern disciplinarian. He was also a very big man with an equally big voice. There was no talking not even to your partner who sat next to you on the bench.

I never heard of a paper airplane or spitball until I began teaching years later. My classmates and I had only seen airplanes in books, so it would have probably been difficult for the boys to design one that would fly. No airplanes ever flew over Drakes.

Our core subjects were reading, writing, and arithmetic. We learned the three subjects well. My two years in the Catholic school in Brooklyn put me ahead of many of the other students, especially in reading and writing. Reverend Venable also taught us history. We had to memorize a lot of dates and places.

A favorite classroom activity was a spelling bee involving all three classes. I never could spell very well, so I never won the spelling bee. I covered up my lack of spelling skills by writing illegibly. This even worked in college and graduate school. Reading was my favorite subject, and even back then, arithmetic was my least favorite subject. I got through high school algebra only because I was one of the teacher's favorite students. My algebra teacher took pity on me. He hoped and prayed that there would never be a day when I would need algebra. I never understood the relationship of numbers being expressed and analyzed in terms of letters and abstract symbols. I wish I could remember that teacher's name. I am glad I have been able to get through life without algebra. I usually do not substitute in mathematics; however, a couple of years ago Marilyn Coates, in charge of substitutes at Oakton High School, asked me to take a calculus class.

"Remember, I don't do math!"

"You won't have to do any math. All you have to do is give an exam."

The teacher left me explicit directions. At the top of her plans she stated, "No calculators!" Each student who walked into the room sat in his assigned seat, and put all notes and books away except for his or her calculator. The teacher had instructed me to place cardboard boxes between each student. The calculators were placed in the middle of each desk.

"Put your calculators away, please!"

"We are allowed to use our calculators!" they all responded in unison.

"Well, today you won't be using your calculator!"

Not only had the teacher written this directive on her plans, she had also written in bold type— "No calculator" on each copy of the tests. I also stated at the beginning of class that I knew nothing about calculus or math in general, so I could not answer questions concerning the test. One student piped up and said, "But I'll ask you in French." "I won't know the terminology to explain whatever you want to know—meaning I don't know calculus in any language." I answered.

The other day, out of the blue, a student in Claire Knight's class asked if I were a *test proctor*. I responded, "No, I just know how to give tests."

All the classes at Organ Hill took recess together. There was one recess in the morning, one hour for lunch, and another thirty minutes break in the afternoon. A bathroom break meant that you had to go to the toilets, one for boys and one for girls, at the edge of the woods behind the school. No one dared to ask for a bathroom break during class. "If you did not have to go to the toilet during break, then you can wait until the next break." The teacher would ring a bell to come in at the end of recess. We would all scuffle to take our place in line. This meant fifth grade at the front, then sixth grade, and last, seventh grade. Our place in line represented the seating arrangement in the classroom. I guess that is why, even today, I have a thing for seating charts. There was absolutely no excuse for being late for class. If you were, there would be the wrath of Reverend Venable.

There was no grass around the school. A large area of sandy red clay surrounded Organ Hill. Our games during recess were typical of the time—*Ring Around the Roses, The Farmer in the Dell, Blind Man's Bluff, Hopscotch, Dodge Ball, Marbles, and Jump Rope*, and the dangerous game called *Crack the Whip*. *Crack the Whip* involved a group of girls and boys joining hands and forming a rope-like line. The person at the end of the line would gradually build up momentum starting with a slow trot and building up to enormous speed resulting in people losing their grip and being thrown to the wind. There were also a couple of swings hanging from the tree in the school's front yard. I stayed away from the swings because the boys would do the pushing. While pushing the girls, they would touch them inappropriately, while other boys would stand around and watch as their dresses flew up in the wind. We didn't know about sexual harassment back then.

My friends and I would often find a corner where we would play hopscotch or marbles. For the game of marbles we would dig three holes about fifteen or twenty inches a part. The object of the game was to make all three holes. The person who finished first would win the marbles of the other players. The player with the widest and longest hand span would have an advantage because the shot is started from the end of your hand span. My fingers were not big but were longer than the other players. People used to tell Mama that I had the fingers of a pianist. I may have had the fingers, but I did not have the talent. When I went off to college I left behind both my collection of marbles and my collection of comic books

When I was in seventh grade a basketball court was added to the backyard of the school. "Added" isn't really the right word. Two basketball goals were put up at the ends of a court designed on the sandy dirt by Reverend Venable. After teaching the rules of the game, the Reverend pretty much left the playing to us. The biggest and bossiest girls in the class would choose the two teams and would act as coach and player. According to the old rules of women's basketball, guards would play on one end of the evenly divided court and the forwards on the other. There was no referee except for the girl in charge. The captain of each team kept score.

I always played the guard position, as I was one of the tallest girls. The boys and the girls took turns using the basketball court. When we were not playing basketball we returned to our old game of softball on a grassy field next to the school. The hard ball could be dangerous. I sprained my index finger trying to catch a ground ball.

After seventh grade at Organ Hill, we went on to Central High School. From 1939 until desegregation in 1969, Central was Charlotte County's black high school. The adjoining county, Prince Edward, closed the public schools rather than integrate. The white students went to private school and the blacks had no school. When I came to Fairfax County in 1959, there were a number of students from Prince Edward County living with family and attending Luther Jackson Intermediate and High School. After integration Central High School became a middle school until the early nineties. Today it is an early childhood development center.

In 1997, a group of concerned black citizens of the county organized and began plans for a museum. At the present time, the museum is housed in the old Central High Library. The purpose is to highlight major contributions by blacks in Charlotte County, particularly the contributions of former students and graduates of Central High. The room is filled with, among other things, championship trophies, yearbooks, and items made in art class.

Much of the memorabilia had disappeared when the school integrated. Helen W. Dennis, a former student of Central, stopped at a gas station in Richmond, Virginia. She saw a man wearing an old Central High band jacket. She offered to buy it from him for twenty-five dollars. He took off his jacket and handed it to her as a gift. My class picture of 1954 is in a display case on the right as one enters the room. I never thought our class picture would be found in a museum. I am proud that my county did not choose to close the public schools rather than integrate, though some of the white parents did decide to establish a private academy. Some whites were more open-minded than I thought.

Many of the extracurricular activities at Central High took place during school hours. Among these activities was the annual talent show. The outstanding performer from my class was Inez Braxton, who would do her dramatic reciting of Paul Lawrence Dunbar's narrative poem, *When Melindy Sings*. The only competitive sport was basketball. Sometimes I would catch a ride to the games with Myrtle and Frances Watkins. Their boyfriends would let Elaine and me tag along. On other occasions, my cousins Octavia and Ulysses would come by and take me to the games.

The biggest event of both elementary and high school was the May Day Festival, known back then as just plain *May Day*. There were folk dances, games, and food. Every student in the school had some part in the activities. The finale was the wrapping of the Maypole and choosing the queen from among the girls on the court. The pole was twelve to fifteen feet tall. Twenty to twenty-five strips of crepe paper of various colors were attached to the top of the pole. The children selected to wrap the pole practiced for days. The objective was to completely cover the pole while performing an intricate dance pattern to music. When the dance was finished the pole was completely decorated from top to bottom in a beautiful and intricate pattern.

The May Day queen was always the girl with the lightest complexion and the "good" hair. In the black community there was a distinction made between light and dark-skinned Negroes. Light-skinned students were given more privileges when it came to special activities. The one exception was the annual talent show. No exception could be made for special aptitude or ability. My neighbors and friends, Carol Jeanne Cousins, Joyce Ellis, and Anne Gilmore performed a dance routine that would rival the Jackson Five. At all assembly programs and sports events we sang the Negro National Anthem *Lift Every Voice and Sing* by James Weldon Johnson.

I had a part in the senior play. I was all dressed up in a gray dress that I had ordered from *National Bella Hess Catalogs*, and white high-heeled shoes that had been given to me by one of the ladies Mama worked for. I can't remember the title or the part I played except that it was a teacher or some other professional. I do remember my English teacher, Miss McCray, who was also in charge of dramatic performances, telling me in rehearsal to speak louder.

I have always had a problem with speaking on stage—before I went out to do my student teaching. (That's what they called it back then.) The professor in charge of student teachers at Bennett sent me to the drama teacher, so that she could give me a lesson in projecting my voice. I still have a problem speaking in public, but no problem relating to students in the classroom. I guess I am still a child at heart.

I went to the Junior-Senior Prom with Theodora Dusenburg's oldest brother, Gerald. My friends Theodora, Clara, and Dorothy set it up. Gerald was like a big brother, but he could have at least pretended that he was my date. I knew Gerald was too cheap to buy me a corsage so I made a pink corsage out of two or three roses from Mama's garden. I not only had to worry about the straight pins but the thorns as well. To the corsage I added a dash of "Evening in Paris" perfume. My sister Eliza Etta sent me all the way from New York a beautiful blue lacey prom dress with a lace stole to match, and silver wedge-heeled shoes. I went to Miss Taylor's beauty shop, the only one in town, for a new hairdo.

The one nice thing Gerald did do was to take me by his house on the way to the prom to show his parents and his sisters how beautiful I looked. I know they had demanded that Gerald do this, because they all rushed over to the car as we drove up to the house.

Once we arrived at the prom in the school gymnasium, we sat side by side in the chairs reserved for the wallflowers. Gerald was either too shy or felt he had been forced to take me to the prom because his sister was my best friend. I had to ask him for my only dance. This was the first time I had ever danced with a boy. This was my first date! Theodora went to the prom with Clara and Dorothy's older brother, Alec. Clara and Dorothy did not attend the prom. There were no more brothers left. Either Clara or Dorothy could have had Gerald, but one sister would not have gone without the other, so Gerald was given to me.

When I returned home at the appointed time—that is, before midnight, Mama asked, "How was the prom?"

I replied, "It was wonderful!" It really was.

I didn't go to the prom my senior year and neither did Theodora, Clara, and Dorothy. Gerald had moved to New York, and neither of the boys I had a crush on asked me—not even Louis Gregory. Our senior year, after lunch, we would take a walk around the school. Louis helped his father clean the white school in front of our house. He had heard me yelling at Miss Mable and thought it was really funny. Harold Johns and I had exchanged Christmas gifts. He had jokingly said that he was going to give me a Christmas present. I can't remember the circumstances in which he made the remark, but I thought he was serious. On the day before Christmas break, I gave him his Christmas gift. I think it was a tie. Stupid me! I should have waited to see if he were really going to give me a gift. He didn't have a gift for me, but sent me one through the mail during Christmas break. What a gentleman!

Louis and Harold were never real boyfriends, but boys who were my friends. I was sure one of the two would ask me to the senior prom, especially Louis. My prom gown and shoes didn't go to waste though. I lent them to another friend, Edith Gilmore. Her big brother was Curtis, the same Curtis that George Robert hit over the head with my lunch box. Edith returned the dress in excellent condition. I took it to college where I wore it to formal parties and dances during the next four years at Bennett College.

Lunch boxes and prom dresses. Two worlds. A world of innocence and simple joys, and a world of adolescent sophistication, mistaken for the real thing, and a first high-heeled step into the world.

I still think back to that day George Robert hit Curtis over the head with my lunch box. It draws a smile from me as I savor the gallantry of it. And what girl does not remember the prom, whether she went or didn't? The exquisite pain of adolescence. For some girls, a dance on a crowded excited floor. For others, of whom there are many, dances occupying their reveries on quiet and perhaps lonely nights.

Before the beginning of my senior year in high school, my mother once more went to live in Brooklyn, New York. I was left home alone. She wanted to earn more money than she could in Drakes. She wanted me to get through high school without a lot of financial worries. Money was needed for a class ring, senior dues, and an outfit for baccalaureate, college application fees, and my senior class trips.

Our big trip was an opportunity to visit the Agricultural and Technical College (A & T College) in Greensboro, North Carolina. I have no idea why this particular school was chosen. I did not ask why and neither did anyone else in class. Not a single person in my class applied to A & T. I suppose the college had invited us down for senior day, and Mrs. Binford took the offer. We wanted to take a trip out of the state and we didn't care why, when or where. I surely wasn't interested in either agriculture or technical studies.

The day's journey to Greensboro required that I would have to meet the bus in the center of town at six. My three friends and I dressed alike—white athletic sweaters, white blouses, and navy blue skirts. None of us had earned a letter in sports, but athletic sweaters could be ordered from a variety of catalogues. A & T is located a few blocks from Bennett College, the school I was to attend in the fall. I only saw the school from a distance.

We spent the morning visiting A & T's campus and attending lectures concerning the courses the school offered. As I look back I don't understand why I wasted my time attending these activities, including a football game in the afternoon. I didn't even like or understand football. I still don't understand the game very well. I could have simply sneaked over to Bennett and learned something about that college and its programs. On the other hand, I guess I didn't want to get into big trouble with the chaperons. I was grateful just being on a college campus, any college campus.

The last day of May we took a special trip to Prince Edward County Regional Park. The park had a beautiful lake, several picnic areas, and a small amusement park. It was the last time that all members of the class of 1954 would be together. All, especially the class clown, had a great time. We had all boarded the bus for the twenty-mile trip back to school.

The class clown yelled out, "We have left MANY!"

"Minnie who?" We all responded.

"Many people!" He replied.

I graduated second in my high school class. A new student moved from the north and joined our senior year. This student (I can't remember her name) was valedictorian and I was salutatorian. Harold Johns was ranked third. At commencement I gave my first oration. I don't remember the title or the subject of the speech. Perhaps it was because the principal was the speechwriter. A couple of weeks before graduation, he would have us practice in his office.

What I remember most about that evening was that I could not find the collar to attach to my robe. Mrs. Binford had instructed the speakers to bring their collars back to school for safekeeping after we had washed, starched, and ironed them. On the night of graduation someone took my perfectly ironed and starched collar even though I had my name attached. I searched frantically for it but to no avail. I went on stage without my collar, but with a soiled one that Mrs. Binford found for me. I remembered every word of my speech, and was told that I performed superbly. I just pretended only Mama and my father were in the audience. Mama, along with my little niece Johnnie, came down for commencement activities a few days earlier.

Mama got a job in Cedar Hurst, Long Island, working for Mr. and Mrs. Greenfield. I spent the evening and nights with the neighbors, Mr. and Mrs. Samuel Cousins. Mr. Cousins was the owner of Cousins's Tailoring in town. During rainy or bad weather Mr. Cousins would take Carol Jean and me to the bus stop. Sometimes we messed around in the morning and missed the bus. One morning, just as Mr. Cousins rounded the corner, we glimpsed the back of the bus. Mr. Cousins made a quick turn and my door flew open. He came to a screeching halt and never caught up with the bus. Luckily for me I was sitting in the middle of the seat. Carol Jeanne and I both arrived safely at school, in spite of Mr. Cousins's erratic driving.

After getting off the school bus in the afternoon. I would go home and prepare my own dinner, which usually consisted of something from a can, like Spam or Vienna sausage, and a vegetable. My favorite desert was vanilla ice cream, but I couldn't have that. There was no freezer. Anyway, someone once told me that anyone who likes only vanilla ice cream has no imagination. Now that I am in my sixties, vanilla ice cream is the only dessert my stomach can take. That's truly poetic justice.

My dog Lucky always returned home after I left Mrs. Cousins for school, so I would have to feed Lucky in the afternoon rather than in morning. For breakfast, I would keep a stash of grapefruit sections in Mrs. Cousins's refrigerator. School lunch provided me with a good home-cooked meal each day. The cafeteria staff actually cooked our school lunch of fresh meat, a starch, a vegetable, and a dessert each day. The price was twenty-five cents. There were no free breakfasts or free lunches.

Central High School was a modern school with electricity and central heating. There was no electricity in my home, because our land was land-locked. Our neighbor, that is the person I considered to be a neighbor, would not permit the county power company to put a post on her land that would bring electricity to our house. So much for good neighbors! Mama was wondering why the power company was taking so long to bring power to us. When she inquired, she got her answer.

I don't think Mama ever said anything to Miss Mable. Nevertheless, one day I called Miss Mable out of her house. As she stood on her porch and I on the path leading to our house, I screamed at her. I told her how mean and selfish I thought she was. She yelled back, telling me how I should have been black like my father. She accused me of putting bleaching cream on my skin. That wasn't true. She was wrong about that. I didn't even know what bleaching cream was. Maybe it was what Michael Jackson, the King of Pop, uses.

I am glad I had no idea what she was talking about. I don't understand why Miss Mable was obsessed with color. She was light-skinned, but her husband was blacker than me. She had one light-skinned daughter and one dark-skinned daughter, whose complexion was also as dark as mine. Augustus, whom everyone called Gussie, the light-skinned one, went to St. Paul's

College and became a Home Economics teacher. Bethel, the dark skinned one, completed high school but did not go to college. She was just as intelligent as Gussie. Bethel's lifetime job was doing domestic work for a white family who lived in the neighborhood.

When I was a senior in high school, Gussie taught me Home Economics. I called her Miss Moseley, and she treated me like the rest of her students. She wasn't vengeful like her mother. She gave me the grade I deserved, even though I had yelled at her mother a few months before. A child should never yell at an adult! I never told my mother of the incident, and neither did Miss Mable.

Back then, there were a number of advantages to being a light skinned Negro, or "yeller," as they were called. Most of the college presidents could pass for white. Most of the black teachers and principals in the Fairfax County School system used to be fair-skinned. It was only in the sixties that black skin became beautiful, and it was fashionable to have kinky hair. Kinky or coarse hair, not "good hair," made the best Afros.

I would order dresses, coats, sweaters, undergarments, and shoes without Mama's knowledge. My favorite outfit was a pink sweater set and a grey poodle skirt. This was the rage of the 50's. When a notice of a C. O. D. (Cash on Delivery) in the post office was placed in our mailbox, Mama would always say, "I am not getting that package out!" She would wait until the very last day and at the very last minute, and she would pay for whatever I had ordered. Not once did she let even one of my packages be returned, and she never stopped yelling at me and telling me not to order anything else.

I was one of the best-dressed girls at Central High. I was a pretty good seamstress even before taking Home Economics in high school. My talent was sewing and designing clothes without a pattern. I made clothes in high school, in the summers before college, and before returning to my teaching assignment. Later, when I was married with children, I made identical outfits for Nikki and Pauly.

Gussie taught me the cooking unit in my senior year. The year before, another teacher taught the sewing portion. I sewed much better than Mama. I used to make a lot of gathered skirts without a pattern. When I was required to use a pattern in my Home Economics class, Mama asked Miss Lucy to take her to Farmville, so she could buy all my sewing needs—the pattern, material and thread. Mama searched until she found a pattern much like the skirts that I made. The pattern required that the skirt be cut into three panels with three folds toward the bottom. The three panels would be gathered evenly around the waistband. Without my telling her, Mama knew a straight skirt would not be acceptable. Back then I was known as Skinny Minnie. It must have taken her hours to find this perfect pattern. The fabric Mama chose had both vertical and horizontal stripes, meaning I had to match the panels. The three yards of material she bought didn't allow for the matching. As a result, the skirt was shorter than it should have been. Mama just wasn't perfect!

Nevertheless, I used the same pattern all through college. I used it for my first day of teaching in South Carolina. I made a brown skirt with a brown cummerbund. I wore this skirt with a yellow ruffled blouse. All of the clothes I made in high school were done on the old treadle machine. Mama always called it my machine, and I don't recall her ever using it. This Singer sewing machine was another treasure I lost when we left Drakes.

I wondered for a long time what happened to all the furniture and things we left in our home. Years later, my brother Gilbert told me that Uncle Flood went in and took all the furnishings and sold them. All I have left is an antique lamp. It is a gladiator on a chariot pulling a large lighted globe. It is an electric lamp that Mama traded with Mrs. Paulette for a set of antique chairs, when she had thought we would be getting electricity. I managed to keep this lamp with me over the years. It now sits in my picture window.

During my senior year in high school, while Mama was in Brooklyn and I was beating a path through the woods that separated the Cousins's house from mine, I even managed not to be scared out of my wits when I saw a couple of black snakes draped around the branches of a plum tree like a Christmas garland. Homework that was not completed at school during study hall was finished at Miss Cousins's.

I shared a room with Carol Jeanne who was four years younger than I. She was like my little sister, and I was her big sister. We shared both the room and the bed. I considered her mother, Ethel, my friend. Ethel loved Mama. She was also good at killing snakes.

Several years before, when I returned from school, Mama had an exciting story to tell. She and Ethel had been on the porch. Jackie, my little niece, was in her playpen. A big moccasin came onto the porch from a hole leading to the flooring under the little room. Ethel, who was several months pregnant with Bill, grabbed the hoe and killed it. Mama said the snake probably came out in search of the milk it smelled on the baby. She had just gotten up from the chair, which was close to the hole. Mama said God was at work that day, and she also hoped that the snake would not mark the baby. It was an old wives' tale that an unborn baby could bear the marking of a horrific event. Bill was born perfectly normal.

Ethel was the Cousins's daughter-in-law. She had always lived with her in-laws. The town gossip was that the son, William, or Bill as he was called, had been forced to marry Ethel. Ethel's father had killed her mother and was now out of prison. It was marriage or death.

Bill chose to live. He married Ethel, but he never lived with her. Nor did he ever visit his wife and daughter. Ethel was a beautiful girl, light-skinned with "good" hair. It appeared that Ethel had three sons by different men. The first son, Bill, was said to be the son of her father-in-law. He did have an uncanny resemblance to his grandfather, but Bill also looked like his father. Later, Ethel supposedly had a second son by a young man who came to work on the construction of the textile mill in Drakes. Much later, she had a third son by a man I knew. I can't recall his name. This, I learned by listening to the conversations of grown-ups. Gossip is never reliable. These stories may or may not have been true. In any case, she always remained with her in-laws. They were a happy family. Ethel has always been my friend. I lost my little friend, Carol Jeanne. She died of cancer in 1996.

Clara and Dorothy both moved to Brooklyn after graduation. They lived with an aunt three or four blocks from my sister Eliza Etta. Theodora moved in with family in upstate New York. It was many years before I saw her again. I was the only one among the four of us who went to college. My mother and I had never discussed my going to college or what I planned to do with my life. I used to say I was going to be a policeman or a nurse when I grew up. I never knew a policeman, and I had never seen a policewoman. Cousin Geneva was a registered nurse.

Nevertheless, Mama just took it for granted that I would be going to college, and so did I. I never thought of the responsibility she placed on me at seventeen. I was living completely alone except for spending the nights at the Cousins's. It was my responsibility to budget the five dollar weekly allowance. From this money I had to buy my school lunch, food, and all other necessities. I could no longer order C.O.D. from the *National Bella Hess Catalogues*. Mama wasn't there, but she knew I would be on my best behavior at all times. Best of all, she never knew I yelled at Miss Mable.

My favorite subjects were French and English, and in that order. I now had the school library where I could check out books. I won an award for reading the most books. The prize was a copy of Louisa May Alcott's *Little Men*, the sequel to *Little Women* that I had read earlier.

My French teacher, Miss Triplett, was the reason I decided to major in French. She knew that I loved French, and that someday I would come to love France and the French people as she did. She emphasized the beauty of the French language and the fact that it was the language of many black people and the United Nations.

The textbook we used back then emphasized only the language and culture of France and never the French-speaking world. Recently, Fairfax County adopted a textbook that is multicultural, emphasizing all areas of the world where French is spoken. The textbook *Allez, Viens!* offers students the possibility of learning the French language as spoken by people in Europe, Africa, Asia, Haiti, and South America and around the world. The year after this textbook was adopted, my friend Norma Farbes, an art teacher with whom I worked at Luther Jackson, related this story.

A parent called Langston Hughes, where she now works. The parent complained that this French-speaking teacher from Africa was spending too much time teaching French as it relates to the French-speaking areas of Africa. The year it was adopted, I had the pleasure of using this text for a few weeks during a long term subbing job. The first chapter is entitled *Bienvenue Dans le Monde Francophone!—Welcome to the French Speaking World!* Evidently, this parent had not examined his child's textbook. His child simply had told him that her teacher was from Africa.

I believe it was just plain old-fashioned prejudice raising its ugly head once more in Fairfax County. I have thought for a long time that white Americans believed that blacks could not learn a foreign language unless they were born in a French-speaking country. This parent believed that blacks couldn't speak or write a foreign language even if she were born in a French-speaking country.

On numerous occasions white Americans, learning that I am a French teacher and that I speak French, will ask, "Where did you learn to speak French?" They are oblivious to the fact one studies or majors in French at a college or university just as one does in mathematics, history, sciences, English, or any other course that is a part of an elementary or secondary school curriculum. This just can't be a matter of ignorance. Would one ask a biology teacher, "Where did you learn biology?"

The French never ask how I learned French. They ask instead, "*D'où venez-vous?*" (Where are you from?) . French may be spoken slightly differently, depending on the area of the world. However, I have never had a problem understanding, or being understood by, people from different regions of France, former colonies of any part of the world where French is the official language.

Prejudice is alive and well in Fairfax County. Children come into this world completely innocent—without prejudices or preconceived notions. We adults should follow the lead of our children. I recall an incident in the 1970s. A parent approached me at the end of *Back-to-School Night*. "Susan never told me you were black!" How was I supposed to respond to this comment? I didn't! I just gave this parent my dumb look.

I once did a long-term substituting job at my old school, Luther Jackson. I worked during the teachers' in-service week, so I decorated the trailer like a French café and put up lots of French posters and pictures just as I did when I was really teaching. I even had on the wall a T-shirt from *France: Champion du Monde*—France's 1998 victory over Brazil 3-0. I welcomed the new students to school on visitation day. I began the first day of school like I used to. I did not greet the students by telling them, "I am substituting for your real teacher, Madame Cercone." Instead, I explained, when we begin learning French greetings, it is not necessary to use my last name. I never said what my last name was. I said simply, "*Bonjour, Madame!*" or "*Au revoir, Madame!*" would suffice. The name *Cercone* was listed on their class registration card. However, at Back-to-School-Night, a parent, whose child had had Madame Cercone as her IFL (Introduction to Foreign Language) teacher the year before, did not think I was Madame Cercone. She went to the Guidance Office to ask what was going on. I wasn't the Madame Cercone that she remembered. Laura Reed, the child counselor, responded, "You are absolutely right!" Her daughter had never mentioned that I was black after three or four weeks with me as her French teacher.

Neither did I mention my name to the parents at Back-to-School-Night. My students were surprised when I told them I was leaving at the end of the first quarter. Unfortunately, Madame Cercone's illness returned later during the school year. I again became their teacher for the last quarter. I taught many of the students from that 1998-1999 school year at Oakton High School. Many had four or five years of French, and they always greeted me with, *"Bonjour, Madame! Ça va?"*

The French never come up to Nikki or me and begin speaking English. They take it for granted if we are walking the streets of a French city or town, then we should speak their language. I often ask my students, "If you were walking down the street in the District of Columbia, would you not think it strange, or even be offended, if a French tourist walked up to you and asked, *"Où est la Maison Blanche?"* or *"Où est le Métro?"*

I have heard an "ugly American" yell louder and louder in English to a waitress in a hotel dining room, believing that yelling would make her understand English. The waitress spoke no English! I fully understand why the French will pretend they don't understand English even if they do. The French are no more rude than we Americans.

A few summers ago Nikki and I were going to show our friend Ayanna McFail (Yanni) the Monmartre district and the gleaming white basilica called Sacré Coeur. Within Monmartre are two famous centers of nightlife, the Place du Tertre and the Place Pigalle. Before meeting our friend Charletta for dinner, we had to show Yanni the famous *Moulin Rouge* nightclub.

Much of Monmartre is also a red-light district. I am known as a fast walker. As I walked several steps ahead of Nikki and Yanni, I was stopped and propositioned by a young man. *"Allez au fer!"* (Go to Hell!), I responded.

I never saw a Moulin Rouge extravaganza until 2002. Our tour director, Frederic, got the very expensive tickets for Nikki and me. The seats were excellent and the price of the tickets included a bottle of champagne. One can also have dinner at added expense, but Nikki and I chose the later performance. We had a less expensive dinner in the Montmartre area before attending the performance.

We shared a table with two Parisian couples. It was their first time at Moulin Rouge as well. The gentleman sitting next to me asked if he could smoke. My answer was, *"NON!"* Later, I changed my mind and said it was okay, even though it was not. His response to my question about smoking and cancer was that the French physiology was different from that of Americans. He moved to the end of the rectangular table and lit up. His reaction to my comment about smoking was the complete opposite of a fellow American traveler. When I told Joe that I did mind if he smoked after his asking, he lit up anyway, so I decided to be rude as well. I began talking to Thierry in French about him and his partner, John. Thierry is Nikki's and my favorite tour director. When Nikki caught up at the Moulin Rouge, she asked, "What was that all about?"

"I don't know if I should have been flattered or offended. In any case, I should have given the nasty man a swift kick in the pants."

"Exactly what did he say?"

"You are too young to know. And I am too old to tell you."

The Moulin Rouge, which is built around an ancient windmill, was founded in 1889, the same year the Eiffel Tower was built. Its shows are still sell-outs. The ushers have unique methods of getting a large crowd inside within a matter of minutes, and I got in even faster when Nikki pointed to my booted broken foot. I wasn't able to figure out how the ushers were able to move so many people in and out of such a small and congested club.

The Moulin Rouge is a theater of the "*risqué*" with the women bare breasted and dressed in ostrich plumes and rhinestones. They still dance the can-can at least once. Toulouse-Lautrec, the artist, often frequented the club.

A rival of the Moulin Rouge was the *Folies Bergère Music Hall*, which also featured high-kicking and semi-nude women. It was located further down the hill. It opened in 1868, but closed in recent years. I attended a performance there in 1962, standing room only. The show was basically the same as the one at the Moulin Rouge, however, I think the women were even more nude. While standing in the back of the theater, I was constantly moving out of the way of a strange character that kept inching closer and closer to me. There are perverts in France as well as at home in the U.S. I don't recall anyone smoking in my vicinity at the *Folies Bergère*.

On another occasion I had a run-in with an artist at the Place du Tertre, the square for budding artists that is also located on the hill of Montmartre. I agreed that one of the artists would paint a portrait of Nikki. When he had finished, he handed the portrait to me.

"*Ce n'est pas ma fille!*"

He insisted that I buy it anyway. "*C'est le talent!*" ("You have no right to criticize my talent!") After a few minutes of our arguing back and forth, I walked away without buying the painting of the girl I did not recognize. Before leaving the Place de Tertre, I bought Nikki a still-life painting by H. Simpson from the studio (now an art gallery) where many of the famous impressionists worked. Maybe H. Simpson will be famous one day.

There were two other places we would have loved to show Yanni, not only from the outside but the inside as well—*La Comédie Française* and *L'Opéra*. The big, classically ornate Paris Opera House is the setting for *The Phantom of the Opera* and where Nikki and I saw the ballet, *Swan Lake*. Yanni had to be satisfied with just seeing the outside of this famous Paris landmark, and shopping at *La Gallerie Lafayette*, within a short walk of the opera house. The *Comédie Française* is the theatre where Molière's plays were, and still are, performed. Molière is considered the world's greatest writer of comedies. He died while he was playing the leading part in his play *L'Invalide Imaginaire* (The Imagined Invalid). His comedies ridicule the weaknesses and foolish actions of the people of his time.

His plays are still read and produced today. My favorite is *Tartuffe* (The Hypocrite). It is the play I had a part in at Bennett College. I also had an opportunity to take some of my students to a performance of the play at Georgetown University during the sixties. They could all fit in my little Corvair. It just happened to be playing the summer Nikki and I were in Paris.

There is a new Paris Opera house in the Marais section of Paris. Many Parisians detest this ultra modern *Opéra de Paris Bastille*. But then they also hated *La Tour Eiffel*. We took Yanni to the new opera house to visit the gift shops that are open during regular business hours. The summer we spent in Marie Jo's apartment provided us with the opportunity to attend many performances that we have no time to attend when traveling with our favorite guide from *Go Ahead Vacations*.

Miss Triplett sparked my interest in France and her language. The class of 1954 consisted of fewer than fifty students, yet the majority of us took the only foreign language offered. We were successful in completing the two-year course. We could not choose Spanish because the guidance counselor said Spanish was easier. There was no guidance counselor. There were no Spanish courses. I advise black students that they should take French because there are hordes of people of color who speak French, as opposed to those who speak Spanish, aside from the native speakers. Our teachers and parents were there to guide us, and what good guidance counselors they were.

The first novel I read entirely in French was Jules Verne's *Around the World in Eighty Days*. My favorite character was not the main character, Mr. Fogg, but his sidekick Passepartout. The word *passepartout* means passkey. He was able to get out of every difficult situation. Miss Triplet would have me stand in front of the room, read aloud, and translate many parts of the novel. Reading about the adventures of Mr. Fogg and Passepartout and the places they visited by train, hot air balloons, and just about every mode of transportation that one can think of, caused me to dream of places far beyond my little town of Drakes. I have yet to set foot on the continents of Antarctica and Australia, but I have taken a rickety boat down the Nile without a life jacket to visit the land of the Nubians, gone whale watching in the Pacific Ocean, and glided over an alligator infested swamp while hot air ballooning in Puerto Vallarta, Mexico. There are still lots of places and things to experience before I am in real competition with Mr. Fogg and Passepartout.

I was also in Mrs. Triplet's home room, and at the end of each six-week period she would proudly place on her blackboard in bold letters-*Honor Roll: Fannie Miles*. I wasn't teased about making the honor roll. Back then, all the students at Central High thought it was a good thing to make the honor roll.

Many years later I was successful in writing and receiving a grant from the *Washington Post* to aid in recruiting black students in Fairfax County into the foreign language program. Students in Fairfax are able to take four or five years of a single foreign language. They may choose from Latin, Chinese, Spanish, German, Japanese, American Sign Language, Korean and of course French. Additionally, there are advanced placement (AP) classes. How much better prepared would I have been for a college major in French if these courses had been available at Central High! We did not need an incentive to learn required courses or to take an elective like French. We took advantage of all that Central had to offer. All students took the same courses, except girls took home economics and boys took agriculture. The best academic students went off to college, found a job in Charlotte County, or a neighboring county, or went North like my best friends Dorothy, Clara, and Theodora. When I return for class reunions, most members of the class of 1954 are there. They are all successful people.

Those who could not make it in school dropped out after reaching sixteen years of age. One of my friends, Edith Gilmore, had a brother who was slightly older than she. In fact, Louis and I are the same age. Louis Gilmore did not get beyond third grade. When Edith left Organ Hill for high school, Louis had to drop out. There was no one to care for Louis. The story that George Robert told was that he was not "right in the head," because one of his brothers had caught his head in a door. I believed that story when I was little, but not any more. Perhaps Curt the mischievous one did mistreat Louis, but he did not cause Louis's problem. He was born that way, but the family did not realize that there was anything wrong until a few years after he was born.

Louis was the sweetest boy I had ever known. He was extremely fond of Mama. He would come to visit her often—all by himself. She always treated him as if he were just another one of the neighborhood children. One of his favorite questions for her was, "Miss Jannie, is there really a man in the moon?" Mama would explain that "The Man in the Moon" was just a fairy tale from many different countries, including tales from Africa. People in Drakes associated death or something bad happening with a full moon. If a dog howled during a full moon, someone was going to die, particularly a family member.

There was also the Mother Goose nursery rhyme that Louis was familiar with:

The Man in the Moon looked out of the Moon,

Looked out of the Moon and said,
Tis time for all children on the Earth,
To think about getting to bed!

No matter how often Louis would ask the question, "Is there really, really a man in the moon?" Mama would patiently give the same detailed explanation.

Louis was also the most courteous person I have ever met. He was, and still remains, the epitome of innocence. I last saw Louis in 2004. He was just the same. He had no difficulty recognizing me when he opened the door for Paul and me. Just as his older brother Tommy yelled out, "Are they Jehovah's Witnesses?" Louis exclaimed, "Fannie Lillian!" His conversation was still sprinkled with, "Thank you!" and, "You are welcome!"

He wanted to know where Miss Jannie was. Sadly, I had to tell him that she had passed on to a better place. He called me "Fannie Lillian" clearly and precisely, just as I remembered. I was a little taken a back by his also answering me with, "Yes, Ma'am!" It's a pity there were no special education classes for Louis.

A few years ago, a young Spanish teacher, Lieu Ha, came to Luther Jackson. She had taught Spanish at Central High, then Central Middle School. Back then, it was inconceivable that blacks and whites would be going to the same school. It was even more inconceivable that a Vietnamese-American would be teaching in Charlotte County. Growing up, I had never seen someone from another ethnic group in Drakes. There were only blacks and whites. People used to talk of Gypsies jumping off the freight train as it passed through town. I never saw a Gypsy except at carnivals. I only saw tramps or hobos around Drakes. They were all white men. They would come by the houses where Mama worked, asking for odd jobs.

When I taught at Luther Jackson Intermediate and High School before integration, there was no shortage of black students in both the French and Spanish classes. There were language classes filled with black students. There were advanced levels four and five. There were also a band, a choir, a National Honor Society, a French Club (*Le Cercle Français*), and many other extracurricular activities. There were all-black casts for the junior and senior plays. Each year the French and Spanish Departments were required to put on an assembly program. There were French plays performed for the entire student body. Students would recite the Lord's Prayer and the Pledge of Allegiance in French and Spanish—not that the pledge made sense in French or Spanish.

When I was growing up in my little town, we said the pledge every morning during devotion at both Organ Hill and Central High. In 1892, Francis Bellamy (No relation to Paul that I know of) and James Upham, publishers of *The Youth Companion*, asked President Benjamin Harris to commemorate the four hundredth anniversary of the voyage of Christopher

Columbus by proclaiming Columbus Day a national holiday. It was on this day that the tradition of schools reciting a salute to the United States began. Francis Bellamy's original words were:

> *I pledge allegiance to my flag*
> *And to the Republic*
> *For which it stands,*
> *One nation indivisible—with*
> *Liberty and justice for all.*

In 1923, a group of World War I veterans began the tradition of placing the right hand over the heart. The following year, "my flag" was changed to "the flag of the United States of America." In 1954, Congress approved adding the words "under God" as Abraham Lincoln had spoken in the Gettysburg Address.

When I began teaching in South Carolina and Fairfax County, students were still saying the pledge each morning before the start of class. I can think of very few circumstances in which I or anyone else would say:

> *J'engage ma fidelité au drapeau*
> *Des Etats-Unis d'Amérique*
> *Et a la République qu'il répresente,*
> *Une nation sous Dieu,*
> *Indivisible, avec liberté*
> *Et justice pour tous.*

But at our annual foreign language program at Luther Jackson Intermediate and High School, students would say the pledge to the American flag in both French and Spanish.

In 1962, I and other Americans enrolled in summer courses organized by the Universities of Bordeaux and Toulouse, were asked to put on a program that represented our country's heritage. We said the pledge in English and sang Woody Guthrie's *This Land is Your Land.*

> *This land is your land, this land is my land*
> *From California, to the New York Island*
> *From the redwood forest, to the Gulf Stream waters*
> *This land was made for you and me.*

The French hold the same ideals as the United States—*Liberté, fraternité, et égalité.*

At one point in time, the tradition of saying the pledge in school ended, but was later revised in the 1990's. It is now a law that all students in the public schools of Virginia must begin the day with a moment of silence and the pledge. There is much controversy concerning the moment of silence and saying the pledge. Objections come from both parents and students. A teacher cannot force a student to say the pledge, but I tell my students that out of respect to fellow students they must stand. As for the moment of silence, they do not have to pray, but there may be others who would like to or maybe just contemplate. In each and every patriotic activity, I renew a solemn promise to the United States of America.

Life at Organ Hill and Central High was never boring. When Mama asked me, "How was school?" The answer was never, "I had a boring day." There wasn't a day that I did not want to go to school. I had my best friends Dorothy, Clara, and Theodora and great teachers like Miss Triplet, Mr. Einhorn, Mrs. Shiver, Miss McCray, and Mr. Roberts.

It was with Miss Triplet that my love affair with all that is French began. Mr. Einhorn turned me on to Shakespeare and England. Mrs. Shiver taught me typing and shorthand. I have found no way I might use shorthand, but typing permits me to use today's computers. My art teacher, whose name I can't remember, taught me to appreciate great works of art. My biology teacher, Mr. Roberts, taught me the little science and mathematics I know. Because of his effort and understanding, I came to terms with my lack of aptitude for the sciences, especially math. The higher sciences, such as chemistry and physics, were not taught.

Almost twenty years after graduating from Central High, I met Mildred Shiver at a cabaret at National Airport. Cabarets were popular during the fifties, sixties and seventies, especially among Blacks. They were dances that were usually held at hotels in Washington and later at hotels in the suburbs. There used to be a ballroom at National Airport that could be rented for social functions. Even Blacks could rent the room. If you were not dancing and having a good time, you could watch the airplanes take off and land.

I was a teacher in Fairfax County and Mildred was now an elementary teacher in Alexandria City Schools. Although I never used her shorthand, I am glad to know what it is. It is a part of the esoteric information my brain now holds, as opposed to the things I really should remember. I met Mildred several years later when we were both members of Alpha Kappa Alpha Sorority. At the present time we work together in a "Reading is Fundamental Program" (RIF). Mildred remembered that I was the little girl from Drakes who applied to Radcliff. Today, I can't believe I did that. I can't believe I did a lot of things back then.

I applied to three schools; Virginia State College in Petersburg, Bennett College in Greensboro, North Carolina, and Radcliffe in Cambridge, Massachusetts. I was accepted by each of these schools. Even though I received a full scholarship to Virginia State College, I chose to attend Bennett College, one of two predominately black women's colleges in the United

States. My daughter Nikki attended the other, Spelman College in Atlanta, Georgia.

I chose Bennett because it was one of the best liberal arts colleges in the U.S., and my major did not require that I take math. I also knew I would not have to compete with men, and I would be free to be me. Nikki also chose a women's college for the same reasons. Her reason for not applying to Bennett was because she did not want to compete with me. This wasn't a valid reason. Nikki and I are very different people. If we were not always together, no one would realize we were mother and daughter. We get along so well together because we are different.

I had no scholarship to attend Bennett, and getting through the first semester was a Herculean task. Even though Mama had gone to New York to work the year before, and with my working during the summer, we still did not come up with enough money for the first semester's tuition. Mrs. Greenfield would not give Mama an advance on her salary.

As a last resort, Mama called Mr. Canada, who owned Drakes' recently opened supermarket. She asked for his help. He agreed to lend Mama two hundred dollars to complete the approximate five hundred dollars we need-ed for me to begin college. Mama took the train from New York to Drakes to get the money. She didn't trust the mail, not even special delivery.

Mrs. Greenfield fired her because she had left without her permission. However, she hired her back soon after I left for college. By the end of my freshman year, Mama had paid the money back to Mr. Canada . He charged no interest. A white man from a little racist town in the south was responsi-ble for my going to Bennett in the fall of 1954. I never personally thanked Mr. Canada for what he did for Mama and me, and Mama has never asked me, "Why on earth didn't you take that scholarship?"

Mama and Eliza Etta presented me with a set of Gray hard-sided lug-gage. It was bought from a salesman who sold household goods on credit, or "on time," by going from door to door. A door-to-door salesman, he was called. Each week he would knock on each door of the approximately sixty apartments in our housing complex. The luggage was a big expense, but for my other college needs I used the money I had made to buy the things on the list Bennett College had sent me.

On the list of necessities were a black dress, a white dress, and a formal evening gown. I used the two-piece suit I had bought for Central High Baccalaureate. The formal gown and shoes, I already had. Most of my other outfits were from the clandestine C. O. D. orders Mama had paid for all through high school, and those I had made on my secondhand sewing machine. An electric iron was also on the list. I finally had my very own elec-tric iron from the door-to-door salesman, in spite of Miss Mable.

I took the train from New York's Penn Station, changing in Richmond for the six P.M. train to Drakes Branch. I stayed with the Cousins for a couple of

nights. I went home and picked up a couple of books and other items that I
thought would be useful in college. I bought a dress I liked at Miss Minnie's
shop, to match the beige shoes I had bought that summer. It was a plain dress
but it had rhinestone buttons. Miss Minnie had an odd taste in clothing. "I
could easily change the buttons," I thought. Two days later, I took the six
o'clock train headed toward Greensboro, with a layover in Danville, Virginia.

I arrived at the Greensboro train station around eight that morning. I
took a taxi to Jones Hall, one of the two dormitories for freshmen. As I
checked in, the dorm matron informed me that breakfast was still being
served in the dining hall. I managed to take my four suitcases up to my room
on the second floor. Before unpacking, I went down for breakfast. I sat with
a group of freshman girls who were not overly friendly. I had no complaints,
because on first encounter I often appear unfriendly.

When I returned to my room, my roommate still had not arrived. I discovered that I had lost my little change purse with my last five-dollar bill. I
returned immediately to the dining hall, but did not find my purse. There
were mostly freshmen on the campus, so I figured that the purse would be
turned in to one of the freshmen dormitories. That evening the dorm
matron called me down. She handed me my empty purse. I doubt that a student would bother to turn in an empty purse.

I knew no one on campus. The first freshman girl I met was Veronica
Shipley. She and a group of upperclassmen passed my open door, and I asked,
"Are you taking a walk?" She turned to the others and asked, "Are we taking
a walk?" Veronica still has this dry sense of humor. I fell in line with them.
When I returned to the room, my roommate Amy Shoffner had arrived.
Amy and I got along well; however, she had a respiratory illness and would
leave school for long periods of time. I spent most of my freshman year with-
out a roommate.

I knew that my mother had no more money to send me. She was still
working to pay for my books and the other supplies that I would need.
Luckily, our meals were included in tuition, so food was never a problem.
There was a snack bar on campus. I never visited the snack bar during my
four years on campus. My mother didn't send me care packages either.
Bennett's dining hall served excellent meals, so I had no need to go elsewhere. I was never a big eater anyway.

I needed the five dollars to buy a tennis racket for my physical education
class. I was lucky. I didn't need money to buy a bow and arrow for archery.
They were provided. One of the things that impressed me about Bennett's
catalog was the picture of a young lady aiming her arrow at a target. I wrote
a letter to Uncle Flood and Aunt Luella asking for ten dollars. My aunt wrote
back immediately and enclosed five dollars. She explained that was all she
had. They hadn't made their yearly income from the tobacco crop. I now had
just enough money to buy the tennis racket. I still have that racket.

Bennett College is a United Methodist Church-related, four-year liberal arts college for women. It was founded in 1873, on land donated by Lyman Bennett as a coeducational institution and reorganized in 1926 as a college for women. Classes were held Monday through Friday and Saturday morning. There was a one-hour rest period after lunch called a "beauty rest." The one and only time I ever missed a class was because I overslept. I didn't really miss the class. I was a few minutes late, and tardiness counted as a cut. Forty-five years later I am still taking my beauty rest in the afternoon.

We were required to attend chapel on Monday, Wednesday, and Friday mornings at nine, and Sunday afternoon at three. There were three full meals served each day. Lunch and dinner were formal meals and we were obligated to take our turn to serve as kitchen help and as waitresses. We also had job assignments in the dormitories consisting of turns at cleaning the bathroom and "beauty work," such as cleaning the brass in different areas of the dormitory.

We were expected to keep our rooms clean and in order. There were no locks on our dormitory doors and the dormitory matrons were free to do their inspection at any time. We were to be in the dorm at ten P.M. Exceptions were weekend dances. No students had cars.

We were taught that a "Bennett Belle" is a special lady. That when she goes to town she wears a hat and gloves. Back then ladies didn't wear pants.

We were assigned a seat for chapel at the beginning of each school year. My senior year I was third row, fourth seat from the center aisle. This seat permitted me to see everything that was happening in the front of the Annie Merner Pfeiffer Chapel, but I was oblivious to what was happening in the back. At the same time, the VIP's were focusing on those who were sitting in the front. There must have been a diabolical reason for having the freshmen in the very back and the seniors as far front as possible.

We were allowed three cuts per year. I never took my three cuts even for illness. I went to the campus infirmary only once during the four years. I was in one of my French classes. I sat there with water running from my eye and streaming down my face. The professor thought I was crying. She asked, *"Qu'est-ce qui passe?" "J'ai mal á l'oeil."* I replied. She told me to go see Nurse Trammel. That was the one and only time I ever went to the infirmary. Everyone knew and loved Nurse Trammel. I caught many glimpses of her as she walked across Bennett's campus. I knew if I really became ill, she would be the person I could turn to.

A student sat in the balcony of the Annie Merner Pfeiffer Chapel and marked a chart that showed the makeup of the student body and the assigned seat of each student. Each year one's class moved forward. The last semester of the school year, seniors wore their robes to Sunday vespers. It was a stately sight to see the seniors walking across campus each Sunday afternoon. We were supposed to wear dresses underneath our robes. Some girls would sneak and wear short pants, or nothing except underwear underneath their robes. One girl even boasted she was completely naked.

Bennett College was a school of many traditions that I came to love and cherish. Our campus life involved socializing with the boys from A & T College. Many of the girls had boy friends, or boys who were friends, from home—homeboys. There wasn't anyone I knew from Drakes Branch, except for John Irving, who was a year ahead of me at Central High. He never recognized me as a student from his old high school. When boys came calling at the dormitory there was an announcement over the PA that went like this: *Anna Ferguson has a guest in the front lobby.* My name was never called over the PA system because I never had a guest in the lobby. When I was called down it was a telephone call from Mama.

I met many unforgettable people at Bennett College. There were the people who gave sermons at our Sunday vespers, weekly chapel, or lyceum programs. At Sunday vespers we heard such notable speakers as Mordecai Johnson, president of Howard University, and Benjamin Mays, president of Morehouse College. At the lyceum programs was William Warfield, the great bass-baritone, whose rendition of *Old Man River* from *Show Boat* brought tears to my eyes. William Warfield had his recital debut in New York's famous Town Hall on March 1950. His career spanned more than fifty years. There was also Mattiwilda Dobbs, the internationally known concert and opera singer, and the third black American to sing at the Metropolitan Opera. And there was the memorable Leontyne Price, whose extraordinary voice had been nurtured by singing in her church choir. She went to the College of Educational and Industrial Arts in Wilberforce, Ohio, to become a music teacher. After hearing her sing in the choir, the president of the college encouraged her to change her major from education and to concentrate on her voice. Later she was to tour all over the world including a triumphant debut at Covent Garden in London and playing "Aida" in La Scala. She married her co-performer William Warfield. She was the second black singer to sing at the Metropolitan Opera in New York. We didn't hear live the greatest of them all, Marian Anderson, but we listened to her music and excerpts from her autobiography, *My Lord, What a Morning* on music appreciation days.

Marian Anderson was a true contralto with a vocal range that permitted her to sing Negro spirituals, popular music, and the classics in German, French, and Italian. She was born in 1897, in South Philadelphia. Her father died when she was a child, and her mother worked as a cleaning woman and laundress to support the family. The black community, recognizing her talent, gave her financial and moral support. She faced overt racism when she applied to a music school in Philadelphia. She was told, "We don't take colored students." She found a teacher from her church who gave her free lessons.

In 1924, she had her first concert at New York's Town Hall. Her lack of knowledge of foreign languages almost caused an end to her career. She did not give up. She went on to study with the great musicians of Europe. Among them were the tenor coach, Giuseppe Boghetti, and Arturo Toscanini, who complimented her for the rendition of *Ave Maria* with, "Yours is a voice one hears once in a hundred years."

After several years in Europe, she returned in triumph to the New York Town Hall. She had mastered the classics in German, French, and Italian. However, she still was not accepted by all of American society. The most highly publicized racial incident occurred in 1939, when Howard University tried to arrange for her to sing in Constitution Hall, the largest and most appropriate indoor location in Washington, D. C. The Daughters of the American Revolution would not allow her to sing there. The U. S. Department of the Interior, with First Lady Eleanor Roosevelt's persistence, permitted her to sing on the steps of the Lincoln Memorial on April 9, 1939. On Easter Sunday, seventy-five thousand people attended the concert and millions listened to her on the radio. She began her concert by singing *America*. In 1955, she was the first black person to sing with the New York Metropolitan Opera Company. In the early sixties, I heard Marion Anderson sing in Constitution Hall. It was the truly richest and most beautiful voice that I have ever heard.

Since Bennett College, I have heard and seen many great performers and performances in the Washington area. Among them were Earth Kitt and Yul Brynner in *The King and I*. Eartha Kitt was blacklisted in the sixties because she voiced her view of America's involvement in the Vietnam War during a luncheon at the White House that was hosted by First Lady Ladybird Johnson. Her part in *The King and I* marked her return to grace. I remember her for her sultry recording of *C'est Si Bon*.

Eartha Kitt chose to remain in America, but a contemporary of hers, Nina Simone, who believed she was treated unfairly because of her race, chose to live in Carry-le-Rouet, France. In 2003, this great singer, pianist, and composer died in her adopted country.

France has long been a haven for black artists and writers. In the thirties, forties, and fifties they flocked to Paris. Today it is southern France, particularly areas in Provence, where artists gather.

Mama and I also saw *Camelot* at the Kennedy Center, and Leonard Bernstein directing his *Mass*, that was created for the opening of the John F. Kennedy Center for Performing Arts in 1971. It is a theater piece created for as many as two hundred singers, dancers, and players and dedicated to the slain president. When asked why a Jew would create a Catholic Mass, Leonard Bernstein replied, "We have to educate ourselves about other religions."

Charletta and I saw *The Lion King*, the award winning musical, at the Lyceum Theatre in London, 2001. We had not been successful in getting tickets for the Broadway production.

Mahalia Jackson has been acclaimed as America's greatest gospel singer, with a career that included television, radio concerts, and movies. She was

Mama's favorite, so I bought tickets for Mama and me to see and hear her at Madison Square Garden. Mahalia Jackson was born in New Orleans, Louisiana, on October 26, 1911 or 1912. She was the daughter of Charity Clark, a laundress, and John Jackson, a Baptist preacher. Her mother died when she was five, and Mahalia was raised by an extended family.

Like many black stars, past and present, her singing career began in the church. In addition to singing church music, there was the music of Mardi Gras; but Mahalia was never drawn to jazz, even though she knew such notables as Louis Armstrong, Duke Ellington, and Benny Goodman. In 1949, she won the French *Grand Prix du Disque*. She was featured at Martin Luther King's March on Washington in 1963.

At Mama's wake I played Mahalia's thirty-three and a third high fidelity album of some of Mama's favorites: *He's Got the Whole World in His Hands*, *Walk in Jerusalem*, *The Upper Room*, and *Nobody Knows the Trouble I've Seen*. Mama's great granddaughter Tiffany Jones, a music major, sang *Amazing Grace* at her small funeral service. This was also from Mahalia Jackson's album.

Weekly chapel and Sunday vespers were programs of music appreciation, student performances, guest speakers, or any activity that would enrich us. Sunday vespers was church for me. Dr. David Jones was the president during my freshman year. I remember especially his delivery of the closing words of each Sunday service. He had a voice like no one else. It was his special gift to each one of us. Each Sunday as we left the chapel in our perfectly assigned order, I would think, *Surely, there is a God!* Dr. Jones' resounding voice at the close of each Sunday service would echo until the next vespertine service:

> *Beloved, now we are the sons of god; and it doth not yet appear what we shall be; but we know that, when He will appear, we shall be like Him; for we shall see Him as He is. And every man that hast this hope in him purifieth himself, even as he is pure.*
> First Epistle of John 3:2-3

> *The Lord hath been mindful of us: He will bless us.*
> Psalm 115:12

And *The Benediction*—

> *Now unto God's gracious mercy, and His divine goodness, we commit ourselves, and all our loved ones, wherever they are this night.*
> *The Lord blesses us and keeps us:*
> *The Lord causes His face to shine upon us*

And be gracious unto us.
May the Lord lift up His countenance upon us
And grant us peace,
Both this night and evermore.
Amen
Adapted from the Book of Numbers
                                        Chapter 6, Verses 22-27

After Dr. Jones' passing, Dr. Willa B. Player, the vice-president, became president and remained president many years after I graduated. One morning at the end of my freshman year, I went into her office. She had an open-door policy. I explained to her what an awful time I was having financially. She listened attentively to my story. After I had come to the end of my extemporaneous monologue, she said she would look into the situation. I left her office wondering if she had heard a word I said. For the next three years, I attended Bennett College without financial worries, or any other worries. Dr. Willa B. Player passed away on August 28, 2003.

Mama would send me five dollars each week for spending money and the train fare back home for Christmas. My home was now officially 15 Albany Avenue, Brooklyn, New York. I would save up the five dollars and buy the extra things I needed. I would go shopping for a dress or a pair of shoes, or even take a balcony seat at the Greensboro movie theater once in a while. Greensboro was still a segregated city. It was in Greensboro that the lunch counter sit-ins by students from A & T University and Bennett College took place in the 1960s. The sit-ins spread to other cities, resulting in changes in the laws, including the laws governing movie theaters.

Sometimes, I even had a dollar or two to lend to my friends. There was also an office in the Student Union where I could borrow as much as two dollars. In short, money was no longer a pressing problem, except during my senior year, when it was necessary for me to travel to interviews for a job. For the two interviews I went on, I borrowed money from my English professor and advisor, Dr. Crawford. I paid him back by saving my allowance for a couple of weeks. My job interview involved my walking to the bus station in downtown Greensboro and taking a bus south. I was able to make two interviews in one day by stopping in Red Spring, North Carolina for one interview, and then heading south to Lake View, South Carolina for the second.

At the end of my first year at Bennett, I again stopped by Drakes Branch on the way to Brooklyn. Exhausted, from final exams and from financial woes that plagued me my first year at Bennett, I went to sleep as soon as I sat down in the segregated car. When I woke up I was in Lynchburg, Virginia. I had never heard the conductor as he walked through the car, calling out, "Danville" several times. I was supposed to change in this town. I took a train back to Danville, arriving just in time to make the train that would take me to Drakes Branch.

I stayed with my second family, the Cousins. My dog Lucky was now staying permanently at their home. He still remembered me, and followed me home when I went to check on all the things Mama and I had left behind. After this visit it was a couple of years before I returned to Drakes. This time Lucky did not recognize me. When I reached out my hand to pet him, he grinned, baring his teeth, and would have bitten me if I had not jerked my hand away. Lucky made me very sad.

I was now a junior in college. On this visit I saw a young man, Louis Gregory, who had been in my class at Central High. He was attending Virginia State College in Petersburg, Virginia. I didn't recognize him, and would have walked past him if he had not recognized me. Many years later, I ran into him at a dance in Fairfax County. By then he was married, and I was married to my husband Paul. He was working for the federal government in Washington, D. C., and I was teaching in Fairfax County.

Over the years, I saw my three best friends Clara, Dorothy, and Theodora. They lived for years in Brooklyn, but later moved back to the South—Drakes and Keysville. I also saw another classmate and friend, Florence Henderson, who also lived in Brooklyn. In 1992 I attended my first Central High class reunion. Most of my classmates were there. They had all met with success in their lives. Many were semi-retired like me.

The visit I made to Drakes during my junior year at Bennett was the last time I saw Mr. and Mrs. Cousins, my second set of parents. They were like Mama. They left me to my own devices.

The head of the French Department at Bennett College was Madame Blanche Raiford. She, like Miss Triplet, was my inspiration for mastering the French language. She taught many of my French classes. I remember Alphonse Daudet's story *La Dernière Classe* from her course, called "The Romantic Movement in French Literature." I required my French IV and French V students at Luther Jackson High School to read this beautiful story. The setting is the province of Alsace-Lorraine, which borders Germany in the northeast. The main cities are Nancy, the capital, and Strasbourg. The region is also the center of France's well-developed iron and steel industry. This area has been an issue of dispute between France and Germany beginning with the division of Charlemagne's Empire in the ninth century. As a result of the Prussian victories of the Franco-Prussian, Germany won control of this area from 1771-1899. The teacher, Monsieur Hamel, speaks to the class about the French language. It is the last day that French will be spoken in the provinces of Alsace-Lorraine.

> *C'était la plus belle langue du monde,*
> *La plus claire,*
> *La plus solide,*

118

Qu'il fallait la garder entre nous et ne jamais l'oublier parce que, quand un people tombe escale, tant qu'il tien bien sa langue, c'est comme s'il tenait la clef de sa prison.

Translation: *French is the most beautiful language in the world. It is the most clear and the most permanent. It is necessary to keep it with us (even though we must now speak German). When a people become slaves, they must not forget their native language. Their language is the key to their prison.*

When the teacher hears the trumpets of the advancing Prussians, he turns to the blackboard, and with all his strength he writes in letters as large as he can.

"*VIVE LA FRANCE!*"

He then turns to the class and without speaking he makes a sign,

"*C'est fini…allez-vous-en*" (It's finished…go.)

I visited the Germanic Alsace-Lorraine region in 1962, and Nikki and I passed through the area again in 1987, as we traveled by train from Luxembourg to Paris. The provinces are now firmly in the hands of the French, but German customs and food specialties (Quiche Lorraine) are still strong. Hitler's army occupied it from 1940-1944. Old Germans still speak of it as "the lost provinces." Verdun is the garrison town where the Allies held out against a massive assault by the German army in World War I. In the closing years of the war six hundred thousand to eight hundred thousand French and German soldiers died there. There is a vast cemetery of endless crosses and Rodin's monument *Défense* to commemorate the dead.

From Alsace-Lorraine we headed east, passing through Domrémy where Jeanne D'Arc was born, and on to Champagne. It is an area of pleasantly rolling and sunny landscape. In the center of the area is the old city of Reims, famous for its great gothic cathedral. The impressionist painter Monet has immortalized the cathedral.

We visited one of Reims' famous champagne cellars, maintained in an old cave. The one thing I remember about the visit is the tour guide. I have never seen anyone combine the two languages, English and French, the way he was able to. He alternated methodically, an English word, then a French word. I could not understand anything he said about the making of champagne or the history of this unique wine. Vineyards in the area grow some of the world's best grapes, and for many the world's best wine. In 2004, Nikki, Dave and I retraced my steps of 1962. The cathedral and the town had changed very little. There were a few more tourists, and the entrance to the wine cellars had been updated.

My junior and senior years I also took Spanish I and II from Madame Raiford, so I am not completely ignorant when I substitute in Spanish. But I am indebted to Madame Raiford for sharing with me her love of the French people and their language,

Another teacher was Ingard Roth from Wiesbaden, Germany. I took her course in conversational French. Mlle. Roth left Bennett soon after I did and returned to Germany. We met again in Pau, France, in 1962. I didn't see her just before I left Pau, but she wrote me a note and left it in my mailbox. I found that note in my little gray cosmetic case more than forty years later. I wish I had taken the time to drop in on her as she suggested:

Dear Mlle Miles,

Sorry I did not see you today to say at least goodbye and to wish you an interesting trip through the various European countries. Here is my address, and I hope you will drop in sometime.

Ingard Roth
Wiesbaden
Ruckertstr 2

Sincerely,
Ingard Roth

There was still another teacher from Bennett who influenced my life. She was Madame Zalities, a Jew from Latvia. She had come to the United States to escape the 1949 deportation of many Latvians to labor camps in Siberia. She would often stray from the lessons of the day and go into a tirade against the Russian invaders. Her straying was particularly beneficial to those who had not completed their reading assignments.

Madame Zalities taught me French history and civilization, and any mention of France's tragic history would set her off. Her recollections of what the Russians had done to the Baltic States would bring tears to my eyes years later. My visit to Dachau Concentration Camp brought memories of her tales of members of her family and friends who had been carted off to work in the mines of Siberia and of the other Jews who were forced to flee Europe.

Dachau was the Nazi's first camp. It was established in 1933, and is ten miles from Munich. Brutal medical experiments were performed there. Almost all of the two hundred thousand prisoners who were sent to the camp died there. The United States liberated thirty-two thousand in 1945. The graphic pictures I saw of mass graves, bodies piled up in the morgue, in front of the old and the new crematorium, strewn across the campgrounds, in boxcars, and on nearby railroad tracks, were a reminder of why Madame wept so often in front of her students. My classmates and I were completely disconnected from the stories she would tell of the atrocities of the Russian invaders.

Dinner at Bennett meant a sit-down formal meal. Professors, those who chose to, also had their meals in the dining hall. Madame would come to the dining hall for her meals. Sometimes she would go from table to table and asks politely, "Is this place reserved?" Repeatedly she would get the answer, "Yes." Some of the Bennett girls did not like her sitting at their table because the conversation would inevitably turn to the Russians and the fate of her country. My roommate Albertina Houwen and I would see Madame leave the dining hall deeply hurt and without eating. I had several Jewish teachers at Bennett. They were mostly scholars who had fled the Nazis in Western Europe and the Russian takeover of the Baltic States of Estonia, Latvia, and Lithuania. They were welcomed at Bennett and other black schools throughout the South but were not accepted at white colleges and universities across America.

There was a Jew who taught me English my freshman year and whose name escapes me. He guided me though the writing of my first research paper on Euthanasia. I asked another Jew who taught psychology if I might have a sheet of his poster board. He asked, "Why?"

"To illustrate a poem."

"How well can you draw?"

"Not very well."

"What poem do you want to illustrate?"

"*My Last Duchess*, by Robert Browning."

He proceeded to draw a beautiful portrait of a lady who was clearly royalty.

"Here is your last duchess. Finish your project."

I needed only to copy the poems onto the poster in my best calligraphy. Needless to say, I received an A for this project. I can't remember if I gave the professor credit for his artwork during my oral presentation. I suppose it was like students using pictures from cyberspace to enhance their written reports. There were no computers back then. There was also the Health Education Professor who said in his syllabus that the term paper had to be typed, but accepted the paper I printed by hand—all one hundred fifty pages. For the hours spent on the research and the perfect manuscript, I received an "A-." The paper had to be typed! Mama sent me a typewriter at the end of the first semester.

Dr. Hobart Jarrett, head of the English Department, was my teacher for several English courses. His speech and diction were elegant. He told me that I was always very quiet, but when asked an esoteric question, or some off-the-wall question about English Literature, I usually had the answer.

Dr. Jarrett was responsible for my coming to Fairfax County. After my one year teaching experience in Lake View, South Carolina, I decided I wanted to leave. I was too far from home. I wrote back to the Placement Office at Bennett College. I am not sure how he found out about my wanting to leave Columbus High. (Dr. Jarrett was not the type of person who would be hanging around a placement office checking on his former students.) In any case he had a friend who was the principal of Hoffmann Boston High School in Arlington, Virginia. He thought this principal might need a French or English teacher. This principal didn't, but his friend at Luther Jackson High School in Fairfax County did. Taylor William called me in Brooklyn. I applied for the job.

Each year I returned to Bennett with renewed energy, enthusiasm, and purpose. My classes always went well. I made the honor roll each semester, and each year my scholarship was renewed. My senior year I was inducted into the Alpha Kappa Mu honor society. I graduated with enough credit hours for a major in both French and English. My years at Bennett were some of the best of my life.

Dr. John L Bryan, Director of Religious Activities, was almost as spellbinding as Dr. Jones. He also taught classes in religion and philosophy; however, I never had him as a teacher. But he held my attention at weekly chapel services and Sunday vespers. He presented the class of 1958 with a little book entitled *Prayers to Live By* with a dedication by Dr. Player. This book has remained on my bookshelf over the years. I can find a prayer for just about any occasion in this little book.

> *For Practice Teachers: Less Frills and More Facts*
> *Hear us this morning, O Lord, On behalf of our fellow students and friends. The members of the Senior Class who, are now practice teaching in many strange and perhaps uncomfortable places. Help them to recall whatever good things they have learned and mastered during their student days on this campus. Preserve them from discouragement. Help them to be sensible and sound, as they prepare their lesson plans, and as they shall rely more upon facts, and less upon frills of educational methods. Give them insight when they excel. And that they shall know how to encourage them and mourn with them when they fall.*
>
> *O God of truth, we know that the last frontier that we are called to push back is the frontier of superstition and of ignorance. We know too that we cannot succeed at this if we rely upon wishful thinking and upon mere pious words. We need to work: And we need their help—whatever our brothers and sisters are half-starved, and illiterate, and persecuted. Send us forth to that place, O Lord.*

Dr. Bryan painted a pretty bleak picture of the task we had before us. Evidently, this prayer didn't grab my attention as most of his prayers did. Otherwise I would have had numerous misgivings about going out to student teach. I only had a few!

Bennett College had an exchange program with several other colleges on the east coast. Among those schools were Vassar, Skidmore, and Mount Holyoke. I attended Skidmore College in Saratoga, New York. In 1958, Skidmore was a privately controlled liberal arts college for women. Like Bennett, it offered courses in art, business, drama, home economics, music, nursing, and physical education. Skidmore grants B. S. and B. A. degrees. It is located in a residential area of the city. Many of the dormitories and the buildings where classes are held are single-family houses, constructed of wood siding. There was no wall, like the one at Bennett, enclosing the campus. Bennett's brick wall was my security blanket. Skidmore was my first experience without it.

I attended French classes that corresponded to the courses I was taking at Bennett. The student union and dining hall were located in a modern brick building. There were only a few black students on Skidmore's campus, but I found the predominately white campus much like the one I had left. Bennett had a couple of white students and quite a few students from Africa, India, and South Korea. At Skidmore, I attended classes made up of predominately white students for the first time since Our Lady of Victory. Bennett College paid for the train trip to and from Saratoga with changes in Grand Central Station.

The terminal made as much of an impression on me as the two weeks I spent at Skidmore, the school for rich young women who actually had cars to drive, The interior of the station, which was all that I saw on this trip, was an amazing sight. The vaulted ceiling was painted like an evening sky with gilded stars and constellations.

Since that time, I have also seen the station from the outside. In the 1960s the station was to have been torn down, but Jacqueline Kennedy saved it. It was declared a historic landmark in the 1970s, and has undergone extensive renovations.

Its rival *Gare d'Orsay* in Paris is now the *Musée d'Orsay*, which probably houses the world's largest collection of impressionist paintings. At one time two hundred trains per day used Orsay Station, but modernizing, electrification, and the lengthening of trains made Orsay's short platforms obsolete in the 1930s. It housed prisoners of war after the liberation of Paris. General Charles De Gaulle announced his return to power as president of the Fifth Republic at the Gare d'Orsay in 1958. There was also plans made for razing the station, but in 1971, it was also declared a historic landmark. So often in America, beautiful landmarks are destroyed to make way for a more modern replacement that lacks the beauty of the old.

After my two weeks as an exchange student, I returned to finish my last semester. Before graduation I had signed a contract to teach French and English at Columbus High School in Lake View, South Carolina. The teacher I replaced was also a Bennett graduate. Each time I wore my Bennett blazer students would remind me that their other French teacher wore the same jacket.

There were no hotels in Greensboro where black parents could stay. Bennett opened its dormitories to families of graduates. Only seniors and juniors who had special tasks connected with commencements remained on campus. We had to find our own sleeping arrangements in the dormitories set aside for students. The graduates registered parents and relatives with the college.

I reserved a room for Mama, Eliza Etta, and my little niece, Johnnie. This was really more fun than it would have been if they had stayed in a hotel in town, but Mama, Eliza Etta, and Johnnie should have had the right to choose where they wanted to stay. They came down by bus, and since we did not have a car at our disposal it would have been difficult to go back and forth to the many activities the college had planned for the weekend. Neither Mama nor Eliza Etta had ever been to Greensboro.

Having my family at my graduation from college was an awesome occasion. If I had been able to rent a car my family could have seen more of Greensboro and the surrounding area. Renting a car probably wasn't a possibility anyway. I couldn't drive and neither could Eliza Etta. Mama always said she was going to learn to drive. She never did. There probably weren't any rental car agencies in Greensboro in 1958, and even if there were they would not have rented to blacks. Learning to drive was next on my list of important things to do. It would come after my first year of teaching in Fairfax County, and when I was rooming and boarding with Mrs. Mae Hall.

The tradition of excellence continues at Bennett College, but Bennett, like many traditional predominately black colleges and universities, has gone through difficult economic times. But, thanks to Dr. Johnnetta B. Cole who came out of retirement to save the college, Bennett College is now operating in the black. At Bennett's Washington, D. C. Metro Alumnae Chapter's traditional White Breakfast, Dr. Cole said: *Anyone who ever gets to the top of a field doesn't get there by him or herself. And once there, you should not forget the responsibility to help others join you.* She challenged each and every one of us to give $1,926.00 to our Alma Mater, Bennett College, by April 2003. Bennett became a woman's college in 1926.

During my thirty years of teaching, I have had such wonderful students. I would like to know what paths these students have taken. After retiring in 1991, I saw many of my students at Oakton High School where I most often substitute. One of the students who participated in an *EF Educational Tour* of France and Spain was Elspeth Leech. Elspeth was the only student who became ill on any of my tours. I had a parent, Lyn Pacella, traveling with us. She accompanied the tour guide and the other students on an excursion to the Chateaux Country. I stayed behind, had the hotel call a doctor, and picked up the medicine he prescribed. The next morning, Elspeth was completely cured of her virus.

It was also on this trip that I ever feared that my students might be in danger. We were traveling a very narrow, almost perpendicular, road up to

Montserrat. Montserrat is a mountain and a famous monastery near Barcelona, in eastern Spain. It is four thousand fifty-four feet above sea level. Its name means "saw-tooth mountain." The monastery stands on the very top. Many people visit the church to see the Black Virgin, patron saint of Catalonia. Going up the mountain we were on the outside of a very narrow road. Our tour guide and the bus driver talked continually. I had difficulty believing that he could concentrate on his driving and carry on a lively conversation at the same time. Every time I looked down, I would think, "If we go over the cliff, I won't be around to receive the ire of the parents."

I have seen Elspeth only once since leaving Luther Jackson. I learned from a letter she wrote a couple of years later that she was participating in an exchange program that would take her to Europe. Elise Keely was a student I taught at Luther Jackson. I have seen Elise often at Oakton High School. She is now a senior and has completed the advanced level of French. There are many, many students I shall never forget, even if I can no longer remember their names. Another student with whom I am in constant contact is Marietta Mitsenas. I called her Marie-Christine in the French classroom. Marietta was from Greece. For her excellent work in French, I had given her a French dictionary with my name and home address. She contacted me several years later, and since that time we have corresponded regularly.

25/9/97

Dear Mme Bellamy,

I am sorry about your little accident. I hope your wrist is doing better now. I had no problem reading your letter; so don't worry about your handwriting.

I am glad that you had a great time here in Greece, and that you are thinking of coming again soon. I just hope that my parents and I will have more time to see you. My parents and I were very happy to have you and Nikki here at home. Even for a while. If you are making plans for the future, don't plan anything for the year 2004. We should expect to see you here in Athens for the Olympic games. It is going to be a great event since Greece is their birthplace.

I would like to thank you for your thinking of my meeting Anne-Lise in Paris. It is nice to know someone when visiting another country. Unfortunately, my French is not good. I haven't spoken French for a very long time. I had to stop French in my senior year due to lack of free time. Besides regular school, I had to attend private school in order to have better results on my exams for the university. It's a whole new story, and I wouldn't like to tire you anymore with it anyway. Now that I have got my "proficiency certificate" in English I plan to start studying French again because I don't like leaving things in the middle.

Now, as far as my studies are concerned, I got a 3.35 C. on my first semester report. Then during the summer, I took Biology I and got a B so my C. became 3.23 for this semester. I have five courses: archaeology, sociology, and psychology as a social science, math, and English. I have so much studying to do, and time passes so quickly. Anyway, the good thing is that I enjoy my classes. It's amazing how much knowledge there is out there.

Now concerning the photos. I haven't developed them yet because we lost the camera, and then we found it recently. It seems to me that someone doesn't want these pictures developed, meaning that yours burned out and we lost the camera. Well, we'll just have to wait for the outcome.

It's time to end this letter. Give my best to Nikki. I plan to write her soon. Hope you are all well.

Love
Marietta

P. S. They say this winter is going to be the worst in one hundred or one hundred fifty years.

Nikki and I visited Marietta and her family in Athens in 1995, and in January 2002 we visited her in Leeds, England, where she was attending the university.

In the *Washington Post* article dated Sunday, February 2, 2003, there was an article: *"Old Schoolhouse Has Bittersweet Lesson to Teach: Local Group Plans Museum on Segregated Education."* Laurel Grove was one of Fairfax County's "colored" schools. William Jasper, one of four slaves, founded it in 1884. Phyllis Walker-Ford is a member of the Laurel Grove School Association, whose mission is to restore Laurel Grove and turn it into a living museum.

I taught Phyllis Walker-Ford and her brother Dumont Walker in the segregated Luther Jackson Intermediate and High School. Dumont Walker became principal of a Fairfax County School. He died tragically in an automobile accident while on lunch break.

There was no high school for Blacks in Fairfax County until 1954, the same year I graduated from Central High School in southwest Virginia. It's difficult to believe that rural Charlotte County was ahead of Fairfax County, which lies only a few miles from the nation's capital. Black students were forced to attend high school in the neighboring Prince William County, more than twenty-five miles away, or pretend to live with relatives in Washington, D. C.

Phyllis Walker-Ford and the Laurel Grove School Association are a reminder of the importance all black parents once placed on education. A plantation owner freed Jasper and gave him twelve acres of land. He built a school and a church on his land. Unfortunately in December 2004, the historic Laurel Baptist Church was all but destroyed by an electrical fire. Schools like Central High, Luther Jackson High, and Laurel Grove are a reminder of Virginia's segregated system, and they are also a reminder of how hard teachers and students worked to overcome the many disadvantages of attending schools that were inferior to the white schools.

Black parents have to take the lead to see that their sons and daughters take advantage of the many opportunities that the integrated systems have to offer. They must demand that their sons and daughters take upper level classes in science and math, physics, chemistry, calculus, computer sciences, art history, photography, advanced placement classes, and, of course, foreign languages. Last but not least, black parents have to make their children behave in class. There are too many black students in special education classes not because they belong there, but because they haven't been taught how to behave. They do neither class work nor homework. No teacher, black or white, can teach a student who does not want to learn. The Federal Government is never going to give us a good education! It's there for us to take! Parents must take charge and be responsible for their children's education. There are many black students who are doing well in school, but those who do poorly often overshadow them.

George Felton, a retired Fairfax County teacher and principal, in a 2003 Martin Luther King address, spoke of the lax attitude too many parents and students have toward education. One of George's former students, Charles Grimes, from the old Luther Jackson High School, is a top attorney, like Johnnie Cochran.

Charles Grimes, whose wife Eloise Duncan was one of my best French students, made this observation: "This country is building a large number of post-grad institutions for black males between the ages of seventeen and twenty-eight. Education must be re-infused with a sense of moral and racial responsibility." Mama would simply say, "Do your work, and behave yourself! I'll take care of the racist principals and teachers!"

Though there are many excellent black students in the Fairfax County School System, there are many who are failing to take advantage of its excellent schools. It is true that blacks are suspended or expelled disproportionately in most school systems. Perhaps this is true of Fairfax County as well. Parents must assume a larger disciplinary role in the education of their children. If a child comes home day after day with no books, the question, "Why?" must be asked. There is no study hall at school, so it is impossible to complete all assignments there. If a child has no assignment, then parents must give them assignments to be completed each evening at home. Take away the telephone, television, and computer during the weekdays. Let them amuse themselves by reading books. Nikki, Pauly, and Chanty looked forward to the weekend. If nothing really exciting was planned, they looked forward to watching television. Teachers now have web sites where class and homework assignments are posted, at least at Oakton High School they do. "Forty years after Dr. King's March on Washington, has his dream become a reality?" George Felton asked.

The end of summer for me has always meant the end of carefree days. When I was in high school it meant the end of my stay in Brooklyn, New York, and supervising my nieces and nephews when they spent the summer in Drakes with Mama and me. When we spent the summer in Brooklyn, we would go to Coney Island or Jones Beach. One time each year we would take a boat ride up the Hudson River to Bear Mountain for a day visit. We would have cookouts at Cousin Leroy and Aunt Geneva's house in South Ozone Park, Long Island. It also meant the return to another exciting year at Bennett College. No matter what school I was returning to, for me it represented a return to a year in a wonderful and fulfilling job—the best in the world— *professeur ou étudiante*—student or teacher!

Chapter 4

A teacher affects eternity; he can never tell where his influence stops.

Henry Adams, *The Education of Henry Adams*

"This is my daughter, Fannie Lillian. She's a French teacher!"

"Mama, would you please stop introducing me as your daughter the French teacher!"

"Don't you teach French?"

"Yes, but..."

"But what?"

"It's embarrassing."

"You don't like teaching French?"

"Yes, I do, Mama. But it sounds like you are bragging."

"I am!"

In the spring of 1960, I began looking for a car. I began my search by using the advertisements in the *Washington Evening Post*, a now defunct Washington paper. I wanted a small car with good gas mileage. After a couple of months, I settled on the Corvair, the car described by Ralph Nader as the car that was "unsafe at any speed." I made the loan and all financial arrangements by telephone and without seeing the car beforehand. Just imagine buying a car over the telephone! However, I chose to buy a brand new car because there would be few mechanical problems. I kept the Corvair for ten years. There was no haggling over the price. I simply agreed to pay the sticker price. If I had had some experience in buying a car, I would have known that one need not pay the sticker price. Marshall Gordon, Mrs. Hall's son, took me to pick up the car that I had bought sight unseen. Marshall later drove the car home to his mother's house.

129

Dee Weaver, Mrs. Hall's daughter, and her husband gave me a few lessons during the couple of weeks the car was parked at the house. I had no problem getting someone to help me practice driving in my car. I obtained a special car insurance for owners who cannot drive. I can't imagine this type of insurance existing in today's complex society.

At the end of the school year, Dee and her family drove me to Brooklyn. That is, Arvayne, her seventeen-year-old daughter, drove my car. Dee and Blake, along with Gary their ten-year-old, rode behind us in their car. We stopped overnight at her sister's house in New Jersey, and continued on to Brooklyn the next morning. After the Weavers dropped my car and me off at our apartment on Hancock Street, they returned to Virginia.

Mama and I had rented the apartment the summer after my teaching job in South Carolina. I had to telephone my brother Willoughby immediately, as the car had to be moved to the other side of the street early the next morning. In Brooklyn alternate sides of the streets are cleaned each day, and my car would be on the side to be cleaned. Willoughby came over straight away to see my new car and me. He drove it back to his home, and said he would return the next morning for my first driving lesson. He was having trouble with his old car, so my new car really came in handy. Willoughby was a very big man, so he often got funny stares when this gentle giant was driving the little Corvair. Willoughby also worked the evening shift on the Brooklyn Waterfront. This was another plus for me. He had even picked up a New York driving manual before I arrived.

One of my students had taken me to get my Virginia Driver's Permit before I left Virginia. Using this permit in the state of New York must have been completely legal back then, I suppose, because I had Virginia tags and insurance. Additionally, the police never stopped me while I was learning to drive. Later, when I would drive around by myself, they would stop me because I would forget to turn my lights on in the "city of lights." I only got warnings though! Today, I am sure this would not happen with all the concern about terrorism. I don't fit the profile of a terrorist, but since 9/11 I have been searched and prodded as if I did.

Willoughby would drive over (in my car) each morning around nine o'clock. Mama was working several blocks from our home, so all summer long we took her to work. We would then drive out to Long Island to our cousins Geneva and Leroy's house. They lived in a quiet residential area without much traffic. In this neighborhood we began our driving lesson.

My brother was unbelievable as a driving instructor. He was patient and always encouraging. The most difficult task was parallel parking, and maneuvering the car and giving hand signals at the same time. After a couple of weeks I began going out into traffic. I would drive from Long Island back to Brooklyn. Back then there wasn't much traffic on the Long Island Freeway or Rockaway Boulevard.

By the middle of August I had studied the driving manual and felt that I had enough experience behind the wheel. I took my driver's test out on Long Island and passed on the first try. This was largely due to my brother's skill as a teacher. I was also proud that this country girl who had never been behind the wheel of a car had gotten her driver's license in New York no less.

Even though I now had a valid driver's license, Willoughby and Mama rode with me back to Virginia, for the beginning of school. After dropping my things off, introducing them to my landlady, and stopping for dinner in Georgetown, I drove them to the bus station. Driving back home alone from the Greyhound Bus Station in Washington to McLean was my first experience driving alone in the city and Northern Virginia.

The Corvair had no seat belts and no air bags. It would spin completely around on the slightest bit of ice or snow. It's a wonder I didn't go through the windshield at least once. I did skid into another car while entering the beltway. There was minor damage to the other's person's car but no damage to mine.

Nevertheless, the Corvair served me well. I used it to transport students to and from basketball games, French plays at Georgetown University, to the National French Exam, and to any worthy cultural activity, and of course for my enjoyment. I was now able to go out on my own. The Seven Corners Mall had recently opened, where I could shop whenever I wanted to. My only regret is that Paul and I sold my little car for a big four-door Chrysler.

My children's driving experiences were quite different from mine. Pauly learned to drive by backing the family car backward and forward in the driveway. We had a pretty long driveway with one entrance. He perfected his driving by moving the car, so another could get out. In seventh grade Pauly got the bright idea that he and his sister should take on the job of delivering newspapers. After calling the *Washington Post* about an ad he saw, and speaking with the manager of the routes in our area, Phil Hambrick, he and Nikki received their assignment. Their delivery area was as follows:

Left out of our driveway on Courthouse Road to Blake Lane and another right—left into the townhouse development of Cyrandall Valley—back out to Blake Lane and left on Platten Drive to the Oak Creek and Oak Plank Drive Housing Development, then down to single family houses neighborhood on Platten Drive,

We then would return to Blake Lane, and I would drive down to Cyrandall Valley Road. This delivery area included:

A group of townhouses and single-family houses on Cyrandall Valley Road—I would then drive a couple of blocks to Bushman Drive and turn left to the Vistas Apartments, now a condominium complex. The apartment complex consisted of twenty to thirty entrances, which ran from Bushman Drive to Borge Street. I would then take a left on Borge and right on Blake Lane and home.

The paper route required Nikki, Pauly, and I to rise at five o'clock. The stacks of newspaper would always be at the end of the driveway. We would use a dolly to bring them to the carport where we would pack them, using rubber bands and plastic bags during inclement weather, or when rain and snow was in the forecast. Rubber bands made for easy packing. It usually took no more than thirty minutes for the three of us to pack from 150 to 200 papers and place the papers in our shoulder bags.

I would drive to the designated area that we had divided into three almost even sections. The first part of the route was pretty easy, and I could park the car in one spot. The second part was a much larger delivery area. Pauly was much faster than Nikki or me, so in the area of Bushman Drive he would move the car from place to place. It was only now and again that Nikki would finish ahead of Pauly and move the car to the next pick-up spot along the route.

In the 1980s the neighborhoods around Blake Lane were deserted at five in the morning. We never once encountered a policeman in the six years we delivered newspapers. Like the pony express in rain, snow, or any kind of weather, our customers received their newspapers. If we ran out of newspapers and needed one or two more, we always carried a couple of quarters in the car to buy what papers we needed from the machine at the bus stop on Blake Lane.

During an ice storm I skidded into someone's parked car and dented it slightly. I left a note with my telephone number on the windshield. I was called later in the day and the problem was solved. That was the only mishap we had, and it was I who was at fault. On Saturday we would sleep until seven before starting the paper route. On weekends we had even more papers to deliver, complete with inserts, and there were customers who took only the Sunday edition. Paul would help us on Sundays.

Weekdays we finished the delivery by six. We returned home and usually napped for about fifteen or twenty minutes. I was at school by seven-thirty. Nikki and Pauly had the responsibility for getting up, showering, getting their continental breakfast, and catching the school bus. Pauly overslept only once. He missed the school bus because I had left early to take Nikki to Bishop O'Connell High School in Arlington. Lucky for him, he was able to get our retired neighbor, Ridgeway Fortune, to take him to school.

The children were also responsible for collecting the money for delivering the papers. We would prepare an envelope for each customer a week before the money was due. As the paper was delivered the kids would attach the envelope to each subscriber's door. A note was written on the envelope indicating that the subscriber should leave a check in the envelope provided for pick-up the next morning. If the payments were not left the very next morning, they were usually left before the due day.

This procedure worked extremely well. I would drive Nikki and Pauly to the areas to finish collecting from the few customers who did not follow directions. Pauly took the responsibility for balancing the books at the end of the month. We had to pay what was owed to the *Washington Post* whether the customers had paid or not. Of course if we got a customer who was a couple of months behind, his paper would no longer be delivered.

Pauly evenly divided the earnings among the three of us. Both Nikki and Pauly built up quite a bank account. Pauly used some of his money to buy a moped, and Nikki spent a lot of hers on Parisian fashions during the summer we spent in Paris. I just had extra money to do as I wished. Christmastime was a windfall because of all the Christmas presents.

Back then, it was boys and girls who delivered the paper and collected the payment. Today, we never see who delivers our paper. We know that it is delivered by car or truck. The paperboy, and later papergirl, are, for the most part, a thing of the past. This tiny job, which was often a gigantic one, taught our children responsibility and that hard work brings results. Their names along with other boys and girls were listed in an issue of the *Washington Post* as outstanding newspaper carriers. They also received a silver plaque. Paul took Driver's Education in high school and to this day has never received a ticket, nor has he had an accident with another car. He once slid into a concrete wall while attending graduate school at Rutgers University. He has driven the mountainous roads of Guadeloupe and the circumference of France without one driving infraction.

Nikki also took Driver's Education in high school. Her driver's record is a whole different story! I knew we would have some problems with Nikki's driving when we stopped at the end of the driveway to get the mail. She put the car in *R*. When I screamed because she was about to back into the street without looking for oncoming traffic, Nikki replied, "I thought the *R* stood for *RUN.*"

Both Nikki and Pauly received brand new cars when they graduated from college. Nikki a red Subaru XT, and Pauly a black Honda Accord. However, they both drove our family car in high school, sometimes having to drop me off at Luther Jackson. In many ways, the eighties were the good old days. Parents could drive juniors and seniors to school and they would even ride the school bus. Teenagers did not have to have their own personal transportation. At least in our house, they didn't.

It was my students at Luther Jackson who decided that I needed a boy friend. Rogia Teal, one of my French students, was instrumental in finding me my first boyfriend. Before integration, black students from all over Fairfax County attended Luther Jackson Intermediate and High School. The enrollment there included children from Fort Belvoir Army Base off Route 1 in Alexandria. Rogia was a friend of Marianne, who was also one of my French students. Marianne lived on the army base. Rogia, Marianne, and Marianne's father arranged a blind date for me.

One Sunday afternoon I picked up Rogia, and we drove to Marianne's home. We all then drove to the Officers' Club. There we met Julius McNair and had dinner. I never thought blind dates worked out, that is, if you can call dinner with two of my students and a couple of parents a date. This blind date did work out, and really well. Julius called me the next weekend for a movie date. After that, we dated seriously for the next year until he was transferred to Germany in 1962, and until Paul Lawrence Bellamy Jr., the student teacher, came into my life.

My own experience as a student teacher was another unfamiliar and challenging journey. Once more Bennett and my professors were my support system. There were several prospective teachers who wanted to be placed in the Greensboro area. Some of us went to the black high school in the city. Cynthia Eddy and I went to Sedalia, a small town, outside Greensboro. It was as if the Education Department knew that I had come from a small school like Sedalia, and I would feel right at home.

Bennett College arranged both our transportation and our bag lunch, which we picked up at breakfast. Mrs. Bethea, a social studies teacher, who worked at the school but lived in Greensboro proper, picked us up in front of the Student Union. She also dropped us off in the afternoon. Sedalia High was much like Central High. I taught three classes of French I and II and one class of English. This meant that I had two separate sets of plans to prepare each evening for two different supervisors.

Mrs. Bethea asked me to type skill worksheets for her students for which she paid me twenty-five cents per page. This was unexpected money for me to buy paper and other materials for the classroom. I was also taking Spanish II at Bennett. I could only attend the class on Saturdays. In order not to fall behind, Mrs. Raiford gave me assignments for the week. My supervisor and my students provided me with the support and the feedback to fulfill my dream of becoming a teacher. I set about learning everything I could about managing a classroom and imparting the knowledge I had to my students.

By the end of the nine-week period I had probably learned more from my students than I had taught them. As a gift the students gave me two sets of clip-on earrings that I still have in my jewelry box. My ears are pierced. Anyway I usually wear the same earrings and necklaces all the time. I am told I am the fastest dresser on the planet.

All my life people have pushed me to succeed. They have made it impossible for me to fail. Aside from the people who have personally touched my life, the most impressive and memorable person whom I have ever met was Martin Luther King Jr. In 1958, Dr. King spoke at Bennett College. It was the spring of my senior year, and several weeks after I had completed my student teaching. Because he was not able to speak at any public facility in Greensboro for fear of reprisal, our president Dr. Willa Beatrice Player invited him to speak at Bennett College. Dr. King spoke to a packed crowd of about two thousand people in our Annie Merner Pfeiffer Chapel. The crowd spilled over into the basement. He began his speech as follows:

*You would have never have of heard of Martin
If it hadn't been for Rosa Parks and the humble
people of Montgomery, Alabama, who decided to
walk in dignity, rather than ride in disgrace.*

Those were Martin Luther King's words that many have forgotten. A few years ago, members of the library staff found a reel-to-reel tape in the archives of Bennett College. Though badly damaged, the tape was restored and can still be heard on *The Washington Post* web site. The seventy-two minute oration was given at the birth of the Civil Rights Movement.

In 1958, many people were leery of the activities of civil rights groups and any person connected with the movement. None of the churches, black or white, in Greensboro would agree to have this now famous minister speak. Our president offered our Annie Merner Pfeiffer Chapel to Dr. King when North Carolina Agricultural and Technical State University (A & T) refused because of fears of economic reprisal. Black church leaders did not want to alienate the white establishment. None gave Dr. King permission to use their pulpit.

The Greensboro Record reported the speech with the front-page headlines: Live as Brothers or Die as Fools, Negroes Told, with a subheading Segregation is Dying Noisily.

The speech had the crowd applauding repeatedly, myself included. Some of Dr. King's phrases in this nationally unpublished speech were immortalized in later speeches and have become famous such as:

*"We aren't in the Promised Land yet, but we've broken
through the Egypt of segregation, and we're moving...
toward the Promised Land of integration.
And we are going in.*

Our chapel was opened to all people that evening, but Bennett students had to enter last only if there was space left. I have an uncanny knack for slipping through small spaces, but by the time I inched through the crowd outside, there were no seats or standing room left. I managed to squeeze into a tiny space on the floor in the back of the chapel. Nevertheless, I had a view of Dr. King as he stood at the podium. Though he had not yet become the great historical figure, his dynamic gifts as an orator mesmerized me.

At the end of his speech, I excitedly pushed my way through the crowd, and finally reached the front of the chapel where Dr. King was standing. I stretched out my hand holding the program and asked pleadingly, "May I please have your autograph?" He graciously signed my program. I later put

the program with Dr. King's autograph in my trunk that was kept in the basement of Pfeiffer Hall. At the end of the school year, I shipped the trunk filled
with clothes to my Cousin Geneva's home in South Ozone Park, New York.
The trunk stayed in her basement until I moved to Virginia. I still have my
trunk, that Nikki also used at Spelman College. But I never saw the program,
or Martin Luther King's signature, again.

Early in the spring of 1958 I signed the first contract I was offered. I was
to teach French and English in the Dillon County School System. The contract read as follows:

DILLON COUNTY TEACHER'S CONTRACT
(Teacher's Copy)

Article of agreement made and entered into this <u>19</u> day of <u>May</u> in the
year of our Lord, one thousand nine hundred and <u>58</u>, between the Board of
Trustees of Lake View District. No. 1 party of the first part, and Fannie
Lillian Miles, Brooklyn, N. Y. party of the second part.

WITNESSETH:

That the party of the first part has duly appointed said party
of the second part to the position of teacher in the <u>Columbus
High</u> School for the scholastic year of <u>1958-59</u> at a salary of
<u>$6,000.00</u> of state plus supplement on Group, class, and Grade
for Dillon County.

That this contract is made and accepted subject,
absolutely in the full acceptance by the party of the second part of the following provisions and conditions:

I shall carry out to the best of my ability all instruc-
tions of the District Superintendent or School
Principal and will cooperate to the fullest extent with
all members of said organizations.

I shall endeavor to place the school's welfare above
personal interest and to keep physically fit to render
efficient service.

I shall conduct myself with due decorum, both in
school and out of school which becomes the position to
which I am elected.

I shall uphold the high ethical standards of the
teaching profession in all my contacts with pupils, parents, school officials and other members of the community.

I shall submit my resignation, if in the opinion of
the District Superintendent and a majority of the
Board any of these conditions or provisions be violated.

Resignation to be submitted upon request of the Superintendent and the Board of Trustees. Thirty days notice is to be given by the Board of Trustees before the services of said teacher are severed from the school.

I shall attend all meetings upon request of Supervisory and Administration Personnel, unless providentially hindered.

I shall make an effort to visit (if teaching in the Elementary School) the home of each pupil in my class between September and January

I agree that this contract shall become null and void, at the option of the party of the first part, if funds or appropriations are ended under the provision of Section 21-2, 1957 Cumulative Supplement. 1952 code of Laws of South Carolina.

The party of the second part hereby agrees that <u>she</u> will accept the said appointment named above under the provision and conditions named above.

Our nation's welfare rests heavily upon the shoulders of those who serve in the field of education. Your strict adherence to this contract will better enable us to carry out our mission more efficiently.

Fannie L. Miles

_____

Witness: _____ Board of Trustees of District No. 1
      S. D. Smith, Principal   by

_____

T. W. Eatman

In late August I took the Greyhound Bus down to Lake View, South Carolina. I totally underestimated the number of changes and the connection times from New York to Lake View. I arrived one day late for the battery of teacher's meetings. Mr. Smith, the principal of Lakeview High School, picked me up at the filling station at the end of the teachers' in-service day. The Esso Filling Station was the town's bus stop. Luckily for me, my room-mate, Mary Jamison, who taught English, had arrived on time and was able to fill me in on what had transpired in the first teacher's meeting.

Mary and I shared a double bed at the Fords, who lived a very short distance from the school. We were also in close proximity to the principal, who lived in a newly built brick house directly across from the school. He could keep tabs on his newly hired teachers. I know this to be true because our landlady was an informer. One morning I got up very early to catch an early bus to Lumberton, North Carolina. I did not tell my landlady where I was going. She was never a very hospitable person.

On the bus ride down I had jotted down the name and location of a black-owned beauty shop located on the main route through Lumberton, North Carolina. The following Monday, Mrs. Smith, the principal's wife, informed me that Mrs. Ford was concerned about my leaving so early on Saturday. She couldn't imagine where I was headed.

On one of the Saturdays after I had flagged down the bus heading toward Lake View and stepped on board, I saw no empty seats in the back. I sat by a woman on the third or fourth seat from the front. The woman screamed, "Get up you, black bitch, and go to the back." I responded, "I'm not moving , you white one!' She yelled to the driver, "Stop this bus!"

The driver pulled over, got up from his seat and told me to go to the back of the bus. I said I wasn't moving, and I had paid the same fare as everyone else. He kept insisting for a couple of minutes, but I stuck to my guns. He then told the woman to move to another empty seat closer to the front. I arrived back in Lake View safely and in one piece.

Our room was twenty dollars per month for each of us. We had use of the kitchen, but neither Mary nor I was much of a cook. Our breakfast usually consisted of cold cereal and a glass of Tang. Our big meal was eaten in the school cafeteria. The principal's wife was the Home Economics teacher and the supervisor of the school cafeteria. Needless to say, our fee of six dollars per month for lunch was a bargain. We usually had a light supper. Grits and sardines became my favorite evening meal. Today, I can't stand grits or sardines. However, Mary was a better cook than I. She would sometimes cook a special meal and share it with me. I was introduced to okra for the first time.

I was again living in a house without indoor plumbing. Each morning Mary and I would take turns getting up and starting a fire in the wood stove, and heating the kettle for our morning wash-off. The one who stayed in bed longer could catch at least a half hour more of sleep. Our most modern convenience was electricity, that provided us with light and an electric stove for cooking. We took turns taking out the chamber pot. The outdoor toilet was located a short distance from the house, but almost directly in front of the home of another Ford family.

The lowly chamber pot. These hours in the night and gray dawn. What a great leveler the chamber pot is. All our aspirations for sophistication, being in fashion, laid low by the simple and so necessary chamber pot. And the cold nights!

While my mind is not fixated on chamber pots, I do sometimes look at the students today, with their Palm Pilots and calculators, their cell phones, and Internets. I think about how Mary and I survived and studied. No rancor or jealousy here; just a bemused look at the times we lived in, our aspirations for learning, and our careful movements in the dark hours to find that cold pot, which above all other thoughts was the answer to our needs....

There were lots of "Fords" in Lake View. One of our French and English students lived in the house in the back. Each of us tried to time when the student would be getting up, so we could take out the chamber pot without being seen. There was also the problem of just going to the toilet for regular visits. Both Mary and I made good use of the bathroom facilities at Columbus High.

I was ecstatic that we had electricity instead of oil lamps. Having just this one convenience made reading and preparations for class much easier. Other modern conveniences were no longer a part of our lives. We went back to the antiquated method of washing clothes using a tub and washboard, and taking a tub bath only on the weekend.

Mrs. Ford, in addition to being a spy for the principal, was very strict with her roomers. When she said anything at all it was usually a complaint. I don't recall Mr. Ford ever saying more than two words to either of us. The two words were, "Good morning!" and "Good evening." We were not allowed to use the living room. In fact, the living room was never used by anyone.

Our time at the Fords was divided between the bedroom and the kitchen. After our first paycheck, Mary bought a tiny black-and-white television. I saved enough money to buy a record player when I went home for Christmas break. Mrs. Ford complained if I played my Harry Belafonte records too loudly. Listening to records and watching television was the extent of our entertainment away from school.

Some evenings we would walk a couple of yards down the road to visit two other young first-year teachers. One of the teachers, Louvenia Jackson, and I became close friends. All of the other teachers at Columbus High had cars and lived some distance from the school. The four first-year teachers did not have cars. Heck, I did not even know how to drive. Mary could drive but she didn't have a car. Sometimes, Mary would get a ride to Orangeburg, her hometown. She would invite me to come along.

At least twice a month I would go home with Louvenia, who was from Florence, South Carolina. It was no longer necessary for me to go to Lumberton to get my hair done. I went to Louvenia's beautician. I never hit it off with Louvenia's roommate, Mary Downing, perhaps because we never hit it off from our very first conversation. She asked if I were gay, because of my choosing a women's college, and because I did not comment on her bawdy stories of her sexual exploits in college.

Columbus High School had been built just a few years before I arrived. It housed grades eight through twelve. Next door was the older clapboard building that was once both the elementary and the high school. It was now the elementary school for grades one through seven. Mr. Smith was the principal of both schools.

I, a first-year teacher, was a sponsor of the junior class. A number of fund raising activities were necessary to raise money for the Junior-Senior prom. We had weekend dances in the old school building, fish fries at the homes of students, and sold refreshments at the basketball games. At all of these activities I was the sole chaperon, something that would be unheard of now. At the time students were well behaved and courteous, even to a young first year teacher, just as they were at Organ Hill and Central High School.

In 1950s Dillon County, cotton was king. Most of the students came from homes where their parents were sharecroppers. At the beginning of the school year, September and part of October, more than half of the students were out of school picking cotton. By the end of year the white farmers were complaining to Mr. Smith that too many tenants were asking for advances on the next year's crops to pay junior class expenses.

Thinking back, I am again bemused by what the students have today compared with the students from these early days. Think about it: farmers complaining about cotton-picking students wanting advances on next year's crop, so they could afford the junior prom. Social pressure there, but how different to the kids today. Cuts on hands some healed, some not, from picking cotton. Today, we have fortunate youngsters with fancy cars and an upscale way of life. Not many, I wager, pick cotton! And yet, come prom night, they would have a lot in common: smiling faces, excited eyes looking around, as they moved one step closer to their lives as adults.

The junior prom was held in the gymnasium, which was decorated like a cruise ship. Back then there were catalogs where sponsors could order a variety of packets that contained everything needed for just about any prom theme. Thus, for the cruise ship theme, there was a sky complete with a moon and stars and gangplanks for entrances. For everything else that was needed—paper plates, cups, etc., a group of students and I left school one afternoon for a buying spree in Dillon, a town with more stores than Lake View, even a five and ten cents store. The student driver borrowed his father's car.

Mary's boyfriend came up for the prom. She asked him to bring along a friend as my date. He did. We corresponded for a while after I came to Virginia. I can't remember the young man's name, though.

I was also responsible for directing and producing the junior class play. Both the junior prom and the play were successful. My classes were filled with great students who showed me much love and respect. Nevertheless, I decided that I did not want to return to Columbus High School the following year. When I informed Mr. Smith that I was leaving, he tried to convince me to stay. He even told me that I could move up as sponsor of the senior class. I would be working with the same students.

I agreed to stay but only because I didn't want to deal with his hassling me for the rest of the school year. I was a coward! If I had not made up my mind before, I definitely would have after the year ended. All of the teachers in the county were forced to stay around for a week after school closed. The county ran out of money. The county was permitted to do this because *The party of the first part agreed that the contract is null and void if funds are ended.* Nevertheless, we were told to hang around and hope that the county would come up with additional monies. After a week they did, but we were not reimbursed for the extra money we had to spend for rent. There were rumors that the white teachers in the county had been paid on time, and it was only the black teachers who were forced to wait until the county found the money.

A lot of good came out of my decision to leave South Carolina. I came back to my "Old Virginny" to stay, and Fairfax County never ran out of money to pay us after we had worked the entire school year. Fairfax County divides the yearly pay into twelve equal payments. South Carolina paid its teachers according to the number of days we actually worked, so at the end of the school year, the Dillon County School Board owed me a good portion of my six thousand dollar salary.

In spite of my very low yearly salary, I was able to send Mama most of the money I made each month. Cousin Geneva took us to look at houses in South Ozone Park that summer, but we gave up on the idea of buying a house. Instead, with the money we saved, Mama and I rented an apartment on Hancock Street, a few blocks from Eliza Etta on Albany Avenue, and Willoughby on Decatur Street.

After a few years, Mama came down to Northern Virginia, where we rented an apartment together. The apartment was on the main floor of a house that Blakely Weaver had renovated and divided into four apartments. Two of the apartments were rented to coworkers, Annette Dillard and Virginia Major. A former French student, Connie Ellis, and her family occupied the fourth one. Annette was my best friend at Luther Jackson High. She married Adolphus Coward, the shop teacher. We all became friends when I married Paul, the student teacher.

Mrs. Greenfield had written Mama a good reference, so she had no difficulty getting jobs, mostly babysitting and light housework. I would take Mama to work before school and pick her up after school.

Fairfax County Annual Teacher's Contract was similar to Dillon County's. However, there was no mention of *Lord* or *God* and no requirement that elementary school teachers visit each student in her class by the end of the first semester. Visiting each student's home would have caused great difficulty for me. There was mention of "the party of the second part" many times in the contract.

I received a call from Taylor Williams, principal of Luther Jackson High School. He asked me to come down for an interview, which was set up with the supervisor of higher education in the county. I am not sure of her title. I think her name was Mrs. Ford. I took the Greyhound bus down from New

York for a ten o'clock appointment. In Washington, I changed for a local bus to Fairfax City.

Fairfax County School Offices were located in the old county courthouse. The bus put me off at the filling station directly in front of the courthouse. Needless to say, I got the job. After the interview, Mrs. Ford made a call to Luther Jackson and asked if someone could come and pick me up, so that I could visit the school. Assistant Principal Robert Tate picked me up. I took a tour of the school and met the principal and the office personnel, Jeanne Minor and Loretta Berry. Mr. Tate then took me to the Greyhound Bus Station in Washington, D. C. I had left Eliza Etta's apartment at two o'clock, taken the subway to New York City, and the bus down to Virginia. On the way to the Washington Bus Terminal, I dozed off in the middle of the conversation with my now assistant principal. I was embarrassed, to say the least.

I returned in late August to Luther Jackson, a relatively new school. It had opened in 1954. The 1959 enrollment did not reach expectations. After a few weeks at Luther Jackson, I was reassigned to Drew-Smith Elementary School, off Route 1 in Alexandria. *"The said party of the second part"* had the right to transfer me without warning for just cause. I had no car and could not drive. By the time I learned that I would be transferred to another school, the principal, Taylor Williams, and assistant principal, Robert Tate, had made all arrangements for the transfer.

After interviewing with the Fairfax County Personnel Officer and signing the contract, there were other people who worked out my housing arrangements. I am not sure who—probably the principal, Taylor Williams. Fairfax County was segregated in all respects. There was no possibility of my finding an apartment available for a black teacher. In fact, there were few apartment buildings available to any teacher. Fairfax County, though not as rural as Dillon County, was rural. Route 7 and Route 50 were two lanes. Seven Corners was the newly built shopping mall. Nutley Road, which crosses Route 66, was a two-lane road with a one-lane bridge over a small stream.

For three years I roomed and boarded with Mrs. Mae Hall on Lewinsville Road in McLean, Virginia. Mrs. Hall was a cook par excellence! Luther Jackson was about ten miles away. There was no walking across the street to school, as had been the case in South Carolina. Mr. Griffin, the band teacher, lived down the road, so I would ride with him to and from school.

After my transfer to Alexandria, I rode with Mr. Lacey who lived in the neighborhood. He was also a teacher at the elementary school. Mr. Lacey picked up Beverly Taylor at Luther Jackson. I always sat in the back seat and listened to Beverly gossip about every other teacher in school, especially about what lousy teachers they were. I was sure that if I were not in the car that I would be the subject of conversation.

I never missed a single day of school that year. Mrs. Hall told me that she heard I was having a difficult time. I was not certified to teach elementary school. This assignment was made more difficult by my having to teach two classes in the same room—sixth and seventh grades. It was necessary to recall the success of Reverend Venable, who managed quite well with three grades in one room.

I had no problems teaching the core subjects of English, social studies, and even physical education. For May Day I taught the students to do a polka. It was one of the dances I learned in my folk dancing class at Bennett. Mathematics or arithmetic were always my weakest subjects. I would go to Mr. Lacey when I needed help.

I especially needed his help at the end of the year when I had to balance the dreaded *Teacher's Registry*, an exact accounting of the days students were present or absent. Mrs. Taylor never offered a helping hand.

Corporal punishment was still legal in the state of Virginia. One of my students made a paddle for me to use when necessary. I got in trouble with a parent for striking her son for being a smart aleck.

Each afternoon, I rode back with Alice Williams who lived a couple of miles down the road from Mrs. Hall. Alice is still a dear friend. The year 1959-1960 is a year to remember during my "illustrative years" of teaching. Saunders B. Moon, the principal of Drew Smith, was also of tremendous help during my year of teaching elementary education. His son was in my sixth grade class at Drew-Smith. Evidently, Saunders, Jr. did not tell his father "tales from the classroom." I received no criticism from him—only helpful suggestions.

It was Dee and her family who began calling me Lil instead of Fannie. Most of the teachers from the old Luther Jackson still call me Fannie. However, when I married Paul I officially changed my name to Lillian, and took my maiden name as my middle name. "Fannie" just did not go with "Bellamy."

At the end of the year, I was again offered the job of teaching at Luther Jackson High School. This was the year the *intermediate school* was introduced to the county system. Some educator came up with the bright idea that seventh and eighth graders needed to be housed in a separate building. Seventh graders were, "too mature for the elementary school, and eighth graders were not mature enough for high school." Thus new intermediate schools were built in different parts of the county to house those two grades.

These schools were traditionally named after American poets. Because of the Fairfax County system of segregation, the seventh grades from the different black elementary schools were moved to Luther Jackson. Luther Jackson, the name of a black educator, was kept in spite of the desire of the white parents to change the name to that of the poet, Carl Sandburg. The change was attempted when the school was integrated in 1965.

After integration Luther Jackson became an intermediate school like all black high schools in Virginia. In the late 1980s, another educator decided that the intermediate school concept was wrong. Sixth graders should be with the seventh and eighth graders, and the intermediate school should then be designated as *middle schools*.

Because the intermediate schools had been built to house only two grades, most sixth graders in Fairfax County remained in the elementary schools that should have housed only kindergarten through fifth grade. The term, intermediate school, is no longer used—except by forgetful me. The schools between elementary and high school are now called middle schools, even those that do not have sixth grade.

In the late 1960s and early 1970s, someone else came up with the idea of the open-school (classrooms with no walls) for grades seven through twelve. These schools were called *secondary schools*. Classrooms with no walls proved to be too noisy for the other classrooms with no walls, so now the classrooms with no walls have all been walled up, except for the door needed by the teacher and students to enter and leave.

Oakton High School was also built in the 1960s. It is built directly in front of the house where Paul and I used to live. The architect must have also been a teacher. Most of the classrooms are traditional ones. Oakton High has a number of classrooms with removable walls that can accommodate team teaching and large groups of students. Fortunately, open schools are now a thing of the past.

Oakton High School has a relatively new concept, that of *block scheduling*. It is like the system the French have always had. The schedule is also much like our college or university class schedule. The students attend most classes on alternate days, except at Oakton there is one class they must attend every day, seventh period.

When Marilyn Coates or Lisa Ludeke gives me the teacher's *Substitute Folder*, the first thing I check for is whether or not the teacher has a seventh period. Seventh period is always the most rambunctious class of the day. I don't understand why, except this is the only class that meets every day. Luther Jackson follows the same plan, except on Monday the students go to each of their classes. I like this system better. Not all intermediate schools in Fairfax County follow block scheduling. It works well in high school, but for intermediate students I prefer the shorter periods. Seventh and eighth graders are just too fidgety for close to two-hour classes of instruction. However, I didn't have a problem with my French students. There are just so many ways to teach the skills of listening, speaking, and writing a foreign language. On the other hand, I guess I am just prejudiced. For me, teaching a foreign language is just pure fun, whether it is done during long or short periods.

When I returned to Luther Jackson, there were a number of students from my sixth grade class who were now in my *ALM (Audio Language Material)* French classes. *ALM* was a method of teaching students to speak the foreign language before learning to read and write the target language. *Speaking* was taught through dialogues, by having the students mimic the teacher and native speakers on tape. The end result would be that the students would memorize the dialogues.

Each dialogue dealt with a particular subject such as "School," "Home" and "Shopping." The problem was getting the students to use the vocabulary of the dialogues in other contexts. The grammar of the foreign language was taught by a series of oral drills in which students would fill in the blank with a subject, verb, adjective, or whatever grammatical structure was contained in the dialogues.

My fellow language teacher was Mayme Holt. She not only spoke fluent Spanish, but her physical appearance would lead one to think that she hailed from Spain. She had beautiful olive skin and long black straight hair that she wore in a chignon. Mayme was a great role model for an inexperienced teacher, and to an inexperienced supervisor of a student teacher.

A week before the student teachers were to come to Luther Jackson, the supervising teachers met at Virginia State College. At the meetings were the department heads who would be sending students to Luther Jackson. They would also make observation visits and monitor their progress. We, as the supervisors, would be working with the student teachers for a nine-week period. My first meeting with Paul left no lasting impression. But after a couple of weeks of observation, he took over my French classes. I thought he had the attributes for becoming a teacher. Needless to say he received an *A* for his effort.

After Paul returned to his hometown of Suffolk, he began writing regularly. He knew I had plans to take my students to the 1965 New York World's Fair. Paul asked if he could be one of the chaperons, and since my students knew him, I thought it was a good idea. He brought his mother, Mrs. Anita Bellamy, along.

Paul also had the bright idea of chaperoning the Junior-Senior prom, of which I was co-sponsor, along with Harriette Hemby. The most pressing reason for his returning to Northern Virginia was to interview for a job.

My protesting that I did not want to date him seemed to have no effect. He even tried to give me his fraternity pin. While I was at Bennett, it was a big thing for a fellow from A & T College to give a Bennett Belle his fraternity pin. We even had a song or chant that we performed for the occasion. I had been there, but hadn't done that, but I still wasn't interested in Paul's fraternity pin.

Evidently, Out of sight, out of mind, is true. His persistence soon made me forget Julius, and we began dating the summer of 1964. Even Mama's adverse reaction to Paul did not deter him. He took a teaching job at Booker T. Washington High School in Suffolk, Virginia, the school he had attended. He would come up at least once a month, and we corresponded by mail at least once a week.

Mama and I had planned to go to Brooklyn for Christmas. Paul came up to accompany us. He gave me my Christmas present, an engagement ring, before we left for the holidays. When I showed the ring to Mama, she became very upset. At this point, she had become very possessive, or maybe she thought Paul just wasn't the man for me. For so many years, it had been just Mama and me.

I had gone away to college and I had spent a summer in France. Mama and I were now living together in Virginia, and Paul was an intrusion. Nevertheless, we drove to New York in an uncomfortable silence. While we were in Brooklyn, Eliza Etta gave us a small engagement party, just friends and family. Mama continued to show her displeasure. She promptly announced that she was moving back to Brooklyn. Eliza Etta suggested that to make things easier Paul and I should get married immediately.

On Saturday, January 23, 1965, we were married in the Vienna Presbyterian Church. Cousin Geneva brought Mama down for the occasion. Other members of the wedding party were Dee and Blakely Weaver. Paul's brother Ralph was best man, and his girl friend Carolyn was maid of honor. Later, after Mama and Geneva returned to New York, Paul and I went to the Weaver's for dinner. We returned to the apartment around eleven o'clock.

The next day I took Paul to the station as customary, and on Monday I returned to school. I had told no one at school that I was getting married, but everyone knew! I have never figured out how they knew. Vienna was still a very small town back then.

Mama never visited us until a couple of years later. After we were married, Paul continued to come up only on weekends for the next year and a half. By that time Mama had come for a visit, and Paul was now working in the area. We had bought land, built a new house, and I was expecting our daughter, Nikki.

The schools in Fairfax were completely integrated in 1965. I was transferred to Longfellow Intermediate, in McLean. In preparation for integration, black teachers were thought to need special training sessions for teaching white students. For these in-service seminars we were given a stipend. One of the training sessions was a course in speech. Imagine me, a French teacher taking lessons on how to speak English from a white teacher from the Deep South.

Nevertheless, I encountered no serious problems during my two years in the newly integrated Longfellow. However, at Back-to-School Night a parent asked for my credentials for teaching French. On another occasion, a parent wrote me a letter on his business stationery containing his name and the members of his law firm—for a total of about ten names. At the time Fairfax County was using the *ALM* textbook. He wanted to know why I wasn't teaching the traditional French grammar.

Back then, a teacher was not allowed to teach if they were pregnant—that is, if "they were showing" as Mama used to say. I became pregnant in January of 1967. Paul and I planned it that way. I could finish the rest of the year since I had not put on much weight. My students knew I was pregnant before I told the administration. Also back then, students were not supposed to know where babies come from.

For the next three years, I stayed home with Nikki, who was born October 12, 1967, Columbus's Birthday. The night before Nikki was born, Paul and I were in the Annandale Theater watching the Julie Andrew's film *The Sound of Music*. The next day was spent in hard labor, until Dr. Brandt knocked me out with chloroform.

When I awoke, I was alone in my room asking for my baby. Chloroform is no longer used in a normal delivery, if at all. Mama would say the circumstances surrounding Nikki's birth had something to do with the child and woman she became.

When she was finally brought to me, I thought she was the most beautiful baby I had ever seen. She had her father's face, including large and beautiful eyes. The only odd thing about her was her hairline, which extended to her eyebrows. Happily, this hair disappeared after a few days. Perhaps the strange hairline was a symbol of her strength and determination just as Columbus, whose birthday she shared, was strong and determined. The beautiful story told in *The Sound of Music* symbolizes her beauty.

While I was away from teaching, Paul and I decided to have a second child. Pauly was born fifteen months later. His delivery was easy. I felt very little pain. Dr. Brandt gave me an epidural, but I was awake and remember his birth. The most noticeable thing about Pauly was his cleft chin, just like his father's. For the next two and a half years I stayed home, content with being a wife and mother.

I had planned to return to teaching when both children were eligible for nursery school. Colonel Fairweather, who was the principal when I left Longfellow, had moved to Luther Jackson, my old school. He had told me when I left Longfellow to let him know when I wanted to return. I called to tell him that I would be ready to return to school in September 1971. He informed me that he would have an opening in English at the beginning of the second semester. I didn't want to take a chance of losing the opportunity to return to teaching by waiting until the following school year. I called the Fairfax County Schools Personnel Office. I told the receptionist that I wanted to apply for the English position at Luther Jackson.

"There is no opening at Luther Jackson."

"Yes, there is! I just finished talking with Colonel Fairweather, and he said there is a position available."

There was a pause while the receptionist went to talk to someone else. When she returned she took my name and address and said she would send me an application.

I returned to the integrated Luther Jackson at the beginning of the second semester, 1971, as an English teacher. I wonder for whom the director of personnel was saving the job. I am glad Colonel Fairweather wanted me as a teacher on his staff. I would be returning to the school where I began my sojourn in Fairfax County. "Fairweather" was a perfect name for this principal. This experience with the personnel office shows how easily a person in authority can misinform, for no apparent reason. I often do not take "no" for an answer.

Returning to work after a two-year hiatus was difficult. Nikki and Pauly had to learn a completely different schedule. I had to keep up with all my teaching duties as well as the work at home. I had begun visiting nursery schools a few months before actively seeking a job. We had pretty much settled on Small World at the corner of Kingsley and Park Street. I chose Small World for the love and care given to the children, as well as the teachers centering the lesson around the theme of a different country each month. It was also very convenient because the school was on my way to Luther Jackson.

Paul would get Pauly up and dressed, and I would do the same for Nikki. I would do her hair in cornrows on the weekend. This hairstyle would last for a week with only a brushing or so. I would drop both children off in the morning and pick them up in the afternoon. It was Pauly, the little one, who caused the least problems. Nikki would cry for her mommy.

The children remained at Small World for two years, then transferred to Creative Day School, which I thought had an even better program. After kindergarten, they both transferred to Our Lady of Good Counsel Catholic School in Vienna. Back then, parents were expected to help in the school cafeteria a couple of times during the year. I would often get my friend Dorothy Hall, a retired teacher, to substitute for me.

When I worked briefly as an assistant librarian, Colonel Fairweather would let me leave school during my lunch period to take care of my responsibility in the cafeteria. He also permitted me to pick up Nikki when OLGC began closing early on Mondays. Nikki would do her homework in the library.

One good thing, among many others, for parents having their children attend private or parochial school, is that there is no decision to be made about what the children should wear each day. Students are not concerned with the best dressed girl or boy. Schools in foreign countries require uniforms. This rule has also been adopted in many inner city schools. For the 2003-2004 school year Fairfax County instituted a dress code. Girls are not allowed to show their midriff, or to wear their jeans so low that their thong undies can be seen. I hope this also includes tops that show too much of the breasts. Boys are not to wear jeans or pants that reveal their underwear either.

When I agreed to supervise student teachers, I was supposed to be the model of what a good teacher should be. Recently, a first-year teacher at Luther Jackson, where I still substitute, asked me if she might e-mail me once in a while in order to discuss teaching strategies. I told her that I did not have e-mail, but she should feel free to call me. I now have e-mail, but I can never remember my e-mail address. I can't remember telephone numbers either, except for mine.

I do remember one of my students asking me this question after we had finished a day's lesson with one minute of class time left—"Madame, how can you plan each minute of every class period, so we have no time left for socializing?" I really didn't have an answer.

I have always gotten the best students in school. These exceptional students were in my French classes, English classes, and my Introduction to Foreign Language classes. I guess I have just been lucky that way.

I became certified as a librarian, and for a couple of years I was assistant librarian to Mable Jolly Mosley at Luther Jackson Intermediate. I though it might be fun to work with all the students in the school. It wasn't. I longed for my classroom and my own little group of students. I asked to return to the classroom.

Returning to the question about no time to socialize—I thought of my class as a big stage with a different scene being played each day. My students were the actors and actresses, but I would write the script. The classroom was divided into two sections with students facing each other. They were then able to engage in dialogue in unison or with a partner. One day I was standing on the side of the room closest to the window. A student across the room kept talking out of turn. The student, a boy, closest to me yelled:

"Shut up, Michael! You dummy! We are trying to learn to speak Latin!"

Michael responded, "Who said that?"

"I did!" I said, answering in my loudest normal voice.

The rest of the class giggled. Michael was too shocked to say anything.

Teachers have to have a sense of humor! Most of the stuff I teach each day is in my head, but for the sake of principals and assistant principals or other important people who might drop in, I would write the objectives and agenda to be followed on the board. Upon entering the room some student would invariably ask, "Madame, what are we doing today?" My answer would always be, *"Regardez le tableau noir!"* My blackboards were always black. Today when a student enters the room, he or she says, "Are you our substitute?" My answer is, "No, I am just visiting." Elise Keely wrote what might be a description of me. I was a long-term substitute for the first and last quarter, 1998-1999 at Luther Jackson:

June 1999

Dear Madame,
Thank you very much for teaching me this quarter. I learned a lot. I learned classroom objects, greetings, French numbers, the months, days, seasons, telling time, sports, and foods, how to respond if you like something, and saying where things are, places around the city, the verb "aller," pronouns, and we did a project on Paris. We also wrote mini-dialogues.

149

I think the fact you let us purchase workbooks, so we could write in them helped. I also think it helped when you talked to us in French. You never gave us pop quizzes. You always told us when they were. Thank you for doing that. I like the Paris video you showed us. I am going to Paris (for the first time) this summer with my family. I'm sure I will have a lot of fun. One of my favorite things was the slide show you put together. It was cool. Thank you very much.

Sincerely,
Elise Keely
Period 3

Elise also composed an Acrostic Poem:

Bought us French videos.
Even gave us study guides.
Learned how we learn best.
Less impatient than most.
Always prepared for class.
Made French fun!
You're a great teacher!

With students like Elise, how difficult can it be to teach? When students walked into the *salle de classe*, they sat in their assigned seats because they knew, when I called the roll, I didn't like figuring out in which direction I should look. After learning their names there was no need to call the roll. With a glance I could tell who was missing. I also hated having students wandering around the classroom without a good reason. My standard question is simply, "Why are you out of your seat?"

There is also something wrong with my hearing. Unless students are reciting in unison, I can't understand anybody when several students are talking at the same time. When I get upset, my voice is really strange sounding. Everyone says I have a unique voice, even when I am not upset. I don't doubt that. Students I have not seen in many years recognize me from afar by the mere sound of my voice. Andy Stynchula, whom I taught in the 1970s, recognized me as soon I entered his chiropractic office and said, "Hello!" I would not have recognized him. I remember him as a twelve-year-old boy with a head full of blond hair. He was now a big man and almost bald. People also say when I speak French, I sound completely different—like a different person. I am glad of that, because I would have an awful time with the French people if I sounded American when I speak French.

Students like order, and like most of us they like their own space—thus assigned seats. I never assigned seats the first week of school. I would let them first find a place where they were comfortable. Invariably students would stay in the same seat they had chosen the first day. It still amazes me when a teacher I am substituting for tells me to write down the name of any student who misbehaves. The teacher then plans to deal with the student later. A student who is not on task is going to tell me his name, so he can be punished when the teacher returns?

There are also teachers who think having students sit in alphabetical order will take the place of a seating chart. I am supposed to look down a list of thirty or more students and figure out who isn't on task? Students seem to forget what alphabetical order is when there is a substitute present. The vast majority of the teachers at Luther Jackson, Kilmer, and Oakton High School leave a seating chart. But it's okay when a teacher doesn't leave a seating chart. I simply make one as I call the roll. There are a number of rules and guidelines that always worked for my students, parents and me:

Bienvenue mes élèves! (Welcome students!)
Le Français I—Salle de classe 26—Mme. Bellamy (Belle Amie)

Objectives

- To help each student attain an acceptable degree of proficiency in the four skills of listening, speaking, reading, and writing as presented in Units 1-8 in French for Mastery.
- To present the language within the context of the contemporary French-speaking world.
- To improve the study skills of each student.

Class work and class Participation

- Daily class participation is extremely important as it helps to improve your comprehension and speaking ability in French. You must be alert and ready to answer when called on.
- If new material is unclear to you, don't hesitate to ask for clarification.
- Oral preparation and class work will determine a substantial part of your grade.
- Only French will be spoken in the classroom. Learn immediately the phrases "*Comment dit-on*? And "*Anglais s' il vous plaît!*"

Homework

- Your homework assignment will range from, twenty to thirty minutes each evening and will be given each day.

- Each assignment must be done on the day assigned, or you will have difficulty participating in class the following day. If you find you do not keep up with your daily work, you will soon be so far behind that you will understand little or nothing.
- Vocabulary words should be written at lease five (5) times each (Or until you can spell each word correctly) in your notebook. Study vocabulary for meaning as well as spelling.
- All class work and homework should be kept in divided sections in your notebook. These notes and exercises will be available when you study for quizzes and tests.
- Your workbook and notebook may not be taken up and checked each day; however, they will be taken up and graded at the end of each unit and the end of each grading period. Assignments will also be checked periodically during the quarter.
- Your notebook should be arranged according to the Table of Contents.

Quizzes and Tests
- Quizzes on vocabulary, grammatical structure, and cultural notes of each lesson may or may not be announced.
- All major tests will be announced in advance.

Make-up work and retest
- All work (homework, quizzes, test) missed because of an excused absence, must be made up within the allotted time—one day for each day of absence. Mondays are set aside for work that must be completed after school.
- If for some reason you fail a quiz or get a lower grade than you would like, you may take the quiz again. The grade recorded will be an average of the two quizzes. Therefore, it is certainly to your advantage to do well on the first quiz. If the retest policy is abused, it will be revoked.
- All quizzes must be retaken within a week of the day they are returned to you.
- No test may be taken over.

Final grade (Approximately 20% each)
- Daily average (class participation, quizzes)
- Notebook (homework/class assignment/activity sheets)
- Workbook
- Projects or special assignments
- Unit tests

Fairfax County Grading Scale
94-100 = A
90-93 = B+
84-89 = B
80-83 = C+
74-79 = C
70-73 = D+
64-69 = D
Below 64 = F

Student's Signature _____

Parent's Signature _____

Date _____

BONNE CHANCE!

At a county teacher meeting many years ago I picked up a simple *Discipline Plan*:

IF YOU BREAK A RULE—
1st *TIME: NAME ON THE BOARD*
2nd TIME: CHECK BY NAME
3rd TIME: DETENTION
4th TIME: CALL TO PARENT
5th TIME: CONFERENCE WITH ASSISTANT PRINCIPAL
SEVERE DISRUPTION: ?

In the late 1980s Fairfax County Superintendent Spillane instituted a *Merit Pay Plan*. Teachers who wished to participate had to undergo a year of minute and critical observation. Most teachers had one preparation such as history, English, mathematics, or physical education. They were also involved with only three evaluators. I, on the other hand, had three different preparations and five different evaluators, including the principal Leslie Kent, critiquing me in three different areas—French I, Introduction to Foreign Languages (French, Spanish, German, and Latin), and English. In addition to the class preparation and seeking to be classified as an exceptional teacher, one had to show that he or she was involved in a myriad of duties outside the classroom. Even though I qualified for merit pay I think it is a system that tends to be subjective. The list that follows is an example of extracurricular activities that were a part of a typical school year:

Beyond the Classroom

- Worked on a committee with the curriculum specialist and other Fairfax County teachers in designing and implementing a Latin unit for Introduction to Foreign Language classes (IFL).
- Prepared personal Handbook for substitutes.
- Attended stress management workshop—January 30, 1988 at Marshall High School.
- Attended chairperson's meeting (Foreign Language), February 17, 1988.
- French and IFL students participated in Fairfax County Foreign Language Poster Contest—took posters to and picked them up from the Lacey Center.
- Served as proctor for National French Exam—Saturday, March 5, 1988—8:00 AM to 9:30 A.M.—Took students without transportation to and from site.
- Took Scantron Machine to Marshall High School on March 4 for use in grading the exam—picked up machine before school the following week.
- Participant—Minority Achievement Colloquium, George Mason University, March 11, 1988.
- Prepared a display (Teacher Handbook, Student Test, Calendars of Events, and grant proposal). Purpose was to share Luther Jackson's special program for minorities with other Fairfax County Teachers.
- Received Certificate of Appreciation from Area II superintendent.
- Attended George Mason buffet for Luther Jackson teacher working with Education Course 569 on March 18, 1988.
- Last quarter worked with George Mason Student Jill Latell and Social Studies Department on drama unit having to do with the 1960s.
- Appeared on "Teacher Feature"—discussed *Faisons Français* shown on cable channel 21—week of March 15, 1988.

The interdisciplinary focus of the group called *Faisons Français* was to have students gain a knowledge of history and geography of the French-speaking area through a variety of activities. The activities included weekly meetings, with lessons dealing with the skills of listening to and speaking the language. There were field trips to the French Embassy and embassies of other French speaking nations, a French restaurant, the museum of African Art, and the National Gallery of Art. Additionally, they learned the contributions French-speaking peoples have made to art and science, and the influences they have had upon the United States. Native speakers were invited to come and talk to the students. A French snack was served at each meeting. The students planned the culminating activity.

A few months ago, a friend asked me where I got my Master's Degree. I responded, "I don't have one." I could have gotten a Master's from George Washington University, but I didn't. The program was too time-consuming and rigid. I just took whatever course in French, English, or education that I thought would make me a better teacher and permit me to renew my Virginia Teaching Certificate. When I retired I was at the top of the pay scale for a Bachelor's Degree, with more than sixty graduate credit-hours. Merit pay added to this pay schedule.

I never knew exactly what I should be getting paid anyway. Teachers do not teach because of the great salaries they receive. As a substitute, I realized I wasn't getting paid as a retired teacher, only when I worked seven hours (one day) during a pay period. It was easy for me to do the math. Fairfax County, after a little hassle, gave me my retroactive pay of a couple of thousand dollars—enough for another trip to France. At the present time all teachers new to Fairfax County must pass a mathematics test. Why? How stupid is that! It would make more sense to require all new teachers be proficient in one or more foreign languages.

In 1962, a summer in Europe gave me more of an education than I could have ever gotten in any graduate course. I made a complete circuit of France, visiting many of the ancient provinces. France is traditionally divided into twenty-two provinces. However, modern government and mail delivery and automobile registration is based on ninety-five departmental regions, including Guadeloupe and Martinique. I started off the summer by taking a transatlantic voyage on *Le Flandre*, one of two large post-war French liners. All announcements were first in French, then in English. The crew was French, as were most of the passengers. I was also in an environment where the color of my skin didn't matter.

I took my students to countries whose languages I was teaching were spoken. During spring break, 1976, I took my first group of students to France. We went with an organization called the *American Institute of Foreign Travel*. One of the students' grandmothers and Nikki, who was nine at the time, went along. The group also included the daughter of one of my sorority sisters.

Seven of us flew on a chartered airline called World Airlines. We landed at Orly Airport, France's second largest. There our bilingual English guide, named Alice, and a French driver of our thirty-eight-passenger bus, named Michel, met us. The nine-day trip included guided tours of Paris, Normandy, and Brittany. In Paris we did the usual tours of this fashionable city, the Louvre, the Eiffel Tower, and Versailles. We then journeyed to the beaches of Normandy, and stopped at the site of the nine hundred-year-old Bayeux Tapestry (which is really embroidery) created by "la Reine Mathilde," the wife of William the Conqueror. The tapestry, the most famous in the world, depicts the events of the Battle of Hastings and the conquest of England.

We discovered the monastery of Mont St. Michel, perched high on a rock and guarded by quicksand and changing tides. At the top of the rock are an ancient abbey and town. The town is now a series of souvenir shops that cater to tourists as they wind their way to the top. Nikki enjoyed counting, *un, deux, trois*, and up to ten, the steps up the Grande Rue as she hurried to be the first of our group to reach the top. When she reached "*dix,*" she would start over again. When she got to the top she said, "Mommy, there are a million steps." After reaching the summit of Mont St. Michel we were able to take a guided tour of the abbey, which was founded, in the eighth century by St. Aubert, bishop of Avranches. There is also a museum detailing the history of the site. Mont St. Michel is now connected to the mainland by a causeway.

After leaving Normandy we returned to Paris by way of Chartres, known as the "Stone Testament of the Middle Ages." The cathedral towers above the town. Rodin is reported to have said, "Chartres is the French Acropolis." When I actually visited the Acropolis I was disappointed that the Sound and Light Show was given in English, not Greek. I don't know exactly why. I would not have understood the narrative history of the place because I don't speak Greek. I would just have enjoyed the sound of the language. But then I could have read the story of the Acropolis in my guidebook.

I have visited the cathedral of Chartres at least three times, in 1962, 1976, and 1989. The last time, I joined a tour conducted by Malcolm Miller, who was an author of a guidebook I bought, *Chartres, La Cathedrale et la Vielle Ville*. Students also got an introduction to the Loire Valley.

We stayed a couple of night in Tours. We visited the castles *Azay-le-Rideau* and *Chenonceau* and Leonardo da Vinci's house, called *Clos-Lucé*. Da Vinci lived there for many years. The house is now a museum where one can see his original sketches of paintings and inventions, including his design of an automobile.

In the 1980s Fairfax County had an extraordinary program called *The Humanities*—a study of French, Spanish, and Greek cultures. Students would spend three weeks in class in Fairfax studying the language and culture he or she had chosen, and then three weeks were spent in the country of the target language. The French and Spanish students also had a home stay for one week in England before going to Spain and France. The Greek students went only to Greece. The assignment abroad was to keep a daily journal that accounted for a large portion of the final grade. The students also presented a program for members of the school board.

Youth Travel Associates planned this tour especially for students in Fairfax Schools. It was advertised as *Bicentennial of the French Revolution*. Hillary Bebko, Kenneth Prowell, and I were the teachers leading the group. There was a fourth person from the area office. I can't remember her name. I do remember when I asked how the visit to Spain was, she responded, "It was hell!"

Our itinerary included London, Stratford-upon-Avon, Bath, and Stonehenge. There was a weekend home stay in Basingstoke, about an hour from London. I, along with two other students, Tevy and Tracy, stayed with John and Diane Butler and their children Emily, Simon, and Mark. The Butlers and my family have remained close friends since 1989.

It is a sad commentary that this program is no longer a part of the Fairfax County Summer School program, because of budget cuts. My next Educational Tour was in 1991. I originally had about ten students signed up. Some parents withdrew their daughters from the program because of the Gulf War. Two young men from the mid-west joined my group. Their teacher had had most members of her group cancel because of the war. For a reason that I cannot explain, female students are usually in the majority on foreign study/travel tours. Girls are now surpassing boys in all areas of academic studies, even science and math. Those were the areas where boys have traditionally excelled. Students whose parents permitted them to go as planned spent an exciting Spring Break in Paris, Barcelona, and Madrid without incident.

The yearly evaluation by members of the Luther Jackson Administration, and especially the strenuous evaluation done by supervisors from the County Office, helped me to become a better teacher year by year. During the year I chose to participate in the *Merit Pay Plan*, I was under tremendous stress.

During the second semester of the 1987-1988 school year Mama became deathly ill. One day, during fifth period, I had an unannounced classroom visit from Assistant Principal Dr. Rodney Bowen. Just before lunch, I had received a note asking me to call Dr. Ham Sr., Mama's doctor. He informed me that the procedure used to stop the bleeding from a silver-dollar-size ulcer had not worked. She needed emergency surgery, and if she did not have it she would die. If Mama did have the surgery, she would have only a fifty percent chance of survival.

There was no way I could meet my fifth period class. I needed to make a decision right away. I went into the teachers' restroom and cried. When I composed myself enough to go to class, I found Rodney Bowen standing by the window. My students were all seated and quietly copying their homework assignment from the board. Needless to say, Dr. Bowen did not evaluate my teaching that day.

On another occasion, I took my French I students on a fieldtrip. The substitute teacher did not show up for my Introduction to Foreign Language Class. No one in the front office realized that she hadn't. At that time I was teaching in a trailer located a few yards from the school building. A student runner brought an office pass for a student in the class. She returned to the office and informed Jeannette Doval, the administrative assistant, that there were students and no teacher in the trailer. IFL classes can be rambunctious, and that day the most hyperactive student had taken over. He was now the teacher, and all students had set about following the agenda on the board.

Teaching in a trailer often provided interesting and comical situations. One morning there was a knock on the door. I opened it and was greeted by a lady who asked if I would like to buy some of her Avon Products. I informed her that this was not a trailer park. "I'm sorry, Madam, I don't live here. I am a teacher. These trailers are classrooms. The school over there is overcrowded."

Later, Norma Farbes and I expounded on the program *Faison Français* that began with a grant from the *Washington Post*. *Faisons Français* became the International Club and was funded by Fairfax County Minority Student Achievement (MSA) Grants. The club was open to all students; however, the ultimate goal of the club was to increase minority enrollment in art and foreign languages, particularly French. That proposal may serve as a guide for other teachers desiring to come up with a program for bringing more minority students into foreign language classes.

There is still a need for all students to take advantage of the many benefits offered by studying a foreign language. One of my students, Tyrone Pitts, majored in art at Virginia State University. His artwork, created and photographed in the 1965 Luther Jackson High School yearbook, is a collage of scenes in Paris. Catherine Beavers, a French student who went to France with me in 1976, studied in Clermont-Ferrand and became a French teacher. My students could become all that they wanted to be, and they did!

Over the years, it has been my husband, children, friends, and most of all my extraordinary and loving students, who have made me the person and teacher I have become. While cleaning out the crawl space, I found my little gray cosmetic case from Bennett College. I opened it expecting it to be empty. Instead, I found the love letters of my husband, and a letter from a professor at Bennett College, and a first letter from my first love, Jacque Houdaille, the Frenchman. The art of letter writing is a thing of the past. It has been replaced by e-mails that must be erased after a while.

I had taken a conversation course from Monsieur Houdaille in the spring. I had told him that I would be in Paris in July. He would be there for the summer. A visit to the Eiffel Tower was not on my itinerary. Imagine that! So when I arrived in Paris, I gave him a call. He came over and we went to the Eiffel and to lunch. For lunch he ordered a bottle of red wine. It made me quite dizzy because I was not accustomed to drinking any kind of alcohol.

The main meal was steak and French fries. The steak was too rare for me to eat. I ate a few bites and M. Houdaille ate both his and mine. No matter how many times I said, "*Bien cuit,*" the waiter would come back with the same bloody steak. There was also my dessert of chocolate mousse.

Then we were in a rush because I had to be back at the hotel by two o'clock. I got a good scolding from the tour director. Luckily, I had packed that morning.

While I was in Pau, I received the following letter from M. Jacques Houdaille:

Le 5 Août. 1963

Mlle Fannie Miles
C/O Mlle Kammerlocher's
3 Rue Duplaa
Pau
Basse Pyrénées

Le 5 Août. 1963
Chère Mademoiselle Fannie,
    Merci beaucoup de votre aimable carte que j'ai eu hier en revenait d'un petit voyage á Lyon où m'a emmène un vieil ami de lycée.
    J'espère que vous avez passé un heureux quatorze juillet. Vous excuserez mes fautes, la machine de ma père marche très mal et me fait die de villains mots.
    Avez-vous vu le chateau où est né Henri IV? Je crois que c'est là où est son berceau formé d'une carapace de tortue. Avez-vous gouté le vin de Turaçon. On en vend peu a Paris mais il vaut mieux le consommer sur place.
    Sinon, la vie continue je vais aux rechives où je copier beaucoup de documents pour boudoir travailler l'année prochaine á Washington.
    Déja un tiers des vacances de passées.
    Je ne sais pas trop quand je vais partir en Bourgogne puis en Autriche, j'espère que ce ne sera pendant votre second séjour á Paris.
    Mon telephone est MEN 46-22. Je vais le récrire á la main pour plus de sûreté.

Bonne vacances!
Jacques Houdaille

In the same little suitcase that still bears a Bennett College sticker, I also found a letter from Emma, a white teacher from North Carolina. We traveled together in 1962. Fairfax County National Bank was supposed to send me my July paycheck while I was in Pau. They did send the check; but it arrived after I had departed for Switzerland. Madame Kammerlocher sent the check on to me at my hotel, but I had left for a return visit to Paris. The hotel forwarded the check to my hotel in Paris. It arrived there before I did, and the hotel returned it to what was supposed to be the nearest post office. I went to the post office, and it wasn't there. By that time, I had run out of money. Emma Marston offered to lend me one hundred dollars, which I gratefully accepted.

Emma was another person that I deeply regret not keeping in contact with over the years. The letter from the bank arrived safely back in the United States about a month after I did. It had four or five forwarding addresses.

I wrote Emma in 2002. My letter was returned, "Addressee unknown!" She would have been in her late nineties. Nevertheless, we did correspond for a few years after our return to the States. She even sent me a wedding present, a set of embroidered pillow cases. She wrote:

> *628 S. Fulton Street*
> *Salisbury, N. C.*
> *November 2, 1962*

> *Dear Fannie,*
>
> *It's always good to hear from you. Yes, I wish we were closer to one another for I would love to see you as well as all of your pictures. However, I did see Helen's and Janet's and thoroughly enjoyed them. Do you mean for me to keep those two shots that you sent? If so, I want to pay for them. I'll send money or return the pictures in my next letter. I'll be delighted to keep the pictures if you'll let me pay for them.*
>
> *We missed you at our Raleigh meeting. I guess Jane and Helen told you about our "get together." I just wish all could have been there.*
>
> *I attended a workshop last week in Albemarle. Mrs. Ladu had charge of the afternoon meeting, and Evelyn Vandiver took charge of the night meeting. You can imagine how much I got out of the night one. You should have heard her rave on and on about what a wonderful trip we had.*
>
> *Fannie, I have really decided to retire at the end of this school year. I have already notified my superintendent. I know I shall miss it, but I feel that I have taught long enough. Then too, I feel so poorly prepared for all this oral teaching. My materials are too old.*
>
> *I wrote you about having such a nice meal with Janet and her husband, did I not? Well, I've invited them over for a meal next weekend. As yet, I have not heard whether or not they can come. I really hope her sister is no worse. Although there is no hope for her sister, she has been feeling pretty good.*
>
> *I've been wondering about the check and money sent to you while you were in France. Did you get it back? I hope you did not lose anything. Write me the results. I'm curious.*

160

Let me know about pictures—whether to return or pay, and thanks for your thoughtfulness, for sending these and offering others. Since I can't see yours, I guess I'll just get some from Janet and Helen perhaps. I imagine you have the best ones, however.

Thank you again,
Emma

There was one teacher from South Carolina, Mary. She refused to accept me as part of the group. She caused a scene in a hotel, to the amazement of the French. Only the two of us had single rooms. In one small village no singles were available. Emma, her roommate Janet, and I shared "une chambre pour trois personnes." At the end of the trip Mary apologized for her bad behavior. She said, "That was the way I was brought up."

Over the years, I have kept many letters and notes from my students. I have also failed to keep in contact with most of them. I neglected them just as I did my teachers and friends. Elspeth Leech wrote me a year after I retired from Luther Jackson Intermediate.

May 18, 1992

Dear Mrs. Bellamy,

Bonjour! Comment ça va? *How has the year been with a classroom full of obnoxious teens that don't appreciate the value of teachers? Good, I hope!*

The first year of Falls Church has been okay for me. I've enjoyed the freedom of high school, but at the same time I feel that the true atmosphere a teen needs to develop individuality is lacking at Falls Church. At least I've come to know myself more carefully, so I don't find myself "going with the flow" as so many of my peers do.

My French teacher this year was Marcia Ipsen. I enjoyed her class very much, and I've certainly learned more French, but I feel that Mrs. Ipsen lacked the needed organization and discipline that you had. I was hoping we would see you as a substitute, but I guess that just wasn't possible with your schedule!

I thought you might be interested to know that I have been chosen to be a Student Ambassador for "People to People." I will spend a month beginning June 21st with peers from northern Virginia. Unfortunately, no one else from Falls Church was selected. The countries participating are Czechoslovakia, Austria, Poland, and Germany. I am very excited! There will be home stays in Austria and Germany. That should be great.

Another piece of information, in which you might be inter-

ested, regards none other than the city of Paris. This may seem sort of far off, but I'm already very excited about it. You see, my mother just returned for a week in France, and she decided that she'd like to take me to Paris for a week right after my sophomore year. As long as I don't slack-off next year, she promises that the trip will happen! I just cannot wait to continue from where I left off last spring. It will be wonderful!

I'm so grateful for all this traveling I have the opportunity to do. I am truly a fortunate person!

Love,
Elspeth Leech

P. S. Si je vous écrive bientôt, je promis que je vais vous écrire en Français!

There was another student, Pierre Leroux. He lived in the apartment complex across from Luther Jackson. His father was American and his mother was French; however they were in the process of divorcing. I kept in touch with him and his mother for quite a long time. When they moved to Washington, D. C. Nikki and I went over to help them move. His mother would invite Paul and me over for dinner after the kids had gone away to college. Pierre also had a sister whose name I can't remember. I wonder what happened to Pierre?

One of my students became Paul's and my foster son. In 1986, Chanty, a Cambodian, came to me while his class was doing research in the library. Chanty, Meline, his mother, and his sister, Socheata, had come to the United States after escaping from the Khmer Rouge reign of terror in Cambodia. Meline reminded me of the Jewish teacher at Bennett whom the Russians had persecuted. She too would go off on a tangent at the least provocation about the atrocities she and her family suffered under the Khmer Rouge.

She had escaped from the capital, Phnom Penh, along with Chanty and Socheata, by walking to a refugee camp in Thailand. Her oldest son had been killed, and her middle son, Panny, had disappeared. She was reunited with Panny when they ran into each other in the refugee camp in Laos.

Chanty and his family were living with a sponsor who was treating them badly. His mother was in the process of finding lodging in Fairfax, but locating suitable and affordable housing was difficult. They finally found an apartment just across the Arlington County line. I gave Chanty my telephone number and told him that I would come to see his family. I did as I promised when I received his call.

Chanty was very unhappy with his living situation, and especially with his new school. His mother and I became friends over the next few months. Chanty was dreading the next school year in Arlington County, so Paul and I offered to take Chanty. In order for him to enroll in a Fairfax County school, he would have to become my foster child. I filled out the necessary papers, and we went before a judge. The court procedure took about fifteen minutes. The judge simply asked Meline if she were willingly giving up her rights to her child. He asked me if I were willing to take on the responsibility of a teenager. Pauly was leaving for college and Nikki was returning to her second year at Spelman College in Atlanta. Paul and I would have an empty nest. Chanty was just what we needed.

He is now married and has a son, Andrew, who thinks of me as his second grandmother. Chanty became a United States citizen several years ago. He now works in the White House as a computer expert. Paul and I unofficially adopted Chanty's little sister Socheata and later Chanty's wife whose name is also Socheata.

"And gladly would I learn and gladly teach!"

Chapter 5

Between the dark and the daylight,
When the night is beginning to lower,
Comes a pause in the day's occupations,
That is known as the Children's Hour.

Longfellow, *The Children's Hour*

ikki and I have been to France dozens of times. To have a daughter is a
dream come true. To have a daughter who loves France and her people
as I do is a wonder. My memories of each visit are pleasant ones, and I think
about our trips often, and especially "La belle France," and her extraordinary
people. A number of things bring each visit to France to mind. One of them
is flying, the other is any kind of food identifiably French.

My first visit to France was in 1962. I was four years out of college, had
begun graduate school a couple of years before, was in my third year of
teaching in Fairfax County and had no man in my life. I decided that it was
time to visit the country whose language I was teaching. Originally, I had
planned to go along with a group of teachers from my school who were participating in a National Educational Association Tour (NEA). However, later
during the school year 1961-1962, I received a brochure from the supervisor
of foreign languages for the State of North Carolina, Evelyn Vandiver.

After reading the itinerary, I found the trip of my dreams—two months
in Europe. More than a month in France, plus a trans-Atlantic crossing, was
offered for the sum total of one thousand dollars. The trip also included several language courses offered by the Universities of Toulouse and Bordeaux,
and a home stay in the French Basque Country at the foot of the Pyrenees.
I can swing it! I thought.

The Basque Country, called *Eyzkalerria* in the Basque language, strad-
dles the western end of the Pyrenees Mountains. Its French and Spanish

coasts are washed by the Bay of Biscay and the Atlantic Ocean. The seven Basque Provinces are divided between France and Spain. More than a million people live in each area. The Basques have retained their own language and culture and to some extent their physical characteristics. They are of medium height, and have prominent noses and narrow faces. Most have a dark complexion. The language they speak is a puzzle to the linguist. It is neither French nor Spanish.

Many Basques moved to the United States to herd sheep. Most settled in Montana. The immigrants, who came to the States via Ellis Island, after weeks on the Atlantic Ocean, were not sure that they would be admitted to the United States. The Basques are brave and freedom loving. They have kept some control over their local affairs in both the French and Spanish areas.

The French Basques appear to be content being a part of France. However, for many years the Spanish Basques have sought to have their area independent of Spain. They often resort to violence. The violence includes the assassination of government officials in both Madrid and the Basque Country. The separatist group is known as *ETA*.

Guernica is the Basque town immortalized in Picasso's work. Francisco Franco permitted Hitler's German bombers to use the town and its citizens for target practice. The first thing the Basque immigrants saw as they approached the waters of the U.S. was the Statue of Liberty—a gift that France gave this country in 1896. The French artist, Federic Auguste Bartholdi, sculpted it.

Memories of my first trip arouse and release a great warm flood of often-suppressed thoughts and ideas. It is something like walking along a deserted beach in the wintertime and being reminded of high summer in Paris or Marseille. There are the fragrances from perfume shops, the mysterious odors of the street vendors produce, the open-air markets, the Mediterranean, and the fast speech of the French, the excited shrieks of the children, the distinctive skyline of the city in the noon sun, and the foreign talk of the tourists. These are details that still stand out, forcefully redefining themselves. They grow repeatedly sharper, more vivid, and more beautiful.

Four weeks in Europe really did make a difference for Nikki and me. She was then sixteen, and she was just at the age of the three-year cycle, thirteen to sixteen, which I believe are the most difficult years for mother and daughter. This is the period where parental values and ideas clash with the values and ideas of their children and the ideas that their peers thrust upon them.

We fly over through a deep Atlantic night; the air in the tourist class of the 747 is too cool for the light sweaters we were wearing. Stars seem to float and tumble all around us, and I am thinking that there must be a few proud ocean liners below us. I imagine these magnificent ships are full of lovers, revelers, husbands and wives, single men and women in ballrooms, dining halls, thick with perfume and smoke. I am remembering when I had crossed the Atlantic thirty years ago unmarried, but perhaps secretly in search of a husband.

The 747 seemed to sail without thrust, as though when it left the coast it had begun to sail. We sailed and coasted, and I recall expecting the plane to buck and fight its way over the ocean like the great ships going along beneath us. But the plane sailed and glided easily, on and on.

I thought of the *Flandre* on which I had sailed in July of 1963, before I knew my husband Paul, before Nikki, and of course before Paul III. The French ocean liner with its palms in the foyer, and the walks along the wide esplanade giving onto the grand dining halls and ballrooms of the tourist class, and the even more elegant and luxurious elevated first class decks.

I got a glimpse of these as I clandestinely walked through the many barriers that separated the first class from the tourist class decks below. Left to my own devices, one evening I decided to explore this French liner. I imagined the sleek young men showing their profiles to advantage as they descended slowly to the dining and dancing salons. I would dance energetically, the foxtrot, the cha-cha, and the waltz with them. When I was jolted into reality by a friendly *"Bonjour, Mademoiselle,"* I realized that no one had attempted to stop this skinny, ordinary, black girl as she wandered among the rich ladies adorned in diamonds and sequins.

Freedom—I learned the true meaning of this word on the French ocean liner, *Flandre*. Freedom was not what I had experienced in my country of birth. I was able to walk into the beauty salon and have the coiffeur say, without batting an eye,

"Bonjour, Mademoiselle! Qu'est-ce que vous voulez?"

I told him I wanted to get my hair done. He proceeded to go through each step: shampooing, cutting, setting, drying, combing, and styling. When he finished, and I complimented him on his excellent job, he said, *"Pourquoi, les cheveux ne sont pas bouchés?"* (Why didn't your hair become kinky?)

I informed him that I had a permanent. You see this Frenchman knew, even though the permanent had been invented years before, most black people still straightened their hair with a hot comb. When it is washed, it again becomes coarse or kinky. In fact, it was in the spring of 1962 that I learned from an acquaintance that a permanent was my best bet for traveling. The "Afro" hairstyle had not yet become popular with black Americans. The coiffeur just couldn't figure out the method I had used to keep my hair from returning to its natural state.

France became the fashion center of the world during the reign of Louis XIV (1638-1715). Louis and the aristocrats of his court greatly influenced hairdressing. The men wore long curly wigs. Supporters of the French Revolution of 1789 opposed all things connected with the aristocracy. Short, and often untidy, hairdos became the vogue.

In one of the courses in Pau the little professor would come in, and step up on his platform (In all of the classes the professors stood on a little platform.). He would begin, *"Maintenant, le style de Louis XIV."* During this session we learned all about the style (life) of Louis XIV. Wigs became popular in the 1960s. Another young black woman on board the ship, not realizing just how accommodating the French are, wore a wig. I am sure if I had brought along my hot comb and curling iron, the coiffeur would have found some way for me to heat and use them, but a permanent is much easier!

But it was now 1985. There was a new kind of social currency in the world. The button-down shirt had long penetrated to all corners, and the old malarkey that I used to live with was gone, all of it succeeded by woefully debased new rates of exchange. In college we had listened to Chubby Checker and Fats Domino, and we had our generation of assassinations and the nasty little Vietnam War. Coming home hooked on cigarettes was the worst new found trait our parents could expect us to acquire.

There were girls at Bennett College who took up this bad habit, but I didn't. When I began teaching at Luther Jackson most of my colleagues went to the smoking lounge after lunch. I didn't want to be left out, so I asked my landlady's son to buy me a pack of Kools. I tried blowing smoke in the air, but after a couple of days I realized that my trying to learn to smoke was a waste of time and energy. After a couple of days of trying, I decided it was better just to return to my classroom. There were always students with whom I could spend the rest of the lunch period.

Nikki had a problem in high school, which I did not have. By the time she reached high school, the attorney general had issued the warning, "Cigarettes are bad for your health." I knew at some point she bowed to peer pressure. I resorted to putting "No Smoking" signs in the cars she drove to Bishop O'Connell High School and cutting into tiny pieces any cigarettes I found in her book bag. She took up smoking again while working on her doctorate degree in Salt Lake. She has since broken that habit. Even though I suspected Nikki smoked at times, I have never seen her with a cigarette in her hand.

I dozed, the plane sagged, and I woke to the muted crackled of static. The captain was telling us that our descent would soon begin, and that we were now over Luxembourg City, the capital of Luxembourg. We took the shuttle bus into the city and got off in front of the old train station in the center of Luxembourg City. Leaving Nikki with the bags in the train station, I took a trek across the street to inquire about hotel accommodations for the night. After two inquiries at hotels on the main thoroughfare, I settled on the first one because it had a view of the main street. Luxembourg City is a magnificent city where a quick visit of substance can be taken in a couple of days.

Luxembourg is one of the smallest countries in northwest Europe, covering an area no larger than our state of Rhode Island. It is a beautiful country, with many castles dotting the landscape. We could tell that both Luxembourgs, the country and the city, had a high standard of living. Within the commercial area, it seemed that every other door was an entrance to a bank. But the city is more than a dull and expensive financial center; iron and steel are its most important industries.

There are three official languages—Luxembourgeois, French, and German. Each person we met would begin speaking to us in Luxembourgeois, but converted easily to French when I responded in French. We spent the first day touring the capital Luxembourg, particularly the ancient ruins.

On the second day we decided to cross the border into Germany, since neither of us had visited that country. After inquiring at the train station which German city close by would be worth a day's adventure, we were advised to visit the city of Trier. The next morning after breakfast, Nikki and I walked across to the station where our train was waiting and we jumped aboard a second-class car. Within minutes a conductor was asking to see our passports and inquiring the reasons for our going to Germany. Before we could put our passports away we had crossed the German border and a German conductor was asking the same questions.

Luck was with us; we arrived in Trier in the midst of a weeklong festival on the traffic-free Simeonsstrasse. Trier, the oldest city in Germany, has many traces of Roman history including the famous Porta Nigra, the massive city gate. The gate is the biggest and best-preserved Roman gateway in all of Europe, and so named because of the black appearance of the gigantic blocks of limestone from which it is made.

We had a schedule listing the departure of several trains throughout the day that would take us back to Luxembourg, so we could have a few more hours there. We ended up taking the very last train because we could not tear ourselves from the hustle and bustle of shopping, eating, and all of the activities of the festival, plus a brief visit to the house where Karl Marx was born in 1818.

Nikki and I had the bad habit of pilfering souvenirs from the restaurants where we were eating—a fancy menu, a glass, or even a carafe. The proprietor or waiter would give us a strange look but never accused us of anything.

Some of the menus were placemats with colorful maps of France, or of a particular area of a country. If I asked, the waiter would give us as many as we wanted. These I could use when my classes were doing a food project on France, Spain, or Germany. We made no exception while visiting Germany for the first time. I came back with a couple of colorful menus for my Introduction to Foreign Language (IFL) classes, and a few souvenirs we had bought at different booths at the festival.

Arriving back at the Luxembourg train station around ten o'clock we had a strange encounter with a well-dressed middle aged lady. She asked in French where we were staying.

I replied, "*L'hôtel á travers la rue.*" (The hotel across the street.)

She then asked, "May I share your room?"

I replied, "Sorry, our room isn't even big enough for the two of us."

We just couldn't take a chance of being robbed while we slept, or worse. I conjured up a scene of waking up the next morning and finding all of our money and clothing gone. That is, if we didn't wake up dead! We are always aware of the signs, "Beware of pickpockets (that may also include children)!" They roam the streets and transit system of Paris and sites like the Louvre, the Eiffel Tower, and Notre Dame. They block you off as you enter the stalls at the train stations. Women should hang on to their pocketbooks with both hands, and never carry valuables—large quantities of money and passports— anywhere except inside the underwear.

The pickpockets, purse-snatchers, and just petty thieves in general are much worse in Florence and Rome. Paul almost lost his carry-on to a child while waiting for the tour bus in Florence. It was the fast hands and feet of our tour guide that prevented the loss. Paul didn't believe me when I told him that he should not carry his wallet in his back pocket. However, he soon realized that his wallet could be lifted without his knowing it, after hearing firsthand from fellow travelers of the magic fingers of the pickpockets.

Paul visited France for the first time in 1987. United Airlines had a special two-for-one flight to Paris. Nikki joined us in Paris after taking a cheap Icelandic Air flight to Luxembourg and the train to Paris. Paul and I were staying in a hotel near the Place de Châtelet. Nikki called from Charles de Gaulle Airport, and we agreed to meet on the square. I worried that she might have difficulty following the directions from DeGaulle to the center of Paris. She said the French managed to understand her mixture of French and English. We spent the next couple of days showing Paul the major sights.

Paris, at the time, was in the middle of a series of terrorist threats. The military was out in full force at the airports, the transit systems, and all tourist spots. All bags were searched upon entering department stores. Any odd actions were questioned, even those concerning food. One afternoon we stopped for lunch at a cafeteria. There were certain rules as to what consti- tuted a meal. Paul could not make up his mind as to what he wanted, or fig- ure out how many different items he was entitled to get for the fixed price. His indecision caused a small disturbance, and the armed guard was called inside to give us a closer look. He watched us the entire time we were eating. I guess he thought we were causing a diversion, so we could blow up the place. Neither one of us fit the description of an Algerian, Tunisian, or Moroccan nor anyone else that the French at that time thought might com- mit a terrorist act.

After a few days in Paris, we took the *Train de Grande Vitesse (TGV)* to Nice. This "train of great speed" is also know as "*Le Mistral*," like the fero- cious wind that sweeps across Provence in the south. France has an excellent railroad system, *Société des Chemins de Fer (SCNF)*, operated by the state.

Leaving our bags in a locker at the train station, we went in search of a hotel room. The one and two-star hotels were dumps, so we settled on a three star not too far from downtown Nice and L'avenue d'Anglais. We were short of money, so the next two days were spent just walking around Nice, rather than taking in the numerous museums and shopping in the boutiques on the Avenue de Pietons. We did take the bus for an afternoon in Monaco. It is nestled around a natural harbor in the northeastern part of the French Rivièra. We were able to see the famous Monte Carlo gambling casino and the palace of Prince Rainier, Monaco's ruler.

We took a sleeper and accompanied Nikki back to Luxembourg. For some reason Paul thought we would have four bunk beds to ourselves. No such luck. Just before the train left the station, an Arab in Arabian attire invaded our cabin. At bedtime, he proceeded to undress and put on his nightclothes. Nikki, Paul and I spent a restless night in our street clothes. We arrived safely in Luxembourg and in time to give Paul a tour of the city and dinner at a rather expensive restaurant. The next morning Nikki took a cab to the airport and her flight home. We took the train from Luxembourg to DeGaulle, arriving in the nick of time for our flight back to the United States. Nikki had arranged for her friend Joseph Hastie, to pick her up at Washington-Baltimore International Airport. What a whirlwind vacation for Paul!

But there is no other city in the world quite like Paris, and to get there Nikki and I took the train from Luxembourg. Our ticket to Paris had included a roundtrip on Lux Air, the tiniest passenger plane we have ever seen, to and from Paris to Luxembourg. Preferring to see the countryside close up, we took the train instead—having to change in Metz. We just managed to climb aboard the last car before it pulled out for Paris. As we descended on the platform of La Gare de L'Ést the conductor informed us we were in a first class car. Nevertheless, he took our second class tickets without even a warning or reprimand. It was not our fault that no one had bothered to come and collect our tickets. That was just the first of our many adventures aboard the French transport system in years to come.

Paris is the most beautiful city in the world. It grew up along the Seine River with its beginning on the Ile de la Cité more than two thousand years ago. In Roman times, Paris was a small fishing village called Lutetia. The town became known as Paris about A.D. 300. It was named for a tribe call "Parisi" who lived there. There are at least three or four historical places worthy of a visit or a casual glance within a single block of every single street in Paris. One can walk over the whole city, not in a day, but in a month as Nikki and I did. We wore out two pairs of shoes to prove that it can be done.

When necessary we also used Paris' excellent *Métro*, which has an abundance of maps to show which way to go. However, with Nikki as a guide, I never needed a map of my own.

Close to the Seine and le Pont Neuf sits Notre Dame on the Ile de la Cité, a huge Gothic cathedral, whose two hundred fifty-five steps I had climbed to reach the towers twenty years earlier. I didn't find Victor Hugo's Quasimodo, but I did get a clear and up-close view of the gargoyles and a panoramic view of the city. Notre Dame is the great masterpiece of the Middle Ages.

In front of Notre Dame is *Point Zero*, a brass compass star, from which all distances in France are measured. A short distance away there is La Saint Chapel, the supreme example of Gothic architecture, which is hidden behind the Conciergerie which also includes the Palais de Justice.

During the Revolution, the Tribunal took over the palace of the Conciergerie. It became the antechamber to the guillotine during the reign of terror. Marie Antoinette, the Austrian queen, when told about the hunger and suffering of the masses retorted, "Let them eat cake." Interestingly, she did not mean our understanding of "cake"—she was referring to the bread strips and crusts left from bread baking in ovens. (I gleaned this tidbit from a well-read friend.)

Shortly thereafter the tribunal executed her husband, Louis, XVI. A few days later she was taken from her tiny cell, walked down Rue de Paris to the Place de la Concorde, where her head was placed between the jaws of the guillotine.

On the front of this huge building complex is the Tour de l'Horloge, a clock tower dating back to 1334. The clock still keeps perfect time. Just across the Seine east, within easy walking distance is the Hotel de Ville, a splendid example of a medieval town hall, and the seat of the city government. We never found the town hall open to the public. However, the hotel is located on a magnificent square where one of the first mayors of Paris incited a mob in 1357 to rise against the monarchy. He was later killed, not by the king, but by a deranged fellow Parisian.

Walk a few more blocks west and we will arrive at the Louvre, the largest and most famous museum in the world. One visit to this museum will never suffice. Nikki and I have been to the museum dozens of times, but we are still ignorant of most of its holdings. It has two hundred twenty-four halls, and its Grande Galerie is longer than three football fields. The Louvre is one of the most ancient monuments in Paris, dating back several centuries. Entrance to the museum is free on Sunday.

In the same area is the curious anomaly, the Tour St. Jacques. The church was destroyed in 1802. The only remnant of the church is an ornate tower that now doubles as a weather station. At the tower base is a statue of Blaise Pascal (1623-1622) the philosopher, mathematician and scientist. He developed the theory of probability and was one of France's first weather forecasters.

Having our fill of history for a while, we became familiar with some of the restaurants that dot the streets of Paris. There are the quaint little cafés in the Quartier Latin, Marais, St. Germain de Prés, and Montmartre where our menus were presented on a tiny chalkboard. There are also many expensive restaurants, along the Champs-Elysées, where Nikki and I would splurge once in a while. The most interesting of all our eating-places was "Le Drug Store," modeled after our old American drug store, thus the "Franglais." If we so desired, we could both eat as well as shop for expensive souvenirs for those back home.

Artists, oddballs and the homeless frequent St. Germain. Nikki and I are not members of these groups, but in the area of St. Germain we seemed to fit well into the lively atmosphere. St. Germain des Près is the oldest of the city's largest churches, and the area takes its name from the church.

If we were not interested in sightseeing there, we would again window-shop along the Champs-Elysées, Rue Rivoli, Boulevard Haussmann, and other streets of Paris. Something or someone of interest would always come upon us, or we upon him, her, or it. We never met a single Parisian who could not answer our repetitive questions—

"*Qu'est-ce que c' est? —Où est-t-il? Cést loin ou près d'ici?*" However, most could not tell us whether we were on "La rive gauche," (the left bank) or "La rive droite," (the right bank).

The French usually gave us more information than we needed—that is, when our question did not concern directions. We only found a couple of rude people that summer. One was a ticket agent in the Metro, whose rapid explanation of the final destination of a train, I didn't get. After the third try, I got it when she yelled at the top of her lungs, "Porte de Claignancourt!" I promptly replied, "*Merci!*" at the top of my lungs.

•   •   •

"*Dog Poop!* Watch it, Mommy! You are going to step in the poop again! Why can't you watch where you are going?"

"If I keep my head down like a dog on the scent of his prey, I won't be able to see what is ahead, to the right, or to the left."

"Nice try at a pun or a metaphor, Mommy!"

Keeping a safe distance from the defecation of the Parisian canines was a continual battle, and one that Nikki, for some unknown reason, is able to avoid. At least two or three times a week I would be trapped in some muck or unsavory slime, and Nikki was continually accusing me of not watching where I was going. I maintained I did not walk any differently in Paris than any other city. It was the fault of the Parisians for not curbing their dogs. Nevertheless, I seemed to be the only one constantly plagued by the stench and having to waste time by going in search of a W. C.

Excitement never eluded us that summer of 1984. Three days after arriving in Paris, we were lost in a cab for about two hours. Our friend Marie-Josée, in her informative letter about her apartment, its location, and dealing with the concierge, forgot to stress one important matter. We would have to be back at the bus stop by nine o'clock when we ventured into Paris. Nadine, another friend of ours, gave us the same information when she picked us at the Gare de L'Est. Nine o'clock was the last bus from the Métro stop to Malakoff, our district.

On one particular dark and rainy night, we did not make it by the skin of our teeth as we had the days before. Just as we rounded the corner, the bus was pulling out. Rather than telephone Marie-Jo's sister, Georgette or Nadine, we decided to take a cab.

After waiting about thirty minutes at the taxi stand, one small taxi appeared out of the darkness. We hailed him down by jumping and screaming anxiously. He screeched to a stop, and we jumped in. As we were in the process of giving him a confusing set of directions, and just as the cabby was making a U-turn, a man ran up and began knocking on the cabby's window, and shouting in French, "My wife is going to have a baby! My wife is going to have a baby! Now!"

Now, I almost never have an occasion to use the French term "To be in labor," but out of the distant past or some long forgotten French novel came the expression "être en mal d'enfant." To make doubly sure, and before we gave up our cab so that the gentleman could get his wife to the hospital, I checked with the cabby. Sure enough I was right. He needed this cab, and he needed it now! And as it is not in the realm of possibility for a French cab to hold four passengers, and especially if one is nine months pregnant, Nikki and I climbed out of the cab, trudged back to the taxi stand and waited thirty more minutes in the pouring rain.

Just as we were about to give up and inconvenience one of our friends by calling and asking to be picked up, another cab appeared. At first glance, we thought it was the same cab as before. It was the same type of cab—white cab, black driver. Imagine our being so naïve as to think that the driver had returned to see if we were still there. We soon discovered that he was less knowledgeable than the previous driver. We proceeded to give him the street address—2 Rue de Paul Vallery. He pulled out his map and attempted to locate the street, "*Ah, voilà!*" He then took off at the usual speed of one hundred kilomètres per hour. After about ten minutes of going hither and thither, we asked if he knew the way. "*Bien sûr!*" he replied.

We then informed him that the bus ride only takes ten minutes even with the stops. He turned off his meter, stopped every once in a while to peer at the street signs, and to look at his map. We were of no help as we had only been in the neighborhood for a couple of days. As we drove around in circles we recognized nothing, but we did get a good view of the neighborhood on a dark and dismal night.

We had taken up lodging in a neighborhood on the outskirts of Paris that was composed of single-family houses, attached two and three-story houses, many little shops, and some five or six-story apartment buildings. After nearly two hours of driving across and underneath railroad tracks, in and out of dead-end streets, up and down narrow alleys, and in, out and between every nook and cranny of Malakoff, we came out on a square. There sat our very own supermarket and bakery where Nikki and I took turns fetching our "*petit déjeuner.*"

"We live right near here!" shouted Nikki.

"*Tout droit et à gauche!*" I continued.

Like men in general, the cabby never admitted he was lost. He did prove to be trustworthy and determined to get us to our destination, even if it meant covering every inch of Malakoff. We paid the total of only about ten dollars in American dollars with as generous tip as we could afford.

We also asked Pierre if he could take us to the airport when we were ready to leave Paris, which was in about a month. We figured it would be a straight shot from our apartment to Charles DeGaulle Airport since we did not live too far from the autoroute. Pierre agreed, gave us his home number, and said that we should call him a couple of days before we were to leave. We would not have to deal with the trains.

Each of us had increased our bags by one, me with paraphernalia for the classroom and Nikki with Parisian fashions. I had even scrounged giant movie posters from a worker as he was putting up new ones. We still could not pack all that we had accumulated over the past month into the extra suitcases. We were forced to leave Marie Jo's apartment clad in three sets of clothes and dragging our bags behind us. Pierre was at the agreed-upon meeting place, our morning bus stop.

After the experience of being lost in a cab, Nikki and I decided that we had to find a solution to our problem of having to make the nine o'clock bus at the Porte de Vanves. We were cutting our nightlife short! So, as we rode the bus to the subway stop the next morning, we made note of a couple of Métro signs that were closer to where we lived. After looking at a Métro map we then concluded that if we rode the subway to the last subway stop, we would be able to walk the rest of the way home. So for the next couple of mornings and evenings we made mental notes of what we passed along the route the bus would take to and from the Porte de Vanves.

There was the meat market with its bloody assortment of fresh meats, including a number of hairless ferrets; there was the furniture store with the couch and chair that I would later inquire about having shipped to the States; and there was the pastry shop with mouthwatering delicacies beyond description. There were also the dollhouse row houses and the single-family houses with window boxes filled with flowers, and lastly there was the nursery school with its colorful decorated windows just off the square where we waited for the bus each morning.

Having carefully studied the layout of the route, we were ready to put our plan to work. We spent our usual day walking the streets of Paris and taking in the sights as they caught our fancy. This particular day we spent wandering through the old cemetery of Montparnasse, where we came upon many illustrious Frenchmen, the greatest being Jean-Paul Sartre. His resting place impressed Nikki the most. She had recently completed a paper on Sartre's friend and fellow existentialist, Albert Camus.

We had dinner at a café in Montparnasse, took in a James Bond movie, and then walked leisurely through the Georgetown-like atmosphere that Montparnasse took on in the evening. Finally we took the *Métro* home. We passed the Porte de Vanves as planned and continued on to the very last stop.

We got off, walked down two flights of stairs into a nearly deserted subway station, and went out onto the street. "*Quelle Surprise!*" We were in another world or on another planet! We recognized nothing. The small crowd had quickly dissipated.

We had no idea in which direction we should walk. We flipped a coin. Heads to the north. Tails to the south. It came up heads. We walked for a couple of blocks without recognizing a single landmark. There was no bloody meat with hairless ferrets, no furniture shop with couch and chair I liked. After walking north for a few blocks and then a short distance east and trying not to panic, we suddenly walked underneath a railroad overpass.

Nikki took a couple of turns and stopped dead in her tracks.

"Isn't that the house where the German shepherd always looks over the balcony?"

She was looking toward a row house with French windows that opened out onto the roof of the store below. As we passed this house each morning and evening, a giant of a dog would be standing on his hind legs with his front paws resting on the iron railing surrounding the roof. The dog seemed to have more than a passing interest in the cars, buses, people, or whatever was happening in the street below. There was no activity now; the dog wasn't here. And, all shutters in the neighborhood were closed at dusk. But Nikki was positive that this was the house and street with the dog.

The French have a thing about closing the shutters in the evening. Marie-Jo's apartment had the French windows with the shutters that we had to close conscientiously each evening. After a couple of days, the concierge caught us as we were going out, to tell us that we were not fastening the shutters back when we opened them in the morning. The wind was blowing them back and forth. We hadn't realized they had fasteners. When Micheline came to visit us, she kept asking each evening, "Aren't you going to close the draperies over that picture window?"

"Shall I go and knock on the door, and ask if this is the house with the huge German shepherd"? I said in jest.

Now that we had our bearings, we began to follow the route the bus would take each morning. After a couple of nights we could make the walk in ten to fifteen minutes. Now we could spend the evening in Paris, where we were able to have a leisurely dinner, attend a performance at the Comédie Français or L'Opéra, or do whatever our hearts desired.

Riding the Métro each day, both subway and bus, proved to be both costly and unforgettable. After a few days of our taking the same bus at the same time, the driver became familiar with our routine and would actually wait for us if we were a couple of minutes late. We also soon discovered that the bus driver did not care whether we paid or not. If we had difficulty finding our tickets in our array of pockets, so that we might get them stamped by the machine located midway down the aisle, the driver or chauffeur would say, "Sit down, and forget it."

We also discovered, accidentally, in our mad rush for the bus, that the machine would take any ticket, used or unused! You needed only put one of the ends in the little groove. The machine would stamp it, resulting in a little hole at the end of the ticket. So Nikki and I started using the same ticket for the subway and bus each day. We figured that the subway ticket transferred to the bus, since we were not in the habit of using the bus as a means of transportation when we came to Paris.

Of course, we could never find the ticket bearing the correct date. We were just as sure that we could not get a French Métro worker or a fellow bus rider to explain the French transportation system to us.

We never got really accurate directions by asking just one person. We sometimes had to get lost for an hour or so in the subway system before we reached our destination, even though the Paris Métro is one of the best in the world, if not the best as far as we were concerned. As for the bus system, there seemed to be no rules, even for the French, for riding this transit system. Many passengers would get on the bus and never stamp their tickets. Other would get on the bus at the front, walk past the driver and sit down without paying. Still others would flash a pass that the bus driver could not possibly decipher.

Nevertheless, we knew we were not recognized as tourists because we were often approached for directions—even people in cars would ask us for directions. We gave them freely, if not accurately, and we became masters of this French art.

"*Cést tout droit. A droit. Puis à gauche. Après ça—tout droit.*"

"*C' est loin?*"

"*Non, c'est n'est pas loin. C'est près!*"

The French do much more walking than we Americans. Therefore, nothing is ever far away. Everything is "*près*," even if it's ten blocks away.

Our best set of directions was on how to get to Fontainebleau and back, especially if you arrived on the day it was closed. Nikki and I decided to go to Fontainebleau on a Monday morning. My guidebook dated back to my first trip to France some twenty-odd years before. Nikki and I were in Paris in 1976 when she was nine years old. I guess I didn't use a guidebook back then, or I was using a more recent guide. I chose to bring along the old guide that gave much more detailed information about the monuments of Paris and surrounding areas. We were in Paris to educate Nikki. I was determined that Nikki would learn all there was to know about Paris' historical monuments. However, the opening and closing times were not listed in this old guide.

Eager to explore the Palace of Fontainebleau, Nikki and I arrived at the Gare de Lyon, bought our tickets, and got on board the local double-decker train bound for the south of France. After a few stops, the conductor came by for our tickets and punched them with the usual hole. An hour later we arrived in the town of Fontainebleau. It was easy to locate the special bus stop because there was a big sign in front that read, *"Le bus à Fontainebleau."*

We hopped on board for the short ride to the palace, only to find it closed on Mondays. A guard told us that it was worth our time to take a walk around the grounds, but we should not go into Fontainebleau Forest. We did as he suggested. We had no intention of getting lost in a forest of six thousand two hundred acres of hunting grounds. The guard let us through the gateway of the Cour du Cheval Blanc. It was in this courtyard that Napoleon made his last inspection of the Old Guard before leaving for his exile to Elba.

After visiting the formal landscape gardens, the tiered fountains, and the lake, we began a leisurely walk around the town of Fontainebleau. We stopped for lunch at a very expensive restaurant across from the palace. Then we hiked the short distance back to the train station. A train for Paris was waiting, and with some feelings of disappointment we climbed abroad. Nikki had not seen the interior of the palace. We had wasted half a day.

We sat with tickets in hand for a long while, but no conductor appeared to punch his little holes in the tickets. After a few minutes we put them away, or rather Nikki put them away, and we began people-watching and enjoying the little pit stops between Fontainebleau and Paris.

Since we had been reminded of the importance of Napoléon in French history, this was the time for Nikki to learn more by a visit to the Hôtel des Invalides. It was originally a hotel built by the "Sun King" to house soldiers who were disabled. The building is recognized from afar by its gilded dome. There is a formidable display of cannon on the cobblestone forecourt. Great attention is paid to the Corsican general who was France's greatest soldier. His red porphyry sarcophagus is placed directly on a base of green granite, mined in the Vosges Mountains. Also, in one part of Les Invalides is the greatest war museum in the world.

The next morning after breakfast, we set out for our return journey to Fontainebleau. Once more we took the bus and then the Métro to the Gare de Lyon, climbed aboard another double-decker, or perhaps it was the same one as the day before, and off we went. This time the conductor took our tickets, peered at them a moment, punched the two holes and returned them to Nikki.

We continued merrily on our journey, toured the magnificent palace and learned more of the history of the Fontainebleau Palace. Touring

Fontainebleau reminded me why history and travel mean so much to me. This magnificent palace, lasting through the ages. Here for generations to pass through and admire, and perhaps to hold in awe. Edifices of man through history draw us in and make us feel connected with man's destiny. Where are we? Where are we going? And as we look and gaze in wonder, we feel the sweep of time, and for a few moments feel our place in it. It has been more than fifteen years since I visited Fontainebleau. A speck of dust in its history. But I was back, one of the privileged few, and I knew a profound joy in seeing the palace again.

Under François I, almost all of the medieval building was torn down and replaced with two main edifices. The present day palace reflects the king's admiration for the Italian Renaissance style. Fontainebleau was a summer residence for many kings of France. The apartment of Marie Antoinette has its original furnishings. Also of interest are the Red Room, where Napoleon signed his abdication papers, the Council Room, and the Throne Room. The Royal Room Apartments contain the famous Gobelin tapestries. A wing of the palace houses a summer school in music and the arts. The palace was as I remembered it from 1962, except there were more tourists. After the tour of the palace, we again stopped in town for lunch and shopping. We arrived at the train station about four in the afternoon and happened upon an express back to Paris.

Minutes later, we saw a conductor coming down the aisle. Nikki asked, "Which tickets do I give him this time?" At this point all four tickets *aller et retour* (round trip) had holes in them. The conductor took them, studied them for a while, and took a long look at us. We both smiled at him. He then put two more holes in them, and handed them back to Nikki. We tried to figure our what he was thinking. Did he think we were two idiots who just liked riding the train back and forth from Paris to Fontainebleau each day? He had probably looked at the date and figured we had come out to visit the palace the day before and found it closed. So, if we thought we should not have to pay for a second trip, well, so did he.

The French are very logical people most of the time. On other occasions they use no logic at all, like the time I took a group of students to the Musée d'Orsay. Students may enter all museums without paying an entrance fee. My students had no problems, the cashier took my word that I was a teacher, and that the group of people with me were my students. Why would a lady of my stature be coming to a museum with a motley group of thirteen and fourteen-years-olds first thing in the morning? They could not have been my children.

Pauly attempted to go in behind my students. He was stopped, with "*Un moment, s'il vous plâit!*" Pauly, after showing his student ID, still was not admitted without paying the entrance fee. According to the cashier, "*Il est trop grand!*"(He is too tall!)

Later, a short and a tall student were entering the Louvre. The guard asked to see the taller girl's passport. After the student had shown her passport, her shorter friend remarked, "Actually, I am older than Lisa." Paul entered the Louvre with his student ID and no questions were asked.

Nikki and I could have probably gone to the Rivièra, and perhaps even to Spain and back to Paris, on those four tickets *aller et retour*. The conductor would have probably thought that we just didn't know "where we were going."

When it comes to using the public transportation systems in Italy and France or just about any country, Nikki and I understand the rules governing riding the bus, the metro, and the train. Well, there really aren't any rules!

A few years ago, Nikki and I were taking the train from Florence to Paris. I had gotten the tickets through *Euro Rail* in the United States. We actually pay a higher price, but the convenience of having a train ticket in hand makes up for the difference in cost. This is especially true if you follow the maxim, "When in Rome, do as the Romans do." Put up a good argument even if you are wrong!

When we got on the train in Florence, we did not see the machine for validating or stamping our ticket. Our friend, Cynthia Foster, had dropped us off at the train station with no time to spare. In our mad rush for the train we forgot about the honor system of stamping or validating one's ticket. We jumped on the nearest car and sat in the first available seat, which happened to be near the entrance to the car.

Almost immediately after the train left the station, the conductor came into our car and we were the first he asked for tickets. He took our *Pass for Two*, looked at it closely, and told us we should have gotten our tickets validated before boarding the train. He was speaking Italian, and the polite expressions we knew in Italian did not suffice. Many Italians speak French if not English. This conductor spoke neither.

I knew his comments were about our thirty-day pass, valid anywhere on the continent. We had been traveling for only about ten days. The conductor and I continue arguing with one another—I in English and he in Italian. There were two teenage American girls sitting across from us who spoke English and Italian. The girls began translating the conversation that got quite loud. There were two seats facing each other. Nikki and I were sitting on the same seat. It went something like this:

Conductor: *You have to pay me for your ticket to Pisa.*

Me: *Why?*

Conductor: *You should have validated the ticket before boarding.*

Me: *We were in a rush. Anyway, I don't remember seeing the machine. You can see the pass is good for a month and we have used it only once—from Paris to Florence.*

Conductor: *You were supposed to get the pass stamped before getting on the train.*

Me: *I understand what you are saying, Sir. Are you sure the machine would take our pass? I thought it would take only regular fare cards. I didn't get the pass stamped on the way down. The conductor used a little machine, like the one you have in your hand, to put the little hole in the pass. Look, there's the hole.*

Conductor: *I'll tell you what you can do. Pay me the two fares from Florence to Pisa, and when you change in Pisa, you can validate the pass from Pisa to Paris. You can also get a refund for Florence to Pisa.*

Me: *Are you crazy? I am not giving you any money!* (By this time the conductor had taken the empty seat across from Nikki and me, and the train had made a couple of stops.) *While you are sitting there arguing with me, passengers are getting on and off the train.* (Nikki and I both turned around and pointed to the passengers getting off and on the train.) *I bet most of them didn't even buy a ticket!*

Imagine the conductor thinking we were stupid enough to pay him for two tickets from Florence to Pisa, and then trying to explain to a ticket agent in the next town what had happened. It might happen that way in France, but not in Italy. Then again, I don't speak Italian. After spending fifteen or twenty minutes arguing back and forth in Italian and English and with the teenagers translating, the conductor gave me back the pass without stamping it. I said "Grazie!" Nikki and I made sure we stamped our pass in Pisa for Paris, just in case.

In 2001 my friend Charletta and I were spending a few days in Avignon. I decided to take a train to Cassis to get some information from a realtor concerning property in that resort area. I had originally planned to go alone, but since Charletta had nothing special planned for the day she said she would tag along. I had bought my senior pass the day before, so I knew the procedure for getting a train ticket. I had to get a slip with a number from a machine off to the side of the terminal.

It had taken me a while to figure out why everyone was getting in front of me in line, without even saying, "Pardon." The first time Pauly went to Paris, he had noted that the French would say "Pardon," even if you bumped into them. This teenager was observing that the French are a very courteous people.

I needed to pull a ticket from the machine and wait until a little number flashed on a tiny screen above the teller. It was an efficient method once you figured out the system. I hadn't thought to ask, "Qu'est-ce qui se passe?" (What's happening?) After buying Charletta's ticket we set out on our day's journey.

I felt better about my ignorance the day before when, on the way to and from Cassis, we were constantly being asked about the train's destination and what stops it was going to make. We understood the many inquiries. There was no announcement as to which stop was coming up. Often the monitors in the stations did not give the correct information.

We could not answer any questions. We had to concentrate on our arriving in Cassis, a couple of stops after Marseilles. We knew how easy it was to get off at the wrong stop.

A summer ago Nikki and I were going from Paris to Nice. There was much confusion in the Gare de Lyon as to which track the train would be leaving from. We had reserved seats but by the time we located the correct train we had to board right away. We had to walk through several cars to find our seats. We struck up a conversation with an American couple on their honeymoon. They too were getting off at Nice. They were staying at the Meridian Hotel on the Promenade des Anglais.

By the time we reached Avignon it was very dark, and it was impossible to see the signs indicating the cities and town along the way. Just before we reached Cannes the honeymoon couple began getting their bags together. Before we realized what was happening, they had rushed from the back of the train onto the platform at Cannes. Nikki and I stared helplessly at their bewildered faces as the train pulled away. We expected to see them at least once on the pedestrian walkway in Nice. We never did. Perhaps they realized that Cannes would be better than Nice, and they may have opted to honeymoon there instead.

Cassis is about two hours from Avignon and a shorter distance from Marseille. It is a very small fishing port in a beautiful setting at the end of a bay. It is known for the quality of its fish, shellfish, and other seafood. Cassis white wine is a local delicacy. Cassis is also a popular summer resort with three small beaches. It is also noted for the quarries not far from the village. The valleys of limestone, as they dip below the sea, form a shoreline of inlets or *calanques*. The scenery is breathtakingly beautiful.

Charletta and I had taken a motorboat to see the *calanques* a few years before. Nikki had fallen in love with Cassis the summer she chauffeured Charletta and me around Provence.

The train station is about a mile from the center of town and all downhill. There is a small café in front of the station. We bought a couple of bottles of water from the proprietor and used the toilet. The owner and waiter (They were one and the same.) called a cab for us.

In Cassis I got the information on properties for Nikki. Charletta and I had lunch on the terrace of a café overlooking the Mediterranean. We spent the rest of a leisurely afternoon in this seaside village shopping, watching old men in berets play the game of boule, and topless sunbathers. Whenever we needed to use the toilet we would return to the restaurant where we had lunch. The French are nice that way! We took a cab back to the train station. We used *les toilettes* before boarding the train. We didn't have to buy anything because *le patron* remembered us from before.

The train arrived on time and we boarded it quickly, lest we were left in Cassis for the night. They conductor looked at us coming from Avignon and on our return trip, but never checked our passes. We were back in Avignon before dinner. We ate at a restaurant near the Place de l'Horloge (Clock Square). The owner came out on the terrace, introduced herself, gave us her name and telephone number and said that we should come back to see her the next time we were in Avignon. I forgot to ask the waiter to bring my broiled fish without the head and tail.

Later in the evening, I noticed that the train passes were good until October. It was now July. The next morning after breakfast, I set out for the train station without Charletta. I always get up and have breakfast before Charletta leaves the room. Upon entering the station, I headed straight for the Information Booth. I explained:

"Mon amie et moi, nous avons acheté hier ces billets. Les billets sont pour trois mois, mais nous allons demain à Nice. Nous ne pouvons plus utiliser ces billets d'Avignon à Cassis."

"Allez à la caisse, Madame."

I went to the Cashier and gave the same explanation—that my friend and I would not be able to use these three month-passes anymore, because we were leaving Avignon and would be returning soon to the United States. The cashier opened his drawer and counted out the francs we had paid for the senior passes. The money I got back was equivalent to about fifty American dollars.

I didn't understand why the cashier would have thought that Charletta and I would have wanted to go back and forth from Avignon to Cassis over a period of three months—maybe to the beaches at Cassis? I had asked for round-trip tickets. Nevertheless, I told the cashier, *"Merci!"* He responded, *"Je vous en pries!"* And I went on my way. Charletta who is extremely tight with her francs, was all smiles and delighted with my morning's accomplishments.

On another trip to the south of France, Charletta and I were walking around the Old Port of Marseille for a bus to take us to Notre Dame de la Garde, located on a hill high above the city. We came upon a bus parked near a bus stop. I asked the driver if his bus went to the church. He said "No," but if we hopped on he would take us to the corner where we would be able to get a bus to the church. He dropped us off a couple of blocks in the direction from which we had come.

We got on the bus he directed us to, but there was no driver. We guessed he had gone to *les toilettes.* We waited by his seat. An elderly gentleman sitting close by said, *"Allez-y!"*

"Go and sit down, Mesdames. You don't have to pay. I never pay."

We said, *"Merci!"* and we did as we were told.

Finding a W. C., or toilet, for an American traveling in France can be quite an undertaking. It is for the French as well. Drinking a couple of coffees in the morning, a glass or two of wine for lunch and dinner, and bottles of water during the day forces you to constantly seek out *les toilettes.* Paris and most villages have public toilets on the streets, which I never use. In some remote villages your head and legs can be seen while you are using the facility. I think toilets like these have disappeared for the most part. There are many restrooms that have the toilet flush with the floor. "Ugly Americans" refer to this type of facility as a "hole in the floor."

On our last trip, I asked Nikki why she almost never wears pants while traveling. She replied, "It's much easier to go to the bathroom." I was wearing only dresses on this trip because I was also wearing a big boot on my broken foot. Dresses really do make going to the toilet much easier, especially if you are taking walks in the mountains or the countryside. The French had more than a passing interest in my big black boot. I really don't think the French often experience broken bones. In fact I don't remember ever seeing a man or woman with a broken arm or leg. A young man in his twenties wanted to know where I got my boot. It was as if he wanted one!

In contrast to the "hole in the floor" was the self-cleaning toilet of the twenty-first century found in the Gare de Lyon in Paris. This restroom was tucked away from the busy areas of the station. It was a very large cubicle made of stainless steel and supposedly completely self-service. When I put one euro in the slot, it unlocked a huge metal door that slowly slid open. I walked in and the door slowly closed behind me and locked. I had entered a time machine taken from one of Jules Verne's novels, *Around the World in Eighty Days* or *Twenty Thousand Leagues Under the Sea*.

After the door closed, I panicked; I feared I would be launched into space or worse. No one would hear me yelling and banging. When Nikki realized I was missing, she would have no idea where I had gone. I had entered a large room that contained only a sink and toilet in a world of filth. I turned around, but had difficulty finding the little stainless button to the stainless steel door. I finally returned to the outside world!

Nikki and I were leaving Paris for a visit to our friend, Carmen Jaouen, whom we call Micheline. Carmen has never told us why we should call her Micheline instead of Carmen. Our friend lives in Le Mée Sur la Seine. After my visiting the restroom, we were now in a mad rush to find the track with the RER train going in the direction of Melum. The last time Charletta and I had visited Micheline, she had written out explicit directions to reach Le Mée from Paris. However, I had left them behind. Those directions explained that after descending the stairs we should take the train to the left.

When we came down the stairs, we found the exact same information on the monitor to the right and to the left, with the final destination being Melum. The first train came into the station on the right. I ran up to a young man and asked if this was the train to Melum. He assured me it was the right train. We should have been suspicious when, while we were waiting, an elderly French woman kept coming up to us and asking which train would take her to the destination, Le Vert de Maisons (translated Green Houses). After we had pushed our way into the car, and the train had pulled out of the station, Nikki looked at the guide on the wall. We decided to get off at Maisons-Alfort, just before the train would change directions. The ticket agent at this station told us that it would be a couple of hours before another train to Paris.

Micheline was expecting us at eleven thirty, and it was now close to noon. We decided to call a taxi. After trying the three telephone cards in our possession, the last one worked. In a few minutes our taxi van pulled up. We jumped in and gave our destination as Le Mée. When we arrived in the area of Le Mée, we kept seeing the sign "Le Mée" and an arrow pointing in the direction we should go.

We knew that Micheline lived near the plaza off the train station. We finally reached the train station, but not an area where the cabby could park and put us very close to Micheline's apartment building.

We asked the cabby to let us out and we would walk the rest of the way. It was good that Nikki and I always travel light, because we had our two-week supply of clothes in two small upright suitcases. We paid the sixty-two euros as the meter indicated in American dollars. The cabby was quite happy with the dollars and the tip.

We began walking in the direction of the station. The cabby took off but returned in a few minutes to tell us he found the entrance to the plaza leading to the trains and the apartment complex. We jumped into the cab for the short ride, but what would have been a long walk, to the station. Sometimes signs in France are not designed for travelers to understand, not even the French.

On another occasion Nikki, Charletta, and I were riding around Provence, with Nikki at the wheel. There was a very confusing traffic sign we passed each day as we were returning to Ventabren. The road sign had only a big question mark (?), nothing else. The road did not seem that dangerous to us. It was narrow, but so are many of the roads in Provence. There were a few curves, and in certain places you might land in a gully if you were not paying attention. I suppose the driver was supposed to figure out the danger since the highway department could not.

Micheline lived in an apartment four flights up very narrow stairways. We called her from the train station and she came to fetch us, as I could not remember which building was hers. We also needed help with the bags. She was really disappointed that we were two hours late, and we had missed her son, Jean Claude, and his children Marion, Laura, and Fanny. Jean Claude had stopped by after taking part in his Napoleonic Fraternity performance at Vaux-Le-Vicomte, a chateau built by Fouquet, one of Louis XIV's finance ministers.

It is said that Louis IV was jealous of Fouquet for building a castle that was more beautiful than Versailles. He had him thrown in jail for stealing funds. Vaux-Le-Vicomte remains one of the great masterpieces of the seventeenth century. This castle was the setting for *The Man in the Iron Mask* starring Leonardo Dicaprio.

Nikki and I were equally disappointed not to have seen Jean Claude in his military finery. Micheline had already eaten lunch, but served us the five-course meal she had prepared. The evening meal consisted of as many courses.

Micheline's apartment, or what Americans would call a condo, has two levels. On the first floor are the living room, kitchen, and W.C. On the second level are two bedrooms—the larger one is Micheline's and the smaller one is a guest room. On a previous occasion Micheline had insisted that I sleep in her room. The bathroom with the tub/shower and sink are on the second level. She was going to do the same with Charletta and me. Micheline said she would sleep on the sofa bed downstairs. Upon hearing there was a bed downstairs where the W. C. was, Charletta piped up and said, "I'll sleep on the sofa. I insist!"

Charletta has to go to the bathroom much more often than I do. It is a little difficult negotiating the narrow spiral staircase in the dark. The French have always had unique and excellent ways of conserving their electrical power. In public buildings and hotels lights turn off automatically when one leaves a room or an area. In some hotel rooms you must use your hotel door key (card) to turn on the lights.

When I lived with Madame Kammerlocher in Pau I often got home long after dark. I had to find my way through a very dark courtyard in order to reach the door to her apartment building. Once inside I had to find the hall light. If I were too slow, or had difficulty opening the apartment door, the hall light would go out. I also had to walk three or four blocks from the school through dimly lit streets.

The only complaint from Madame Kammerlocher was my using too much water washing clothes. She never complained about my coming in late at night, or my fumbling around in the hallway trying to find the light switch. I never felt afraid or threatened while walking the streets late at night on dimly lit streets, even when a group of young men asked if I would like a ride home. I refused this ride just the same. Micheline often chastises me for leaving a room without turning out the light.

The French custom of separating the bathroom from the W. C. (toilet) is not just practiced in France proper. We were visiting Marie Josée René-Gabriel in Guadeloupe. Her cousin invited Paul, Nikki, Pauly, Jackie, and me to her home and to a New Year's Eve party at a local restaurant. The New Year's party was much like the parties in the U. S. Lots of food, drinks, dancing and a toast at midnight are a part of the festivities. It was also at this party that I ate goat that I thought was beef.

After the party it was too late to drive back to Saint François, so we spent the night at Marie Jo's cousin's house. Her cousin had recently moved into a beautiful new home. Her W. C. was located in a beautiful water closet, thus the name W. C. However, the bathroom (*salle de bain*) and the W.C. were next to one another. This custom prevents one person from causing an inconvenience for another who might want to take a bath or shower.

In recent years the "bidet" has disappeared from homes and hotel rooms. I am glad that I no longer, when traveling with students, have to explain this fixture that was often mistaken for a toilet. Invariably, they would ask, "Madame, why do we have two toilets in our bathroom?"

Probably the strangest restroom that I have ever seen was at a restaurant in Paris called *La Table de Julie*. Nikki, Dave, and I were having dinner with my old professor, Jacques Houdaille. Dave went to the restroom and stayed an awfully long time. We could not imagine what was taking him so long. I found out why when I had to use the facility. As I entered the door I was facing three urinals. The W.C. which contained the toilet, was at the end of the line of urinals. When I entered and closed the door the light came on. I was accustomed to this manner of saving electricity, but Dave was not. He had taken quite a bit of time trying to figure it out. When he could not, he decided to take the chance of finding his mark in the dark. Of course when he closed the door the light came on. My problem was the possibility of coming face to face with three men using the urinals when I came out of the water closet. Luckily, the restaurant wasn't too crowded that evening.

I am as amused as the French when an American asks a French man or woman, "Where is the bathroom?" The differences in cultures and peoples' outlook on life are a great part of my fascination with the peoples of the world, especially the French.

Our visit to Fontainebleau led Nikki and me to another interesting part of Paris. We returned to the Latin Quarter and the area where Louis IV and other members of nobility had their tapestries woven. This part of the Quarter, the factory, the avenue and the neighborhood, all take their name from the brothers Jean and Philbert Gobelin. They established their famous dye works here. The name Gobelin has become synonymous with tapestry, though the brothers never wove any. They made a special scarlet dye.

Louis IV's minister, under the king's direction, assembled a colony of artisans to rival the Flemish weavers. The Sun King wanted the walls of Versailles to be covered with the finest tapestries. Today, scores of weavers at the Gobelin's factory manufacture tapestries using the ancient techniques. Three days a week there are guided tours of the factory, and we just happened to arrive on a day for a tour. Nikki and I could not afford a wall tapestry, but we did buy a piece of fabric to cover her piano stool. In the same neighborhood, Nikki also bought a beautiful sweater with an equally beautiful design on the front. She took this sweater to college, and considered it to be her lucky sweater.

The workers in this factory were all men. They were in contrast to the young boys and girls we had seen weaving the famous Egyptian carpets in Cairo and Luxor. The children were as young as seven or eight years old. When Paul and I ask about the children doing such difficult work, and the lack of child labor laws, the adult supervisor who was standing around watching responded, "The parents don't mind. The children are learning a trade they can use as adults."

Like any large transportation system, the Paris Métro has its "weirdos." One evening on our journey back to Malakoff we sat directly facing three punk rockers with the usual purple and red Mohawks, the heavy makeup, the tattered shirts and pants, and the multicolored tennis shoes. They were passing among the two of them a plastic bag filled with glue or some other substance that appeared to give them a high. They would take long sniffs or whiffs, and at the same time they spoke a vulgar sounding French. There sat Nikki and I, looking straight ahead, as we avoided eye contact with either of them.

A wise soccer mom had told us as we rode the transient system in Göteborg, Sverige, (Sweden), above all else, never make eye contact with the perfectly dressed and groomed drunks we encountered each morning as we rode the bus to the soccer fields. In 1979, Nikki and the Vienna Raiders Select Soccer Team played tournaments in Denmark and Sweden. In Tokyo I found a very inebriated man as polite as the rest of the Japanese. He sat down beside me in the airport and proceeded to carry on a one-sided conversation all in Japanese. My only response every now and then was, "I don't speak Japanese!"

On still another occasion, we encountered a black man who systematically cursed every passenger in the subway car until he arrived in the back of the car where Nikki and I sat. We had originally thought that he was only cursing the French, but after plopping himself down directly in front of us he proceeded to curse us as well. We stared straight ahead of us for as long as we could, but after a while I just could not take it anymore.

I nudged Nikki, indicating it was time to get off, even though we were several stops before our destination. Nikki strongly suggested that we should continue to ignore him, but I was just too frightened. As we stepped off the train at the next stop, a gigantic blob of spit followed and splattered on the concrete platform and just narrowly missed the bottom of my jacket. Nikki still insisted that we should have remained on the train, and that we just infuriated him by getting off. She was probably right!

Paris in 1998—We were there when France won the World Cup. National pride was shown everywhere, even the *agents de police* showed their exhilaration by painting their faces and cars with the colors of France. The idea for the World Cup was of French origin. Paris was the place to be, and we were there along with our friends, Charletta and Yanni.

Yanni is Charletta's godchild and she accompanied us on this trip. We made our expensive dinner reservations at a not so fancy restaurant near our hotel. We got a ring-side seat in front of a giant TV screen—that is, as far as big television screens go in France. There was a group of Brazilians sitting across from us, but they were no match for the French diners, the people in the street, and us. The French showed class in victory over Brazil.

After the big upset, to my knowledge, there was only one incident of violence in all of France. This involved a woman backing her car over a group of spectators. She said it was an accident.

A group of men and women from Sub-Saharan Africa marched in front of the parade. It was a perfectly peaceful demonstration. They were protesting the type of treatment they received from the French government. For Nikki, the avid soccer player, watching the World Cup in Paris and having the French team win was an experience of a lifetime.

Though Nikki and I have had many memorable sojourns in France, there is one that stands out more than any other—a week in Provence with Nikki as Charletta's and my *chauffeuse*. In September of 1995, Charletta and I decided that we were going to spend a month in France. We were going to use our customary senior citizen travel program, *Go Ahead Vacation*. The name has a special meaning for Charletta and me. It usually means that we are going to *Go Ahead of Nikki*.

In 1995, we decided to take the "Provinces of France and Spain" tour. *Go Ahead Vacations* has offices in many countries and has reasonable prices. We are provided with experienced tour guides who often become friends. They take care of all the planning, but one may deviate from their plans as one sees fit. That's exactly what Charletta, Nikki, and I do. In 1995, Charletta and I decided to take advantage of *Go Ahead Vacation's* reasonable prices and planning, and tour some of the provinces of France and Spain. Nikki would join us later in the south of France.

Our tour began in Paris where we met our guide, Mark DeCote, at Charles De Gaulle Airport. Mark has degrees in several languages from Cambridge University. He described himself as half French and half Bahamian. I could also say he was half black and half white, or racially mixed would perhaps be the best way to describe Mark. He spoke perfect English with an English accent. In addition to being fluent in French and English, he was also fluent in Spanish, German, and Italian.

Brian Haldeman is another extraordinary Go Ahead guide that Charletta and I have had on a couple of tours. In 2004 Brian accompanied Nikki, Dave and me on an optional day trip to Champagne. He is an American living and working in Paris. He was born in upstate New York. He has a comprehensive repertoire of stories of French history and culture that cannot be found in a guidebook. Brian is also fluent in several languages.

The group spent a couple of days in Paris doing the usual touristy things. Since Charletta and I had been to Paris several times in the past, we went off exploring on our own. Charletta attempted to look up a friend who was living in Paris, but she had just returned to the States. I paid a visit to Georgette one evening. After getting off at the familiar Porte de Vanves, I forgot the directions to her apartment. A young Frenchman let me use his calling card. Her son Yan came to pick me up by the telephone booth.

I decided that I wanted to take a day to visit Euro Disney. Charletta, always ready for a new adventure, accompanied me to the park outside of Paris. We found the park interesting, but on a much smaller scale than Disneyland or Disney World.

The rest of the trip included a return visit to Chartres, the Loire Valley, Bordeaux, Biarritz, and a day's journey to San Sebastian in Spain. Pamplona, the city of the *Running of the Bulls* was also on the itinerary. The bulls were not running that day. We missed the bloody sport where young men are chased and risk being gored by bulls.

Touraine is usually visited from Paris, on side trips lasting from a day to three days. It is one of the old provinces of western France. It includes most of the fertile valley of the Loire River, famous for the chateaux. From the fifteenth through the eighteenth centuries, the Loire Valley was the playground of the nobility. Originally built for defensive purposes, the chateaux were later transformed into palaces of extravagant entertainment. The principal town of the region is Tours, with a beautiful cathedral and several famous châteaux just outside the city. Another important town is Blois, where François I built the greatest and most beautiful Renaissance castle, Chambord. It is the largest and most lavish chateau.

Bordeaux and Biarritz, along with Bayonne, are part of the region of Gascony called Côte Basque. San Sebastian and Pamplona are in the Spanish Basque region. Each of the Basque areas has its own capital, Bayonne, and San Sebastian. Bordeaux is located on the Garonne River. It is France's fourth largest city, and an important seaport and industrial center. From its vineyards come some of the finest wines in the world.

Not far from Bordeaux is Cognac. Twice I have taken the scenic tour down the Charente River to the Hennessy Distilleries, once with a group of students and their parents in 1997, and earlier with Charletta.

Susie Smith organized the 1997 parent and student group. After the guided tour, the students and parents were each given a small sample of cognac that Susie Smith confiscated. She kept the bottles of Hennessy until we returned to the U. S. and the bottles were in the hands of those parents who were not on the tour.

Susie Smith and her husband Joseph are model parents. They are not rich, but they realize the value of exposing their children to an education beyond their neighborhood school by being there. Cornelius learned something of English, French, and Spanish history as well as a bit of the language and culture of parts of Europe. This thirteen-year-old showed his knowledge of the three countries by leading lively discussions of places we visited with his group and another group of students from the Midwest.

William Raspberry, in his column entitled *Children Caught in a Deadly Drift*, *Washington Post*, December 6, 2002, writes:

189

> *Thousands of black children are drifting downstream toward a deadly waterfall. And we black adults are standing along the bank reassuring ourselves: "Well, at least it's not our fault."...There isn't any doubt that the trouble has its origins in America's racial history: slavery, Jim Crow, political powerlessness, disproportionate poverty. Many of the effects of this history persist today.*

This is old stuff. What is new is our willingness to substitute self-exoneration for help... Successful black parents in affluent suburbs fail to pass on their success and spend too little time passing along to their children the values that produce their own success and spend too little time tracking their own children's success.

Susie, who does not speak French, took her son back to the Eiffel Tower, so that he could have the experience of climbing to its top. They found their way to the restaurant where we were to meet and have dinner in the Les Halles area of Paris. My worrying about Susie and Cornelius had been for naught.

Both Cornelius and Nathaniel Waddell, his friend, are excellent athletes and outstanding students in academics as well. Cornelius sent me an invitation to his high school graduation. For some reason I could not attend. I sent him a gift that he could use in college. He responded with a thank you card (two in fact) in which he referred to the wonderful summer he had spent traveling in Europe.

Cornelius is now in his second year at the University of Richmond on an athletic scholarship with a major in Business. But at this university freshmen are not allowed to play competitive sports, and even, in some cases, sophomores must wait until their junior year. In order to participate in the sports program athletes must have at least a 2.0 grade point average. Cornelius' grades are above average at the university, just as they were in high school.

I wish more black parents were like Susie Smith and her husband Joseph. Boys need strong men to emulate. If the father leads, the son will follow. Like his father, Cornelius joined the *Kappa Alpha Psi* Fraternity, a group that stresses academic achievement. Cornelius's little sister Ashley is off to college next year. If Susie and Joseph have anything to say about it, Ashley will spend at least one semester studying in France.

Instead of showering our black children with expensive sneakers, jackets, and jeans that are too big, we all would be much better off if they were showered with all the elements of a good education—preferably an education steeped in the humanities. Jean Jacques Rousseau describes in his novel *Émile*, the type of education a young man should receive. It should encourage self-expression but does not exclude literature and the other arts.

Our black boys should spend more time doing their homework instead of spending hours in a chair getting their hair braided, so that we teachers cannot distinguish them from the girls. Most successful black men don't wear earrings and visible tattoos either. Those black basketball players who are drafted right out of high school or before even completing high school will not have the skills to manage their lives and finances when there is no more basketball. I blame this problem on their parents who do not say, "College first!"

As for my expensive bottle of Hennessy, on New Year's Eve of 1999 I discovered the bottle was empty. I first accused Nikki of the dastardly deed. Paul was the culprit. He who would never dream of spending one hundred fifty dollars for a bottle of cognac, even Hennessy, had drunk every single drop and left the empty bottle in its beautiful gift box.

The highlight of the trip to French and Spanish provinces for me was a couple of days and nights in Andorra. When I was teaching geography, I always mentioned Andorra as the little country in the Pyrenees Mountains—the mountains that separated France from Spain. I could never tell my students that I had been to Andorra, one of the smallest countries in the world. Now I could.

It is also a shopper's paradise. After this trip, they knew Andorra as a storybook country, with rolling hills and green valleys. It's a country that covers only one hundred seventy-five square miles, a little more than half the area of New York City. Andorra is the capital of Andorra, as Luxembourg is the capital of Luxembourg. The people speak Catalan, Spanish, and French.

Charletta and I continued our journey into Spain with *Go Ahead*. In Valencia we left the group and took a train back to Marseille, where we were to meet Nikki. Arriving at the border, our car soon emptied of all passengers. At the very last minute we realized what was happening. The front of the train was going to France, and the rear cars were going to stay in Spain. Charletta started to descend, but I suggested that we would make better time if we ran through the Spanish section to reach the French cars. If we had not done this, we might have been stranded on the platform without either the Spanish or French section.

We reached the last car of the train bound for France just before the Spanish section was disconnected. If the conductor had checked our tickets before we reached the frontier, I should think we would have been told that we were occupying the wrong part of the train.

Before continuing to Marseille we stopped for an overnight visit in Montpellier, the city made famous by Nostradamus, only to find that we could not stay in the city overnight because of a doctors' convention. We then took a cab to a beach resort, a few miles from the city, where we had a leisurely stroll through town and a wonderful dinner by the sea. The proprietor of the restaurant gave us a complimentary *aperitif* and *digestif*. Needless to say, the drink before and after dinner, along with a bottle of wine with dinner, made us a little intoxicated. However, the blustering wind from the sea, the dinner, and the drink made for a good night's sleep.

The next morning we returned to Montpellier by taxi, where we got a glimpse of the university where the widely known astrologer, physician, and prophet was a student. I was able to satisfy some of my curiosity concerning this man. François Rabelais, the famous French satirist, also studied at the university. His best-known works are *Pantagruel and Gargantua*. The stories tell of the adventures of Gargantua, a giant with an enormous appetite, and his giant baby, Pantagruel who became the "King of Drunkards." These works satirized politics, the Catholic church, and education.

After lunch near the University of Montpellier, where two great Frenchmen, Nostradamus and Rabelais, had lived and worked, we continued our journey to Marseille where we were to meet Nikki. We booked a room for a couple of days at the Hotel Ibis, located on the plaza behind the train station. Nikki was not expected for another couple of days. She was meeting us for two reasons—to drive Charletta and me around Provence, and to have a free vacation. Charletta and I passed our time sightseeing around Marseille. France's second largest city lies within the region of le Côte d'Azur (The French Rivièra) and next to the province of Languedoc.

Marseille is the chief port on the southern coast. Le Vieux Port (Old Port) is filled with fishing craft and yachts, and seafood restaurants offering the specialty of Marseille, *bouillabaisse*. The Nazis blew up the old quarter in 1943, destroying the narrow streets and subterranean passages and the houses of prostitution.

From the old port Charletta and I took one of the small motorboats to Chateau d'If, the fortress built by François I to defend the city. Alexandre Dumas used the castle as the setting for *The Count of Monte Cristo*. It was late afternoon when Charletta and I arrived on the island. There were only a few tourists around. After we took a short tour of the castle, we returned to the little pier for the last boat at five o'clock. Each time a little boat arrived, we would ask if we could get on board. We could not! They were bringing supplies to the island. We were concerned that we would be stranded on the island. The last boat back finally arrived a few minutes past five.

Nikki had happily agreed to be our driver during the next few days, as she would be spending time in a part of France that she loved. To prepare for this job, Nikki had taken a few lessons in driving a stick-shift car from our neighbor Pegah just before coming over.

Late, as always, in getting to the airport, Nikki missed the Friday evening flight from Dulles to Charles de Gaulle. Imagine my surprise when Nikki called me around midnight. By my calculation, she should have been on *Air France* and halfway across the Atlantic. She had called to inform us that she would now be arriving on Sunday instead of Saturday. What were we supposed to do about the rental car that was supposed to be picked up on Saturday? The rental office would be closed on Sunday. We had reservations in Ventabren, seventy kilometers away where we would be staying the following week. After hearing the news, Charletta turned over in her bed and fell asleep. I stayed awake most of the night trying to think of a solution to our problem.

After about an hour or two of a restless sleep, I got up and set out to find the Auto Europe Rental Office. I arrived at the rental office in downtown Marseille just as Gregoire was opening the door. I explained my dilemma— my daughter had been due to arrive at Marseille Airport today, but she was delayed. She had planned to take the shuttle bus to town where we would pick up the rental car and drive to the village of Ventabren.

However, now she would not be arriving until Sunday afternoon. Of course there was no way that I could get an automatic! I didn't know how to drive a stick-shift, and neither did Charletta. I had to convince Gregoire that he should drive the car the few blocks up the hill to our hotel and park it. I had already asked the hotel manager if it would be possible to leave the car at the hotel. After much pleading with Gregoire and using his name in every sentence, I got him to agree to my plan. Mama always told me there is nothing like being polite, especially when requesting a favor. Calling a person by his or her name as often as possible also helps. Lastly, the key to a Frenchman's heart is to speak his language. Gregoire would drive the rental car to the Ibis Hotel after getting off from work.

Just as he began writing up the paper work, he thought of a much better plan. He could call his office at the airport and reserve a car there. Nikki could pick it up when she arrived on Sunday. Excellent!

Le Mistral? There still was the problem of the reservation at Le Mistral in Ventabren. I didn't want to take a chance of losing our rooms for the week. While I was walking back to the hotel, another plan came to mind. Charletta and I would take a cab to Ventabren. At the train station, I stopped at the taxi stand and asked about the fare for the journey. The fare amounted to about fifty or sixty dollars for the two of us.

The beautiful village of Ventabren is perched at the top of a hill. The ruins of a château loom above. It is ideally situated in the middle of Marseille, Aix en Provence, and Salon de Provence. It was in Salon de Provence, while touring with our good friend Cynthia Foster, that we first met another good friend, Carmen "Micheline" Jaouen. The modern city of Ventabren surrounds the ancient village where we spent a week. In the village you fall under the spell of the little cobbled streets, the stone houses with window boxes filled with red geraniums. Climbing up a steep set of stairs past the *boulangerie*, you arrive at La Grande Rue, which is actually a very small square where sits the village church and the mayor's office.

There is a stone walkway that leads to the top of the village where *Le Mistral* is situated. It is a superb, four-bedroom house surrounded by the medieval village of Ventabren. Lynn McDonald, an American, maintains the charm of the past with the modern comforts of the present. All rooms are decorated in the Provençal fabrics of yellow, gold, and green. Each has a private bath, a telephone, and satellite television. There is a library where guests are invited to leave a favorite book.

Charletta and I arrived in Ventabren on Saturday afternoon. We checked into the bed and breakfast, unpacked, and relaxed until dinner. For our first dinner in this little hilltop village, we chose the less expensive of the three restaurants. Since Charletta and I had been together for almost a month, we decided that she should have the single room and not Nikki—that is, she could have it by paying me the difference in price.

The next morning I arose bright and early in time for the mass. After sitting alone in the church for close to an hour, I realized that France had changed to daylight saving time. Immediately after church, I found the lone taxi stand and the young driver and headed for the airport. During the ride to the airport, I learned that my taxi driver was the mayor's son, and that the whole village knew of the two American ladies who had arrived by taxi from Marseille. On the way over I took copious notes of the route to the airport, so that Nikki would not have difficulty finding her way to the airport the following Sunday.

Nikki finally arrived in Marseille by way of Orly Airport. She had told me she would be arriving at DeGaulle, so I was watching the monitor for flights from DeGaulle. Nevertheless, I was more than delighted to see her when she finally walked down the ramp from the aircraft.

We immediately walked to the Auto Europe Rental Office. Our Renault Clio was waiting. Nikki had difficulty starting the car. The attendant informed her that their rental cars in France have an automatic locking system to prevent theft. There was no problem getting to the area of Ventabren except when Nikki reached a roundabout (a traffic circle) where she had to slow down and change gears.

The road to the village was a different story. She could not get very far up the hill without the car rolling back down. There were a number of people walking up to the village. We later learned why. There was a pottery festival in the village. A couple of young men guided Nikki slowly, sometimes pushing the car, until we reached the top. When we reached the village, all parking spaces were taken. Nikki found a tiny area between two cars and very close to what we were now calling a mountain instead of a hilltop.

We found Charletta lounging in her room. She informed us that she had had a wonderful time at the festival, and she had had a delicious lunch in one of the three restaurants. Charletta also told us we would not be able to have dinner in the village because since the restaurants had been opened for an extended lunch, no dinner would be served. Another dilemma!

"But Nikki and I haven't even had lunch!"

After resting a while, we decided we would try to make it to Aix en Provence and back. We did! When we got to Aix, about thirty minutes away, it was not yet dinnertime. Nikki and I needed something to eat. After walking around Aix we found a brasserie where we could get a *quiche* and a *croque monsieur* left over from lunch. Charletta said she was hungry also, but she didn't want anything with cheese. I asked the waiter if my friend could have a *croque monsieur* without cheese, and he looked at me as if I was completely insane.

"A *croque monsieur* is a *croque monsieur*, and a *croque madame* is a *croque madame*. You can't leave out the cheese."

This reminds me of the time when Nikki and I were traveling in Greece. The waiter in the hotel restaurant was serving the group from a large platter containing the main dish of slices of roast beef and mixed vegetables. When he got to me, I said I wanted only the mixed vegetables. "I don't eat red meat." The waiter said, "I can't give you just the mixed vegetables without the slice of beef." I said " Okay." I sat there with nothing on my plate, hoping I would at least get dessert. A young man across from me spoke up and told me to take the roast beef; he would be happy to eat it. By the time the waiter got to Nikki, she knew exactly what to do. She took the roast beef and the mixed vegetables, and promptly gave her roast beef to the young man. The *Patron* (owner) seeing Nikki and me with only the mixed vegetables on our plates, offered us a Greek salad. "When in Rome, it really pays to do as the Romans do, and in this case as the Greeks."

Charletta couldn't stand watching us eat, so she decided to take a walk. She returned a few minutes later with a plate of french fries. I don't know how she managed to get only french fries. French fries are not a snack food.

Paul and I were in Marseille. I wanted the typical French midday meal, which is like dinner to us Americans. At a restaurant in the Old Port, I ordered my favorite, *Salade Nicoise*. Paul said he just wanted french fries. The waiter said he didn't have any. This part of the conversation was in French. A few moments later, the waiter came out with a bowl of french fries. Paul said, in English, "I thought he said he didn't have any fries!" The waiter promptly responded in English. "French fries are a vegetable!" Then Paul saw a McDonald's in the distance.

This incident with the quiche reminds me of an e-mail sent by my Bennett classmate Geneva Averett-Short. Our President is one of her favorite topics.

Evidently President George W. Bush has no idea what quiche Lorraine is as evidence by a joke that appeared on the Internet during the most polarizing campaign in American history. Then George W. had never visited such capitals as London, Paris, and Rome before his fraudulent takeover of the presidency. How could he possibly know what the Lorraine area's connection is to a world famous dish. Charletta and I agree that this president got all his academic training on the job—his being a "C" student and all. Luckily, he had Dick Cheney as his *mouthpiece*.

George Bush and Dick Cheney are enjoying a quiet lunch at a very fancy Washington restaurant. Their waitress approaches the table to take their order. She is young and very attractive. She asks Cheney what he wants, and he replies,

"I'll have a heart-healthy salad."

"Very good, sir," she replies, and turning to Bush she asks, "And what do you want, Mr. President?"

Bush answers, "How about a quickie?"

Taken aback the waitress slaps him and says, "I'm shocked and disappointed in you. I thought your administration was committed to high principles and morality. I'm sorry I voted for you."

With that, the waitress departed in a huff. Cheney leans over to Bush, and says, "Mr. President, I believe that's pronounced *quiche*."

The above "Bushism" may be a joke, but this one isn't.

"Our enemies are innovative and resourceful, and so are we. They never stop thinking about new ways to harm our country and our people, and neither do we."

After our quiche Lorraine and sandwich, we walked up and down the Cours Mirabeau, looking at menus on the restaurants from which we would choose our dinner. This wide avenue, shaded by tree foliage, is the hub of Aix. The city revolves around this avenue. Restaurants line the north side of the avenue including the *Café de Deux Garçons*. This restaurant was once the meeting place of artists and writers.

Cézanne (1839-1904) was from Provence. He was the son of an Aix banker. Not far from Aix's cathedral is Cézanne's studio where he painted. It remains the same way Cézanne left it. A docent, wearing the dress of his time, tells the story of his life and his work.

On the other side of the avenue are the old hotels, shops, and bookstores that show the intellectual side of Aix, namely the University of Aix.

A couple of days later, Nikki decided to inquire about admission to the university as a doctoral student. After asking several students in the university area, we finally found the right office: the office of Madame Verte, who gave us the information we needed, mainly that Nikki needed to pass an equivalence test to show that she was proficient in the French language. Madame Verte then directed her to the office where she could pick up a brochure, a bulletin, and an application for the university.

We first knocked on the door of a professor, and after telling him our problem he directed us around the corner to a receptionist's office. The receptionist said she could not give Nikki the information she wanted unless she paid for it. As we left that office we bumped into the same professor. He asked if Nikki had gotten what she wanted.

"*Non, ça, c'est trop cher!*" (No, the packet was too expensive!)

"*Venez avec moi!*" (Come with me.)

Monsieur, le professeur walked up to the receptionist and said, "Give her what she wants!" The lady started to object, seemed to have a second thought, then she got up from her seat at the window, put together a packet, and handed it to Nikki.

After all of that, Nikki decided to go to the University of Utah in Salt Lake City.

It only took Nikki a couple of days to become an expert at driving a stick shift. During the week we covered the towns and villages around Ventabren. One day the three of us took the train from Aix back to Marseille, as Nikki had not seen much of France's second largest city.

We were walking down hill from the station when we were accosted by gypsies— two women, one with a baby in her arms, and a boy of about nine or ten years. They surrounded us. We tried to fight them off. We thought we had succeeded, but after walking a short distance, Charletta felt a light tap on her shoulder. The little boy handed her the wallet he had lifted from her shoulder purse. American dollars were the only thing Charletta had in her wallet. The gypsies knew they would have difficulty exchanging U.S. dollars. It was kind that they chose to return the wallet with the money.

Cassis, an ancient fishing port, was Nikki's choice of an ideal village in which to retire. In Cassis there is a small beach, and little fishing boats that share the harbor with yachts and a collection of tourist boats for visiting the *calanques*. After inquiring at a real estate office, Nikki decided that she had better find another village in Provence where she could spend her retirement years.

During the week Nikki would park the car on a small lot quite a distance down from *Le Mistral*. On our last evening, she decided she was going to park on the higher lot, so Charletta and I would not have to drag our bags down the steep, uneven stone stairs. Nikki took a wrong turn and ended up in an area where she could not turn around without backing extremely close to the edge of the cliff. I got out of the car and tried to guide her, but my screaming and yelling only upset her more. She finally got the car turned around without our backing off the cliff and sending us to our demise.

After that ordeal the three of us did not want to go back to Aix for dinner. We had also eaten several times at our favorite restaurant in the village. Charletta remembered that she had seen a sign advertising a restaurant near the Roquefavour Aqueduct. A twenty-six-year-old engineer, Franz Mayor de Montricher, constructed the aqueduct in Ventabren. It was constructed (1842-1847) to transport water from the Durance River to Marseille. The city was in desperate need of water to relieve the droughts. This aqueduct was successful, and the designer received many honors for saving the city from drought. This aqueduct is longer and taller than the more famous Pont du Gard near Avignon. In fact, as we approached the area in our taxi on the first day, we actually thought it was the Pont du Gard, that I had not seen since 1962. The taxi driver set us straight.

We decided to try The *Arquier*, with its magical surroundings, suggested by Charletta. It offers a renowned cuisine of provincial tastes. Nikki and I chose as our main course our usual fish in a cream sauce. Charletta chose the following:

> *Entrée*
> *A mixed salad*
> *Viande*
> *Lamb with Garlic Cream and Tarragon*
> *Dessert*
> *Apricots Gratin with Almonds and Kirsch*

We spent an unforgettable evening in the lovely atmosphere of this provincial restaurant. Just as we were about to leave we were presented with three Santons. Charletta's choice of an eating-place was perfect for our last evening in Ventabren. Provence is our most favorite area of France, after Paris.

Nikki and I spent a week in Provence in 2002. This time our stay was in Nice at the Mercure Nice Grimaldi. Nice is the capital of the Côte d'Azur, home to the rich and famous—Tina Turner, Elton John, and the late Nina Simone to name a few. It offers one of the most beautiful coastlines in the world, with pretty bays overlooked by some of the most expensive villas and blocks of apartments.

In 2004, Nikki, Dave and I saw firsthand the true meaning of the term Côte d' Azur. The area was given this name because of the beautiful deep blue of the sea and sky. Our many trips to the south of France usually included the resort areas of Nice and Cannes, but never St. Tropez. I always wanted to see Brigitte Bardot's city. We inquired at the hotel front desk about getting there. Taking a bus was one possibility, but we would not see much of the coastline. Hiring a taxi would be our best bet. We took the breathtaking scenic route along the blue coast, arriving in St. Tropez just in time for lunch at *La Bastide* one of Ms. Bardot's favorite restaurants. She wasn't there! After lunch our taxi drive and personal guide Denis wanted to get back less we would arrive back in Nice in the midst of rush hour. I just had to have a souvenir from St. Tropez so I rushed into a shop and bought the first item I saw, a mint green cashmere sweater. We took the autoroute back to our hotel. This day's journey was well worth the 400 euros. An added bonus was Denis taking the three of us by his apartment to show us his nine-year old Yorkshire terrier and introducing her to our Yorkies, Chanel and Jacques.

Before taking the TGF to Nice, Nikki and I spent a week in Paris. This trip was a part of our favorite travel agent's itinerary, *Go Ahead Vacations*. This particular tour is called *Paris, City Stay*. You are really free to explore Paris on your own and at your pace. However, there is a tour director who comes to the hotel each morning to answer any questions you might have, to tell you what is happening in and around Paris, and to give suggestions.

Tulip Inn Little Palace in the Marais Section was our home for a week. It was located in the heart of Paris between the Marais and Beaubourg areas. The nearest metro was Reamur Sebastopol, which was only a block away, according to our tour director Frederic Morgand.

After we settled in our room, Nikki and I set out to explore our favorite haunts. A huge billboard facing us covered the main entrance to the Métro. We passed the entrance and continued for several blocks before realizing that either Freddy or we had made a mistake. Of course once we turned around, we came face to face with the entrance to *Reamur Sebastopol.*

Tulip Inn Little Palace is a small three-star hotel of only fifty-seven rooms. A very good continental buffet breakfast is included. It is located in the heart of Paris on the edge of the Marais area. Le Marais, once marshy land, is now in the heart of elegant Paris. It fell into decay over centuries. Today many of its mansions have been restored and its apartments rent at prices higher than anywhere else in Paris.

The Place de la Bastille is the site of the prison for people who opposed the monarchy. It was stormed by the Parisians on 14, July 1789. The column in the middle of the square is in memory of the victims who are buried in the foundations. At the top of the column is the Spirit of Liberty. The new Bastille Opera was inaugurated on 14, July 1989.

Victor Hugo's house is located on a square which used to be called Royal Square, because of Henry IV's and his queen's house. It has since been named the Place de Vosges. The tour of the area with our director, Freddy, who grew up in the area, was well worth the couple of hours. Today le Marais is the gay section of Paris, especially for gay men. There are numerous bars, clubs, restaurants, and shops catering to gay clientele.

Freddy recommended a restaurant called *Le Colimaçon* within walking distance of the hotel. The food was excellent and reasonably priced. Nikki and I ate dinner there two or three times during that week. I suppose our fellow diners thought we were gay as well.

The good food and pleasant atmosphere put us in a good mood. The high point on the calendar is the annual Gay Pride parade. Freddy said we had to see it, so Nikki and I were there in St. Germain along with our friend Thierry Delahousse, who isn't gay. He didn't even know about the gay parade. There was no comparing this parade to the parade we witnessed in San Francisco a few years ago.

On previous visits to Paris we had seen the sign near Les Invalides pointing the way to the Rodin Museum. We decided to spend an afternoon in Rodin's mansion, which was also his studio from 1910 until his death in 1917. Rodin was born in Paris in 1840. He was the greatest sculptor in the second half of the 1800s. Rodin was a realist. From 1871 to1877 he worked in Brussels. He did his *Age of Bronze* there. At the Paris Salon his work caused quite a furor. His statues were so realistic that some people believed that he had cast his sculptures from a living person because of their perfections. But Rodin proved his critics wrong by producing the models who posed for him.

His *Saint John the Baptist* is thought by many to be his finest achievement. His most memorable works, *The Gates of Hell, The Burghers of Calais,* and *The Thinker* are displayed in the front courtyard. He made busts of the great and the unknown. Toward the end of his life he received many honors and became internationally known.

He left most of his work to the French nation. Inside the his house, now a museum, are his sculptures, plaster casts, reproductions, original sketches, and a whole room filled with sketches and drawings by Victor Hugo. Rodin appeared to have a special admiration for the great poet, dramatist, and novelist. Interspersed with Rodin's work is the work of his student and mistress, Camille Claudel.

Dave in Paris: On Sunday, October 11, 2003, Nikki and I first introduced Dave to our favorite city. After going through customs at Charles DeGaulle Airport we were met by a non-English-speaking Frenchman. He was carrying a sign that read *Bellamy-Bellamy-Johnson.* It took us quite a while to get to Tulip Inn Palace Hotel on the edge of the Marais District. Two workmen were repairing holes in the autoroute and causing a terrible traffic jam.

Tulip Inn is the same hotel where Nikki and I had stayed in 2002, so we were familiar with the Métro station, Sébastopol-Réamur. It is also the line frequently used by the pickpockets. Dave had his money safely inside his undershirt. Dave had a lot of fun with our morning waiter, also named David. He was always very polite and friendly toward us. Dave tells the incident he witnessed one morning when he was eating breakfast alone. One of the guests, an American, said, "Monsieur!" David's response was, "I'm busy!"

Nikki had suggested that we go in search of my Frenchman that afternoon. So we began Dave's introduction to Paris by attempting to find my professor of forty years ago, Jacques Houdaille. Our tour director Jean-Jacques Legalle happened to live in the same area, metro stop Galleni. The number 17 is really the entrance to a courtyard containing several apartments. A young man was kind enough to let me into the court as he entered. A code was necessary to enter the door. Once inside I found a posted hand-written list of tenants.

We learned from a neighbor that Monsieur Jacques did indeed still live at 17 Pixérécourt in the twentieth *arrondissement*. He wasn't home. The next morning Jean-Jacques called after checking the telephone directory. The telephone number that I had was preceded by the letters *MEN*. French telephone numbers, like ours in the U. S., are now all digits.

Jacques Houdaille answered the telephone. He wasn't on vacation or out of town, as we had feared. He had actually been in the park across the street on Sunday. After a brief introduction he remembered me. We arranged a rendezvous in the park at six o'clock the same day.

When Nikki, Dave, and I walked through the gate we saw an elderly man walking in our direction. He was much smaller than I remembered Jacques. I called out to him. It was he!

Nikki and Dave went to a creperie close by, while the two of us talked for a long while. I learned more of his life. During the German Occupation, his parents had sent him to live with an aunt and uncle in Provence. He was fifteen at the time and had thought of joining the *Maquis*. He was now seventy-nine. I had guessed that he would be in his eighties. From 1951-1963 he had taught at Howard University and from 1963 to 1966 he had taught at Georgetown University. After returning to Paris he took a job with the *Institute of Demography*.

He had also spent some time in Mexico, where he had married a woman from Guatemala. From that marriage he had two daughters, Elizabeth and Claudine. They now live in Miami Beach. He and his wife had separated years ago, but never divorced. He said he might have had twin sons by the maid of his landlady in Mexico. He wasn't quite sure of their paternity, as the boys were born eight months after his leaving Mexico. Their birth did not correspond with the last time he had been with their mother. Nevertheless, he had sent child support for many years.

I told him a little about my life, and that I would send him copies of the books that I had written. His autobiography would be much more interesting than mine. I apologized profusely for having come to Paris many times and never having looked him up.

Nikki and Dave returned after a while. We spent my best evening ever in Paris at *La Table de Julie*, a Provençal restaurant suggested by Monsieur Houdaille. We walked with him back to his apartment. Dave and Nikki waited at the entrance while I walked monsieur back to his apartment. The telephone rang just as he opened the door. It was his daughters' nightly call. I gave him a kiss on both cheeks and left.

I called him again on Friday, and he called me on Saturday morning. He wanted to know if it were possible we could get together again. I hope I will not regret being too busy to have seen him a second time. I shall call him often from the U. S.

Later Dave mentioned that Monsieur had a much better spring in his step after an aperitif, a couple of glasses of wine, and a digestif. I know he enjoyed the evening as much as we did. Monsieur Houdaille wanted to pay for the dinner but Dave insisted that he pay. I had paid for our plane tickets. Nikki and Dave were responsible for all expenses in Paris. They even insisted on paying for nonessential items such as a nonessential Parisian purse that

I wanted. Seeing Monsieur Jacques Houdaille after so many years of neglect, on my part, made all other visits to Paris unimportant. Once more luck, or God, was on my side!

We decided not to take Go Ahead's city tour. During the rest of the week we introduced Dave to the usual touristy sites. We began with Père La Chaise Cemetery, located in Monsieur Houdaille's area.

After leaving Monsieur Houdaille's apartment on Sunday we set out for the Champs-Elysées, the most famous avenue in Paris. We got off at the Métro stop closest to the Arc de Triomphe de l'Etoile. Old soldiers were having their customary Sunday ceremony at the Tomb of the Unknown Soldier. Dave took a picture with two *Agents de Police* who were near the Arc. We had dinner at the Bistro Romain.

On Monday, and during the rest of the week, Dave visited the Eiffel Tower, Notre Dame, La Sainte-Chapelle, the Palais de Justice, the Hôtel des Invalides, and the Army Museum.

Nikki and I had been by the Conciergerie many times but had never gone inside. The building was so named because it was in the charge of the Governor of the King's House. It was turned into a prison in the fourteenth century. Many famous prisoners have passed between its walls. The most famous of all was Queen Marie Antoinette. During the revolution it was known as the Antechamber of the Revolution.

The following days Dave was to see La Tour Eiffel, and the lively area of St. Germain de Près where he had the best pizza ever. Nikki remarked several times that Dave just had to see L'Opéra. Just before getting off the train, Dave said he really didn't want to see an opera. Nikki said, "You picked a fine time to tell us!" The exterior of white stone marble, and especially the interior of marble of all colors and gilded bronze, fascinated Dave. Dave was in luck. No operas are performed during the day.

On Thursday, we took a *Go Ahead* sponsored tour to Normandy, site of the D-Day Invasion. We walked on Utah and Omaha Beaches, and visited the American Battle Monument and Cemetery. There is also the Garden of the Missing. I had visited Normandy before, but I was not aware that there was also a German Cemetery with beautiful gardens and a monument. The French were equally as generous to their conquerors in death as to their liberators.

We had lunch in Avranches by the English Channel. This seaside resort owes its fame to the gigantic landing operation which took place there in June 1944. We then toured a small museum there and bought a few souvenirs, in particular a few small bottles of the famous *Calvados aperitif* made from Normandy's delicious apples.

On Friday we ventured to Montmartre, an area that is difficult to describe. One has to go there! We showed Dave the Basilica of the Sacre Coeur. It was built in a spirit of atonement and devotion to the Sacred Heart of Jesus Christ. After touring the church, we met our friend Thierry

Delahousse out front. We had lunch with Thierry at a restaurant directly in front of the Place du Tertre still frequented by painters, who work and display their painting in the open air.

Dave and Thierry hit it off right away. Thierry's hobby is collecting old cars, one of which he has in Paris. He intends to start his own tour company, using his refurbished antique car for guided tours around Paris. *Une bonne idée*!

Thierry had given Nikki and Dave a wedding present of two canisters of tea that he bought at the famous *Mariage Frères* teahouse near the Hotel de ville. We had planned to go there after lunch. We had difficulty finding the shop. I stopped to ask an old lady for directions. I made the mistake of pointing to the name of the street on the empty canister. She thought I was begging. She shrugged her shoulders and gave me an evil look. Didn't she think I was pretty well dressed for a beggar? We found the teahouse after a few more "Tout droit!"

On Saturday, Nikki and I set out for a day of shopping. Dave said he was tired and would sleep in. Our first stop was the pet store on the Quai near the Pont Neuf. Nikki and Dave had decided that they were going to buy a dog, a Yorkshire terrier that they had seen the day before. There was no comparison between the size of the dog and the cost of the dog. The cost was much, much bigger.

We had no difficulty getting little Chanel, or Ulca, her given name, on Air France. The French didn't even ask for little Ulca's papers, which were in perfect order. She had had all her shots and was in perfect health. The French love their dogs! I encountered no problems getting her through customs in the U. S. either. I just walked through with Ulca in her carrying case. I thought I would be less conspicuous than Nikki or Dave.

Our last day in Paris was quite an adventure—first the dog and then disappearing Dave. We returned to the hotel about one thirty. Jean-Jacques said Dave had just left a few minutes before. We figured he had just gone out to lunch, as it was getting pretty close to two o'clock when most restaurants close. Jean-Jacques, Nikki, Ulca, and I went for lunch at a restaurant close to the hotel.

When we returned to the hotel, there still was no Dave. By dinnertime we were really worried. Had he gotten lost? Had he been kidnapped? Neither of the above! He had gone to an Irish Pub, which he had seen the day before at the foot of Montmartre. There he met a group of English rugby fans and had one too many beers while watching the brutal game. He had had no problem finding his way to Montmartre, but he got a little mixed up on the way back to the hotel. Nikki and I were so happy to see him so neither of us scolded him for the worry he had caused.

We then took a cab to *Le Colimaçon* on the rue Vielle du Temple. It is the restaurant run by gays that Nikki and I had visited the summer before. It was packed on this Saturday night. There was no more space. A few steps away we came upon a bigger two-story restaurant. Dave ordered his usual steak, and Nikki and I our usual fish. The food was equally as good as the food at *Le Colimçaon*.

We had a happy last evening in Paris after all. When I am no longer able to travel to France Nikki will have Dave as her traveling companion. Dave loves Paris and the French! Especially the food! They will teach their children to love France and her people. That will be their legacy! What more can I ask for?

Cimetière Père La Chaise is a famous cemetery that Nikki and I had not visited. I first learned of the importance of this burial place from my eighth grade student Kasi Pacella who participated in the *France / Spain Tour* in 1991. The cemetery wasn't on our schedule, but Kasi insisted on finding her way to the burial place of Jim Morrison. At the time neither Pauly, who was traveling with us, nor I were familiar with Jim Morrison, the lead singer of the rock group *The Doors*. He wasn't of great interest to Nikki or me, but because so many tourists were following the sign leading to his grave, we followed the crowd. His site is the only one with a guard, because many of his fans either deface his tomb or chip away parts of the concrete encasement. Notes and letters are also left for Jim to read while he is lying in his coffin.

Jim Morrison was a troubled young man with an ideal voice for the rock music of that era. The band was accomplished and creative, years ahead of its contemporaries. Jim Morrison was a great poet, and he wrote the lyrics to many of their songs. He was the son of a U.S. admiral. He died of a heart attack, induced by heavy drug use, at the age of twenty-six. He died soaking in his bathtub. Thirty years old, their music still stands up with contemporary audiences. His poetry is mystical, and he still has a cult following.

Within this cemetery, named after Louis XIV's confessor, are the elaborate tombstones and burial sites of the famous star-crossed lovers, Abélard and Hélöis, Molière, Balzac, Modigliani, and Toulouse-Lautrec just to name a few. We also came upon Eugène Delacroix's resting place, whose house and museum we had visited the day before. With the exception of Arlington Cemetery, we Americans do not place graveyards on a list of places to visit while on vacation. The other exception would be the Cemetery for Americans lost at Normandy, June 6, 1944 during the Normandy Invasion.

France's cemeteries are places of artistic beauty and historical significance. However, they are quite different from the cold and desolate catacombs. Freddy suggested the catacombs to us and another mother-daughter duo from the *Go Ahead* group. The catacombs are not classified as a museum, but I asked the cashier, in French, if we could use our museum pass. I also told her that Nikki's pass had been stolen the day before. The other mother had asked the same cashier about the museum pass in English, and she had shaken her head "No." This is another example of "superior" Americans assuming that the French speak English, their language. She waved Nikki and me through the entrance.

The catacombs began as a network of quarries extending for miles beneath Paris. In 1786, thousands of skeletons were transported from another overcrowded cemetery near Les Halles to the catacombs. They were stacked in neat piles along the underground tunnel walls. As one begins the descent, there is a sign that reads, "Stop! Beyond Here is the Empire of Death." The Nazis must have believed this to be true, as they never discovered that the French Resistance were secretly meeting beneath their feet.

The Panthéon is a temple dedicated to the dead. Louis XV commissioned it as a result of his recovering from the gout. It is a classical building constructed in the form of a Greek cross and resembles St. Paul's Cathedral in London. The crypt is a depressing place where notables like Voltaire, Rousseau, Victor Hugo, Emile Zola, and Louis Braille are buried. Jean Moulin, the great resistance leader, who was tortured to death during the Nazi Occupation, is also buried here. The Panthéon dominates the square of the same name in the Latin Quarter.

On leaving the places of death, we turned to the next phase of our vacation 2002. We took the Métro to the Gare de Lyon for tickets and reservations to the south of France. Buying train tickets is a small adventure in itself. The next day we started our journey to the south of France. Our destination was Nice, and the Mercure Nice Grimaldi Hotel at 6 Rue Grimaldi, around the corner from La Promenade de Piétons and a short walking distance from la Promenade des Anglais. Nice, the modern city of the goddess Nikaia, was founded by the Greeks. It is a city of never ending activities—dining, shopping, sun bathing, parks, and museums. It is a place for Nikki and me to enjoy the best that life has to offer.

Nikki and Dave's Big Fat Interracial French Wedding—I first met Dave when he came over for Thanksgiving Dinner in 2001. I thought he was an acquaintance of Lonica, a friend of Nikki's from New York. The next time I saw Dave, it was Christmas Dinner also in 2001. I thought he was with Amy, an intern who was working with Nikki, and had also come over for dinner.

On the Martin Luther King Holiday weekend of 2002, Nikki and I attended a Vie de France Festival in London. She told me that she and Dave were dating. Imagine my surprise! The summer of 2002 in France, Nikki told me that Dave had asked her to marry him. Thereafter our two weeks in Paris and Nice were interspersed with advice on marriage and plans for the wedding. (On Saturday, April 26, 2002.) I wasn't really surprised, as Nikki had hinted at the possibility previously.

Needless to say, we sort of planned the wedding in France. In fact, I bought my dress and shoes at *La Gallerie Lafayette* in Nice—a very plain dress and shoes, but pretty expensive compared to prices in the U. S. We decided that it would be a Provençal wedding, so we bought some of the gifts for the bridesmaids and favors for the guests in Provence. We also thought that if things went drastically wrong, our guests would think that must be the way they celebrate a marriage in France.

Meanwhile, Dave was asking Nikki's father for her hand—on the golf course back in the U. S. I guess he thought Paul would be more amiable when he was playing the game he is so dedicated to. The only problem was that Paul thought Dave should call him Mr. Bellamy. So for almost a year Dave addressed Paul as Mr. Bellamy, and me as Lil. After the wedding Dave asked Paul if he should still call him Mr. Bellamy, or could he call him Dad. Paul said it was now okay for him to call him Paul.

Paul is like his mom and dad in many ways. His dad once sent a father's day card back because Paul had not addressed the envelope to Mr. Paul L. Bellamy, Sr. His father died of congestive heart failure in 1999. Whenever I send his mother flowers I make sure she is addressed as *Mrs. Anita Bellamy*.

I know many Blacks are hung up on *Mr.* and *Mrs.* because whites used to show their disrespect by never addressing us using a title. If they did have some respect for elderly black folk they would call them "uncle" or "aunt." How silly is that custom? We could be like relatives, but not friends or acquaintances. Or, as in the case in South Carolina, they would call the principal of a school "Professor."

Mama never forgot her name even when she was suffering from dementia. When asked her name she would say, "Jannie Miles," with no title. She would have known when someone was being disrespectful. The nurses and aides always called her "Jannie."

To make a long story short, Call me "Lillian" or "Lil," I don't care—as long as I am not in the classroom. In fact I used to work at Woodies with a couple of students from Oakton High School. All of Woodies' employees were called by their first names. The students called me "Lillian" at the department store, but switched to *Mrs.* or *Madame* in the classroom.

I never call Paul's mother by any name. If I am talking to her, I don't have to call her anything. When I am talking about her I refer to her as "Paul's mother" or "Mom." "Mrs. Bellamy" seems too formal and cold. All the kids in my neighborhood in Drakes called Mama, and all grown-ups they loved or knew really well, by their first name—with the title "Miss" attached.

Most of the people I know from other countries call adults by their first name with no disrespect intended. Jackie, Pauly's first wife, didn't know what to call me at first. So she didn't address me at all. She would just start talking. I told her to call me "Lil." She does. I have told Lela and Dave to do the same. I could never call another person mother or a derivative of mother. There will always be Mama. And my father, well he is just *there*. It's like when Pauly was about four or five, he stopped in the middle of play and said,

"Mommy, is God really everywhere?"
"Yes, he is."
"Is he sitting there on the sofa by you?"
"Yes, he is!"

At Nikki's shower Jackie passed out a suggestion list to the guests. The suggestions were for Nikki. One of the questions was how to deal with your in-laws. My answer was "Always agree with whatever they say and do." Another was "Kissing in public." My answer, "Never do this—only if you are in France."

Recently, I asked Nikki if she had asked for her days off for our trip to France. She said she had, but she hadn't indicated where she was going. She said the last time she mentioned that she was going to Paris with me, the response was, "You travel with your mother?" She said, "Just think what they would say if I told them I was going on my belated honeymoon with my mother."

"What's wrong with that? It's not as if we will all be sharing a room. Whatever we want to do in public, we can."

When Nikki said she and Dave were going to have a small wedding—just friends and family, I responded with "Good! I only have four friends—Charletta, Yvonne, Annette, and Thelma. Those are my best friends." Actually there were lots of friends Paul and I would like to have invited, let alone Nikki and Dave's friends.

There are many people who know Nikki, so for months I had to be careful when mentioning that "Nikki is getting married!" We just could not invite all of our friends and all of Nikki's friends. From time to time Paul would tell me that he saw so and so in the supermarket (Paul does all the grocery shopping.) or on the golf course. I would respond, "Did you tell him or her that Nikki is getting married?" Just a few days before the wedding, I received a phone call from a friend, who said:

"I heard congratulations are in order."

"Why?"

"Nikki got married."

(Silence)

Nikki and I weren't really concerned about gifts. We just wanted everyone to come and have a good time. They didn't register at any department store. They received many gifts, even though when people called I would say, "Really we just want you there." Amazingly, each of their gifts was completely different and absolutely beautiful. Nikki and Dave spent the week after their wedding writing thank-you cards.

I addressed the invitations for Nikki—the number was eighty-nine—of course most of those were couples. We planned a menu for one hundred forty-five to one hundred fifty.

There were snow and ice storms beginning in November. The last bit of snow melted in March. Then came the never-ending rains. That was a good thing. After contracting with *Agro Lawn and Landscaping Service*, by spring our grass was luscious and green. The flowers I had planted around our house and our neighbors' formed patches of lavender colors, Nikki's colors.

However, the squirrels feasted on the tulip bulbs because they could not find their hidden acorns underneath the mounds of snow.

The day before the wedding the tents were set up. *Brooks Rental* was nice enough to bring the largest tent and a smaller one at no extra charge.

I didn't attend the wedding rehearsal, but from the wedding tape, everything seemed to have gone well. I was at Nikki's condo helping my sister, Eliza Etta, and my niece, Johnnie, with last minute details for the dinner. By early afternoon Diane, Thelma, and even John were helping to arrange the dozens of flowers that Nikki and I had bought from Costco the evening before. Nikki had bought plastic vases from the Dollar Store months before.

Diane and Thelma had made beautiful bows for the vases, but the plastic vases would not stand up right with the number of flowers being used. John asked if I had any little stones. I had a bag of leftover garden stones, but when they were put into the water, they turned the water white. John then took to washing the stones, while the ladies arranged the flowers and ribbons.

After taking Eliza and Johnnie shopping for the food I dropped them off at the condo. They stayed there all day preparing an Italian meal of meatballs and spaghetti and a mixed salad, and having a mother/daughter good time. My sister said it was one of the best days she had had in a long time.

I asked them if they had gone upstairs, since they had not been in Nikki's home before. They both said, "No!" I didn't know whether I should believe them or not. It's like when you are in a friend's bathroom, you tend to look in the medicine cabinet.

My sister is a caterer, so it was fine with her that I didn't help with the food preparation. Nikki and Dave had checked with several restaurants about a rehearsal dinner. The prices were much too high, so Nikki offered her condo.

For the Bachelor Party, Dave's friends took him on a golf outing. No worries about women jumping out of a cake there!

They intended to have this wedding without any bills left over, and they did. Nikki had planned to have some of the guests eat on her patio, but it was pouring down rain, so the rehearsal dinner consisted of wall-to-wall people in two rooms from the two families who got to know each other really well.

In addition to the wedding party, Nikki and Dave invited their wives, husbands, and children. The kids were watching TV upstairs, but kept jumping down the stairs and landing in the midst of the grown-ups.

Everyone commented on the delicious food, and had a whopping good time. John and Diane Butler, from England, arrived a couple of hours late. The street leading to Nikki's house is next to the entrance to Route 66, so they turned on to 66 and kept going, almost ending up in Washington, D.C. When they finally arrived in Nikki's courtyard they remarked they knew exactly where the party was because of the chatter of the people.

Nikki has a Ph.D. and Dave has a high school diploma. He is kind, sweet, and intelligent. He has his own construction business and is excellent at what he does. One job brings in more money than I make in a semester of substitute teaching. I really don't like stupid or ignorant people, and I know lots of those who have college degrees. So when my friends and acquaintances ask, "Where did Dave go to college," I say, "He didn't!" That ends the conversation.

Nevertheless, Dave does plan to take a series of summer courses at Oxford University entitled "The English Country House," "Great Britons and their Houses," and "Furnishing the English Country House." Oxford University, no less!

I pride myself on being a judge of character. Nikki said she knew she would be free to fall in love with Dave when I liked him at first sight. I could also add, but do not, that Nikki's brother has had two wives with college degrees, and has divorced both of them. Pauly, because of two divorces, is not in good standing in the Catholic Church, so he no longer takes communion. But he never misses a week of mass. God knows he is really a good person, and in his need for forgiveness he bypasses the priest and goes straight to God. I, on the other hand, feel that I need from time to time the intercession of a priest. I especially like the confessionals in France. I don't have to look the priest in the face.

Paul's first wife, Jackie, was in Nikki's wedding. She also gave Nikki a lingerie shower and later baked the wedding cake, which was the best I have ever had. The shower was only part of the wedding festivities that Pearis was able to attend. Pauly came down for the weekend because Lela, his girl friend, was also invited to the shower. Jackie had gifts for everyone.

Pearis made a diary. Even before she left the reception she began writing about the day. She was looking forward to telling the whole story of her Aunt Nikki's wedding.

Jackie and her second husband are true friends of the Bellamys. Pauly has since resolved the issues of our being friends with Jackie after the divorce—and with her second husband, Sam, and their son, Jordan. Jackie's parents, Bill and Delores Sykes, are good friends. Her sister, Angela, and her daughter, Chloe, attended the wedding and reception. Life is just too short to be wasted on animosity.

We all love Lela, who happens to be Chinese-American. She is great with Pauly's children, a cause for much of the discord with the children's mother. I suppose if Pauly marries Lela, the Bellamys will really be at odds with some of the people in the black community. It won't matter! Those persons would be people who are not our friends, or people we don't even know. Everyone at the wedding thought it was a magnificent and festive occasion. It was, at least the part I witnessed.

The real or imaginary problems:
Choosing the church—no problem. They had already chosen St. James' because of its diversity. Evidently, they preferred St. James' formal service to St. Mark's or Holy Spirit's more contemporary services.

Attire—Nikki had already found her designer gown in *Vogue* magazine. There was no problem purchasing the same gown at Lady Hamilton's in Arlington. Me, I already had my dress and shoes from Nice. Paul had his own tuxedo of thirty years. Dave was going to rent his.

Wedding party—Junior bridesmaid—It wasn't Pauly's weekend to have the kids—at the last minute he and his ex-wife could not agree on an exchange for Easter weekend and the weekend of the wedding. We thought that the exchange had been worked out. Pauly called me the week before the wedding and told me that they were not coming to the wedding. They meaning his son and daughter.

His daughter, Pearis, was to be the junior bridesmaid, and Dave's nephews, Austin and Russell, were to be her escorts. Paul IV was to be the ring bearer along with Dave's nephew, also named Paul.

Nikki and Dave had inadvertently set the date of the wedding as April 26, 2003. (It was also a date the church was available.) I immediately called Nikki after receiving Pauly's alarming telephone call. She went ballistic. I, Paul, and Nikki tried to reason with her brother. "Give your ex-wife what she wants," which was part of his spring break with the kids. Pauly didn't budge, because he believed that if his ex-wife had the kids during spring break, she still wasn't going to let him have the kids the weekend of the wedding.

This may have been true, but both Nikki and I thought he should have taken the chance. It was only a matter of losing two or three days with his children, and they would have memories to last a lifetime. But neither the mother nor the father could understand this. There is also an ex-mother-in-law from Hell involved. Each was thinking of themselves and not the children.

Nikki called Pauly's ex-wife and asked if she (the ex-wife) could bring the kids down. Nikki told her she would put her up in the hotel and give her shopping money—meaning she and Dave would give up their hotel room on their wedding night, plus she could go shopping at Tyson's on them. The Marriott Hotel where our guest would be staying is a short walking distance from the mall.

Kirsten, the ex, said she would think about it, but called on the Tuesday before the wedding and said, "No!"

We had bought a dress and rented a tux for Nikki's nephew, Paul IV. Nikki's cousin, Kim, agreed to let her daughter Amber be the substitute. We went over to southern Maryland with Pearis's dress. Luckily, the dress was in Virginia and not New Jersey. I had to determine how much of the dress I would have to cut off and hem.

Pearis had tried on the dress the last time she was in Virginia. It was a very beautiful dress (Not to mention expensive!) and Pearis looked beautiful. The child was looking forward to being in the wedding. Her brother was excited about having to wear a tuxedo, even though he pretended he would hate it.

The following week, I spent a whole day figuring out the best way to alter the dress and the rest of the week on the alterations. Since Amber is much shorter than Pearis, I would have to cut off and hem the multiple skirts.

Needless to say, Nikki's niece and nephew and our grandchildren were missing what should have been a very special day in their little lives. It saddens me each time I watch the wedding video and look at the wedding pictures, and see that Pearis and Paul IV are missing. I had planned to send a copy of the wedding video to the mother. I had thought Kristen, her parents Alvin and Joyce Pearis (with whom she and the children live) would enjoy watching the video together. Divorce is hard on children!

The very next evening, (After Pauly's call) Nikki's grandmother called to tell me that she wasn't coming to the wedding because she didn't feel well. I reminded her that she had told us a few days before that her doctor had given her a clean bill of health. She then said she would feel, "I am in the way."

I went off the deep-end and began screaming and crying. I told her Nikki was already very upset because her niece and nephew would not be in her wedding—NOW her only grandmother wasn't coming! Paul's mother then said she would come to the wedding if she had to crawl. Paul was already scheduled to pick her up, so she would not have to crawl. Nikki's grandmother was caught on tape having one of the best times of her life!

Originally we were going to have two ring bearers, Pauly's son, Paul IV, and Dave's nephew, also named Paul. Now Paul is the only ring bearer. Dave's nephews, Austin and Russell, escorted Amber.

Kim called just as I was about to leave for church. She wasn't going to come by the house to have Amber try on the dress as planned. She would meet me at the church. What if the dress didn't fit? She and her daughter arrived at the church at one forty-five. I was helping Amber to change into her dress, but then the music started for me to be escorted in and seated. Amber's dress was a little too short, but other than that it was okay.

The church wedding planner had left, and Kim couldn't find Amber's bouquet of flowers. Instead, she gave her one of the leftover corsages. Nikki's flowers were Calla lilies, so the corsage was pretty big. One had to look closely for it because the two escorts were holding Amber pretty tightly.

Paul, the ring bearer, started to cry because his mommy tried to take his stuffed whale away. It would have been pretty difficult for him to carry the pillow with the rings, and the whale. He finally relinquished the whale after his mommy told him that he could have it back as soon as he delivered the rings to the best man, Ken.

It was now a few minutes before two o'clock. The bridesmaids arrived in two different cars. Christine was chewing gum. I told her to take it out of her mouth. She shouted back, "I will!"

Nikki, who is known to be late, wasn't there yet. I had made a bet with Nikki and Dave that they were going to be late for their own wedding. They have a habit of blaming each other when they are late for Sunday dinner. The organist began to play the wedding music, which indicated the bride's mother and grandmother were to be seated. At that moment Jackie drove up in her SUV with Nikki. If I had known that Jackie was bringing Nikki, I would not have been as worried. Jackie is always on time. She would get Nikki to the church on time—five minutes before the hour.

I was really relieved when I learned Dave and his groomsmen had been in the back room where they were supposed to be since one thirty. There was no need for me to worry about Nikki being left at the altar—just— "Will she ever get here?" Meanwhile, Father O'Brien was also worried that Nikki was going to be late. He had told her that she had better not be late, as he had an evening mass.

Soon after I was seated Pauly handed me his cellular phone. "This is it— the disaster!" I thought. The band director just wanted to know if the band could move to an area closer to the dance floor.

As in every mass, three scriptures were read. Yvonne Redcross Jackson and Michael Dinkins (Nikki's cousin and Sam's brother) did a great job of reading the first two and Father O'Brien the third. During the ceremony, Father O'Brien told the guests that only Catholics were to take communion, but Paul's mother jumped up for the communion wafer. Paul started to protest but I said, "Let her go."

I thought Father O'Brien was ungracious in announcing that only Catholics should partake of the bread. The individual should have determined that. If he or she, not being Catholic, had chosen to take communion in the Catholic Church, then who would be committing the sin?

Father O'Brien's pretty long homily was addressed not only to Nikki and Dave, but also to all of the guests who were married and to those who had ever thought of getting married. When he expressed his view of marriage in his sermon, he used the word *sermon* according to its meaning of "a moralizing *lecture* or admonition." That was a good thing. I was able to listen to his sermon and remember the vows Paul and I had taken on our wedding day.

Ken dropped the rings; the guests laughed—the light moment was a good thing. Happily, the rings didn't roll off the altar, down the stairs, and into the sanctuary.

Nikki and Dave presented a bouquet of flowers to the Virgin Mary in honor of Dave's mother, father, and sister who had passed away a few years before—no problem there. Just a reminder that three people very close to Dave were there in spirit.

Our neighbor, Iraque, was washing his black Jaguar as we left for church. He had agreed to bring Nikki and Dave home from the church. Would he have his Jag parked in front of the church after the mass? It was there! The Pooshaghaghi family, Iraque (Ira), Shazzard (Sherri), Pegah (Peggy), and Payment are the best. Whenever the Bellamys have a problem it is their problem, and vice-versa. They helped with all the wedding preparations; they opened their home to the wedding guests.

I had been praying since the snows, *God, please let the rains stop!* I rose very early on the wedding day, April 26, 2003. It was raining. The rain stopped promptly at noon.

The wedding ceremony really was beautiful. Nikki and Dave did not want the wedding taped, but I hired *J Paul Video* anyway. Paul and Pat Tessier are members of our church, St. Mark's. I am glad I contracted for the video. Otherwise I would not have known all that was going on in church and almost nothing of what was going on at the Provençal Wedding Reception. Now both Nikki and Dave are happy about the video, because they also missed a part of the festivities. Nikki consoled herself and me when the stress of the wedding preparations seemed to take over by saying, "The only two people who have to be at the wedding are Dave and I. It would be fun having our family and friends there though!"

The caterer, Chef Joseph, is owner of *Le Petit Mistral* in McLean. Nikki and I tried to share our money equally between black and white. This is a stress we could have done without. We soon decided that we were just going to order the best service for the best price. For a caterer I first called a friend of Charletta's. I made the mistake of calling her on Sunday morning. I just figured she would have a business telephone and I could leave a message. She was very rude. "Don't you have Sundays off? I am getting ready for church."

She said she was going to yell at Charletta for giving out her home telephone. Charletta had inadvertently given me her home phone. I was not sure Charletta knew her business number. They were friends. I begged her not to yell at Charletta. She wanted my number, so she could call me back on Monday. I said "No!" and hung up. Imagine a businesswoman treating a potential customer like that.

All I needed was a caterer who would be rude to our guests if he or she made a mistake with the food. We then checked with a couple of restaurants. Le Mistral turned out to be the most reasonable, and we knew Joseph's food would be good, which is an understatement. It was too delicious!

Joseph is the typical Frenchman. I asked him if he needed electricity. His answer was, "No, Madame." I took it to mean he was going to cook the food in his restaurant and use sterno or candles to keep it warm. I had asked about the electricity, so I could tell my neighbors, if I needed their electricity for cooking, as well as for the band.

Imagine my surprise when Joseph's assistant chef, Christophe, with his two assistants, came into my kitchen with all the uncooked food at eleven o'clock on the day of the wedding. I had wondered why he would be at the house by eleven.

Joseph had never been in our home. He had no idea what kind of kitchen I had or what kind of counter space, ovens, or stovetop. In fact, there was no problem with the cooking of the food, and the chef and his assistants left my kitchen sparkling clean. But Joseph could have informed me—"*Je n'ai pas besoin d'électricité, mais j'ai besoin de votre cuisine.*" (I don't need an outside plug, because I am going to use your kitchen to cook the food.) But that's a Frenchman for you. Answer the question and give no more information than is necessary. Later Lela told me that a caterer always cooks the food on the premises. But I had never had a caterer!

The biggest problem was running out of food. The menu consisted of *Des Plats Froids* and *Des Plats Chauds*—five cold dishes and five hot dishes. The guests were supposed to choose one cold plate and one hot plate. Christophe or one of his helpers was supposed to serve the guests and give them a choice. When I asked why he wasn't doing this, he said the line was moving too slowly, because people could not make up their minds, so he let them serve themselves. Of course, each person or most of the guests took a bit of each, that is—for the hot dishes they had a taste of *chicken, salmon, lamb, filet mignon,* and *penne puttanesca* and for the cold dishes there was a taste of *salade nicoise, pate campagne,* cheese *tarte,* onion *tarte,* and *ragout* of mushrooms. Christophe said he even began cutting the servings in half, but he still thought he was going to run out of food. With twenty-six people still in line, he said he was definitely going to run out of food.

I then jumped in my car that was parked at our neighbors' house and not blocked in. I drove up to the *Whole Food Store* in Vienna and ordered servings of hot pasta and chicken, cold pasta and chicken, and macaroni and cheese. The young man behind the counter was in a tizzy but was very pleasant. He began putting the food in his largest plastic containers. I screamed, "They are too small! Don't you have anything bigger?" He did—a large tin foil pan. "Perfect!"

I ordered four tins of food at an additional cost of one hundred fifty dollars. The Whole Food Store is very expensive. I got strange looks and compliments in the Whole Food Store. I was all dressed up, hat and all, with four large tins of food.

When I got back there were ten persons who had not been served, including Dave. Later, when I told Nikki what had happened, she could not believe that I had actually left the reception to get more food. But she had wondered why Dave's food was different from everyone else's.

I had begun eating a plate of Joseph's food in the kitchen. When I returned, it was gone. When I went to Le Mistral to finish paying Joseph, and to return a couples of glasses and plates Christophe had left behind, I told him he owed me a dinner.

Joseph was the typical Frenchman in another way. He never asked for any money beforehand. I insisted that he take at least a partial payment, because we didn't want any bills coming in after the wedding. He said that he would only require that I pay for the food if the wedding was cancelled within twenty-four hours of the wedding—that is, after he had bought the food. I paid him what he charged for catering, except for the three hundred dollars that Nikki and Dave were supposed to pay.

I was still holding Nikki's credit card from the time she was in Utah, so I paid Joseph with that. I had intended to check to see if it was still active, but I forgot. Joseph's charge machine wasn't working on the day I came by, so he took the credit card number down. Later, I checked the card expiration date and called the company. Nikki had closed the account. I called Joseph and he said, "The card didn't work!" I wondered if he were going to call me if I had not called him. I gave him my credit card number. Nikki and Dave now owe me three hundred dollars I think I can depend on Dave to pay me back!

Nikki and Dave's wedding was a day to remember—a beautiful day! And a magnificent Provençal reception! Another reason it was great? When it was all over, all bills were paid in full! Everyone tells us that it was a beautiful occasion.

At the end of the day, I could say like Mama, "THANK THE LORD!"

Pauly—the sundry statements that follow give a precise picture of Paul Lawrence, otherwise know as Pauly. He was born at twelve forty-four, lunchtime, and has always had a bottomless pit for a stomach. The date was January 11, 1969. He weighed in at six pounds and nine ounces; lengthwise he was eighteen and one half inches. He has since grown in length, but not in width. His most distinguishing feature is a cleft chin that he inherited from his father. As Pauly grew physically he developed a distinct and winning personality. When things did not go right for him, he did not throw a temper tantrum. Instead he refused to talk for several hours, sometimes for days, or even years.

After pitching a perfect baseball game and his team lost because the out-fielder missed all of the balls, his anger and disappointment was shown by his coming home, going straight to his room and reading his favorite Alfred Hitchcock mystery, or rereading the story of Stuart Little.

The kitchen door would fly open at exactly three o'clock. Books would be flung on the kitchen table, and his homework would be completed within an hour. He would start his long-range assignments as soon as they were given, and be finished weeks or days before they were due.

"Five A's and one B! You received a B in the easiest subject you have."

"Good! I don't want to be known as a 'Goody, Goody.'"

He gets an A+ in religion, but hates going to mass. He cries because I won't let him go to school with a strep throat infection.

"I gotta read the Gospel today at mass. Sister George is counting on me!"

Now he is ill only on weekends.

He practices his oral book reports many times at home, so he actually knows them by heart, but he reads them from his notes in class and gets an A-. "My teacher said you didn't have to memorize it."

He irritates his teachers with his often-biting sense of humor. He sometimes misbehaves in class, but never to the extent where he is sent to the principal's office.

He does well in all his endeavors, though not his very best. Now and then, he will slip up and get all A's—in all his subjects, conduct included.

He fights with his sister constantly with both words and knuckles, but has never been in hand-to-hand combat with another child. Both he and Nikki have battle scars on the forehead—Nikki's to the left, and Pauly's to the right. Pauly received his when he was about six, and Nikki received her scar when she was twelve. Pauly took Nikki's jump rope and started to run with it. She caught one end of it and pulled him toward the stairs causing him to hit his head on the banister.

Several years later Nikki received almost the identical wound. Pauly would take the time and energy to tape songs from the radio; Nikki would not. Yet, she felt it was okay for her to go into Pauly's room and get his tapes anytime she had the urge to do so and without returning them to their proper place. Pauly would try to change Nikki's bad habit by pushing and socking her around. During one of these encounters, he pushed her into the deadbolt lock of the kitchen door, cutting her forehead. This get-tough attitude with Nikki hasn't changed through the years. In fact, Pauly's personality has changed very little, and neither has Nikki's.

Pauly's motto is, and always has been, "Never give up!" When he was about four years old, and he was still riding a bicycle with training wheels, his cousin Michael gave him a small bike minus the training wheels. Paul was determined to learn to ride this bike on the very first day. He went out at the crack of dawn the next morning—that is, to the sidewalk in front of the house.

He was out for about two hours, and I would see him from the kitchen window as he rode up and down the sidewalk, falling, getting up on the bike, falling again and again, but determined to master this two-wheeler before taking a break. Around noon he appeared in the doorway. I could not believe my eyes. Both of his legs were covered with blood from knee to ankle. He had fallen numerous times in fulfilling his desire to learn to ride this bike in one day.

"I can ride my bike now, Mommy!"

Then there was the day before the family was supposed to leave for Africa. Pauly had gotten a complete physical examination and all of his shots. He had suffered the side effects, as we all had, of having to be immunized against a variety of possible illnesses including the dreaded smallpox vaccine. Dr. Depoala had warned each of us, Pauly in particular, that we should not go into Africa with an open wound. So for the past week or so, I had kept careful watch over him, so that he would not get his weekly cuts and bruises. One morning I glanced out the window and saw our neighbor, Raquel Martin showing off her mother's touring bike. Pauly was examining and admiring the bike. "Innocent enough," I thought. "He wouldn't dare." I went about some last minute tasks.

"Mommy, look what I just did!"

There he stood on one foot as he held his other knee in a horizontal position. The top layer of skin on the right kneecap had completely disappeared. In its place was a bright red—BLOOD! A price paid for learning to ride Raquel's mother's touring bike. I took him to Dr. Depoala's office immediately, where he received a good scolding and was given a prescription for antibiotics just in case.

His desire to be a football player probably best illustrates his extraordinary will and tenacity to succeed at every endeavor. He made the freshmen football team at Bishop Denis O'Connell High School, even though he was smaller than most of the other players. He also made junior varsity his sophomore year, junior varsity his junior year, and varsity his senior year. There was a rule that seniors could not play junior varsity.

During his years in high school he never got to play very much, and there were many games when he did not play at all. Yet, he never missed a game or practice. He would make a great effort to stay in shape during the summer months as well as attempting to put on a few pounds—which was a Herculean task for him as well as for me. His eating dozens of raw eggs and drinking gallons of milk made going to the store each day a necessity. Watching him practice with the rest of the team and seeing him always coming in last when the team had to run the length of the football field, I would think,

Thank God that boy does not have to depend on his physical strengths and attributes as a football player, or as a participant in any sport to succeed in life. Thank you, God, for giving Pauly the unique brain he has, and for all those other very special talents he possesses.

His close friend James O'Donnell once remarked, "Paul can get into any college he wants to. He has the grades, the SAT scores, and he is black."

His friends in high school were a mixture of the good and the not-so-good. I would call them the motley crew: four or five white Americans, one Latino, one first generation German-American, and one black. When he had to make a choice between the good and the bad, I believe he usually made a wise decision.

One Friday evening, he and his friends were at the local McDonald's in Vienna. They made plans to vandalize the assistant principal's house. It seemed that this gentleman had made a rule that students would have to return to school on Saturday for a lesson on "high fashions" if they were caught out of any part of the school uniform during the weekdays. This group of boys was going to teach that assistant principal a lesson he would not forget.

The plan went this way—they had got a friend who lived in the Vienna area. He just happened to be black, but any color would have sufficed, as long as he did not go to O'Connell High School. This boy was to knock on the assistant principal's door to see if anyone was home. No one was home that evening. The group of O'Connell boys broke just about every window in the house.

The following Monday, all of the boys, Pauly included, were called into the principal's office. They told their story again, including the part about the black boy knocking on the door. At this point the principal stopped…

"Paul, I thought you said that you were not with this group."

"I wasn't, sir."

The principal and the assistant principal had heard the same story several times from each boy. The boys had been called in the first thing Monday morning, before they had had an opportunity to agree on exactly what their story would be. He already knew which students, including the girls, were not involved in the crime. The principal just wanted to put Pauly to a final test.

Pauly had left with the girls who were a part of the group who met at McDonald's. He had taken them home, and then returned to his home. The two boys who actually threw the rocks and broke the windows were expelled from school for the rest of the year. I learned about this incident from one of my eighth grade students. Her brother was one of the boys expelled.

When I confronted Paul about his part in the incident, or rather, his knowing about the plans and not trying to convince them to do otherwise, he replied—"I was just one of many. They wouldn't have listened to me anyway."

Paul has, for the most part, stayed in the middle of the road as far as friends and acquaintances are concerned. The assistant principal at Luther Jackson Intermediate School remarked: "Paul gets along well with everyone. Have you seen him during lunch? He sits with none of the worst troublemakers in school and some of the best students. I like this because the troublemakers seem to be neutralized. That particular table causes no problems during lunch." Pauly's ability to find a common ground with all types of people has gotten him into trouble. He has been married twice; to *the good, the bad, and the beautiful*. I will not define who is who. That is Pauly's story.

Nevertheless, he did outgrow one of the troublemakers in our neighborhood. The door flew open, and true to form his calculus book and the copy of Richard Wright's biography, *Black Boy*, sailed across the kitchen table.

"I'm ready to eat dinner, Mom. I did my homework at work."

Then he noticed an acquaintance from seventh grade, a high school dropout. He gave him a hearty "hello," and that is as far as the conversation went.

How was he able to do his homework at work? He was a porter at Woodies Department Store, where I also worked. During the weekdays, after completing his usual chores of cleaning the restroom and taking trash from all areas, he waited for calls—calls to carry out heavy purchases for Woodies' customers. Many nights there were no calls, and because the managers knew and loved him, none minded if he did his schoolwork.

Pauly never called in late; he never called in sick. In short, he could always be counted on. It was a small price to pay, permitting him to do his homework on the job. During his freshman and sophomore year at college he returned to his job as porter during winter and summer breaks.

The summer after his junior year, one manager was concerned that Pauly had not worked during the previous winter break. She said that he would be paid top dollar if he would return for the summer. I softened the blow. Paul had joined the Army Reserves. He would be away for most of the summer.

He could have gone to any college he wanted to—Morehouse College, the University of Virginia, but he chose a small predominately black university, Hampton University. He wanted to find himself, his blackness. He wanted to be near home, and that's where his best friend Marty Summers was going.

I am not sure that Pauly has always known just who he is. I think this true of Nikki as well. Growing up in an integrated society has its drawbacks. It is difficult to decide who you really are, and what you should be to the people around you. It is really difficult to explain, but I have seen this in both of my children. Each of them has tried to find his black heritage on his own, even though his father and I had always tried to expose them to black culture.

And consider the interracial couples. Nikki married a fine white man, how does this affect my daughter's sense of her black culture, or Pauly's, as he watches this marriage take place? It is indeed a fragmenting experience, a further spin on finding out one's sense of place and belonging. In the end, I think we can but trust in our bedrock of values as human beings. Down in that bedrock there is our common humanity. From this bedrock may spring insight and understanding of black culture, and we can give back to the world much stronger values, because of our contribution to it.

Travel in three countries of Africa and several islands of the Caribbean did not give them the answers they were searching for. To find their roots, Paul chose Hampton, and Nikki chose Spelman in Atlanta.

Pauly had no telephone at Hampton and he only came home during Thanksgiving and Christmas. In fact, he had no telephone during his first three years. There was no such thing as a cellular telephone, so it was difficult to reach him. He called when he had some information to convey. I always knew that he was all right because God was always by his side. He tells of his complete conversion to Catholicism in a paper written in high school on the power of prayer. He hasn't missed a single weekly mass, or a mass on a day of obligation, since ninth grade.

"I love being of the Catholic faith, because it is the hardest religion to practice. It is a true challenge for me."

Pauly's standard response when asked if he liked college was, "It's so boring."

I really think this was his way of saying, "I am homesick." Nevertheless I was worried as to how he was relieving his boredom. The suspense continued until I saw his grades. They arrived in an envelope addressed to Paul L. Bellamy III. I continued my bad habit of opening the family mail as soon as it arrives.

"Four A's and two B's." Surprisingly enough, Pauly wasn't upset because I had opened his mail. He was troubled because he had received the B's. He was adamant about the unfairness of his receiving a B in English when he deserved an A. In high school, he would carry his report cards around in his pocket for days. He would then take pride in taking out his rumpled report card and showing his good grades. It was the same in college.

There were no real clues as to what he was doing in school other than the fact he always had a great number of books around him, and he was usually at work on something of substance. His best friend at college would say, "Paul does study a lot."

His goal at Hampton was to get a 4.0 average for at least one semester. He did so more than once, and he graduated with honors, just as he did from high school. In college he joined the Student Leaders Association, Alpha Phi Alpha Fraternity, and the Army Reserves. Perhaps he had decided he was no longer satisfied with walking the middle of the road, with a group of very different people on both sides of him. But today, he still walks the middle of the road, where he can be a leader of men.

Pauly is like his dad. He likes to go to different parts of the world, and two trips to France is one too many. In 1989, I learned of a special offer by the French airline *UTA* (Unions des Transports Aeriens). It was a great two for one deal aboard a DC-10. *UTA* was beginning a new route between Newark Airport and Bordeaux and Toulouse.

UTA was a superb airline with its gigantic blue tail, green doors, and huge letters that could be distinguished from all other planes on the runways. The flight attendants wore Christian Dior designed uniforms in blues and greens.

Nikki and I, Pauly and his girlfriend Jackie, would take the trip. We would leave the day after Christmas—spending two weeks in France.

We left Vienna about three in the afternoon, picking up Jackie in Baltimore and continuing on to Newark Airport. Our flight was delayed a couple of hours, so we spent the extra time just amusing ourselves. We noticed, too, that the homeless had come in out of the cold. Each little group had claimed its own little area in the airport and set up portable tables with coffee, tea, and sandwiches.

UTA no longer flies from Newark to the South of France. I believe it still operates as a domestic airline. We finally took off about one o'clock. We arrived in Bordeaux around three in the afternoon. Our rental car was waiting for us at the airport. It was much smaller than we expected. If each of us had brought more than one piece of luggage, we would have had to discard a couple of our suitcases.

The four of us fit snugly into the tiny Citroen and we set off to find the hotel. I sat in the front seat to interpret the French signs. We checked into our hotel, but before going to our room we asked directions to the nearest bank. We got the usual directions from the hotel manager, but after a block without seeing a bank we decided that we were lost.

We stopped to ask directions of a man washing his car. He started with the usual:

"*C'est tout droit. A droit! A gauche!*"

Seeing my puzzlement, he said, *"Je vous conduis!"* (I'll take you.)

He jumped in his half-washed car, leaving the rags and pail of water on the sidewalk and instructed Pauly to follow. We wouldn't have been able to find the bank! There were a lot of right and left turns. We found a parking place on the sidewalk in front of the bank and quickly jumped out of the car and rushed inside. It was exactly five o'clock. As we entered the door, the gentlemen explained to the teller that we had just come from the United States, and we needed to exchange money. We got enough francs to last a few days.

That was just one of the extraordinary kindnesses the French showed us as we circled France during this two-week period. We were on our way back to Bordeaux from Spain when we discovered one morning that we had a flat tire. Pauly looked for the spare tire and jack, but did not find them where he thought they should be. We went back to the hotel's restaurant and asked the chef, who was now preparing lunch, if he could help us. He came out wearing his chef's hat and apron and located the tire underneath the trunk along with the jack. He then proceeded to change the tire. We asked if we could pay him for the job. He refused.

However, while in Paris we did not get the same kind of treatment. We arrived in Paris on Sunday evening. We found an empty parking place near our hotel. We toured the sights of Paris by Métro and by walking. The next morning while Jackie, Pauly, and I were having breakfast, Nikki who was always the last one up, came running into the dining room. She had been to the car to get something she had left behind, and had found that they were taking our car away.

I ran out just as this lady in uniform was about to pull off with the car. I screamed for her to stop. She did and got out. I explained that we were from the United States and had not realized that the car had to be moved before the morning rush hour. She said fine, but in order for us to keep the car, we would still have to pay the towing fee. I paid about one hundred dollars in American dollars to get our car hoisted down. We found a pretty economical garage to park our car for the rest of our stay in Paris.

As we were traveling around France, people would always approach Pauly when asking for directions or any other information. They would take it for granted that Pauly, being a male, was the leader of the group. Pauly did not speak a word of French except for an occasional *"Bonjour"* and *"mercii."*

Pauly was shocked to learn how trustworthy the French are, aside from the professional pickpockets, and how much they trust strangers. We were having dinner at a French restaurant on the Champs Elysées. Pauly observed that the waitress kept her money in an unlocked drawer of a little table next to where Pauly was sitting. The whole time we were having dinner, which was the entire evening, she would come back and forth to deposit her cash. She did not have the slightest concern about leaving her cash beside four black people and within reach of Pauly's long arms. This same scene was played out in other parts of France.

After spending a night and day in Bordeaux, we headed north. Our first stop was Limoges, a town in west-central France famous for its exquisite porcelain and enamel works, the latter a medieval industry revived in the nineteenth century. We bought small pieces of pottery at the *Prestige de Limoges*. It sells only Limoges porcelain—much cheaper than Limoges found in Paris and the United States.

We arrived back in Paris late in the evening, where Pauly found himself driving on a street and suddenly meeting bright lights from oncoming traffic. Luckily, he was able to make a quick right turn. In spite of the extreme cold, we spent the next couple of days re-visiting the most famous monuments in Paris.

After Paris, we headed southeast, stopping for a few hours at Dijon, spending a night and day in Lyon and then on to Marseille. It was at Lyon that we attended mass on Saturday evening. Paul spied a nun in full habit. He gave me a quick nudge and instructed me to ask her where the nearest church was located. The church was right around the corner.

After church we shared a sumptuous meal, sharing it with the *patron's* German shepherd dog. As we drove southeast from Paris we would stop at small villages and shopping malls. Prices were much better away from the fashion capital of the world.

We arrived in Marseille on New Year's Eve and checked into the hotel next to the train station. Parking was free and safe from tow trucks, so we could begin our tour of the old port. We learned that an American naval vessel was docked in the New Port. We encountered many M. P.'s. (Military police) and sailors along the Canebière, the main street.

We struck up a conversation with a group of young sailors. They were out of the Norfolk, Virginia naval base, doing maneuvers in the Mediterranean. The sailors invited us back to their ship where they said a New Year's party would take place later in the evening.

We didn't take them up on their offer, perhaps because these young sailors didn't know where they had come ashore, France or Spain. Instead, we had a New Year's Eve dinner of bouillabaisse (a Provençal fish soup with saffron, and white wine) topped off with champagne at midnight as we celebrated the evening in a restaurant along the Vieux Port (Old Port). On New Year's Day we took the train for a day in Monaco.

The next day we set out for Barcelona, Spain, where we spent the next couple of days touring that city. Jackie was an architecture major, so the building designed by Antonio Gaudi fascinated her. After our short trip to Spain, we were now in a big rush to make our flight from Bordeaux back to the United States. We did have time to visit Carcassonne on the way to Bordeaux. We had picked up an extra day after several hours of Pauly's driving at one hundred kilometers per hour in dense fog.

Carcassonne is fifty-seven miles southeast of Toulouse and consists of two towns, the Ville Basse (Lower City) and the medieval Cité. The former has little interest except for us. It was where the chef in full garb changed our tire.

The Cité evokes images of bold knights, fair damsels, and troubadours. It rises against the background of snow-capped Pyréneés Mountains. It is floodlit at night, and it was the Cité that had captivated me as I gazed upon it from my hotel windows thirty years before. It was fairytale magic! In the Middle Ages it was a place of battering rams and mobile towers, inspired by the Trojan Horse, and flaming arrows and lime-filled moats.

Pauly took delight at the speed he was able to drive in both France and Spain.

"Mommy. I have to keep up with the speed of the other cars on the autoroute, or someone will run into my back!"

He asked a young man in Spain about the fast driving. The response was that there were not many accidents at all, but when an accident did happen, it was usually fatal. Nevertheless, Pauly's driving was superb for a first time in France and Spain! He showed the same skill at driving on a Christmas trip we took to mountainous Guadeloupe, France's overseas department.

We left Carcassonne in time to arrive back at Bordeaux Airport for our flight home. Two weeks in France was a whirlwind vacation to remember, with six foot plus Pauly at the steering wheel of a tiny car. Originally we had set off in the old Pontiac station wagon. After going a short distance we decided that we should take the newer Subaru wagon. We were awfully glad we had. The temperature was way below freezing when we returned to Newark. The Subaru started without hesitation. We dropped Jackie off in Baltimore, and the three Bellamys continued south. We were safe and back in school before the first winter snow fell.

In 1991, we took a ten-day trip to Guadeloupe, the French West Indies (Les Antilles Françaises). Pauly was again our chauffeur. This times there were five of us—Paul, Nikki, Pauly, Jackie, and I. Paul just could not pass up the beautiful beaches of this island.

Guadeloupe is a group of seven islands in the West Indies. It is an overseas department of France within the French Community. It is about three hundred miles southeast of Puerto Rico. It consists of two main islands joined by a bridge over the Rivière Salée. These two islands form a butterfly. Pointe-à-Pitre is the largest city, chief port, and the economic capital of both sides of the island. To the west is Grande-Terre with its beautiful sand beaches, rolling hills, sugar cane fields, banana and coconut trees, and its resort areas.

Saint François is the area where Paul, Pauly, Nikki, Jackie, and I stayed for several days. Basse-Terre has a quite different topography. It is renowned for its rain forest, waterfalls, mountainous terrain, and volcanic ash beaches. Guadeloupe's volcano is called La Soufrière. The name comes from the French verb *Souffrir* and may be translated as "to suffer or to put up with." La Soufrière is an active volcano. The last eruptions were in 1976-1977 and caused grave economic disruption to the capital and largest city, Grand-Terre, that lies at its base.

Columbus landed on the island in 1493. He named the island after the "Sanctuary of Sante Maria de Guadelupe de Estremadura." The French established the first settlement there in 1635. Beginning in 1644, with the institution of slavery, the trading of spices, sugar, tobacco, and rum prospered between France, Africa, and the other islands in the Caribbean.

In 1815, the Treaty of Paris designated Guadeloupe as French, and slavery was abolished. Most of the people are a mixture of black and white ancestry. It has been a French possession most of the time, except for a brief occupation by the British in the 1700's. The other smaller islands making up this French overseas department are Marie-Galante, Les Saints, Désirade, Saint Barthélemy, and Saint Martin.

We left Dulles Airport aboard an American flight two days after Christmas 1991, making a change in San Juan, Puerto Rico. By the time we reached Pointe-a-Pitre it was ten o'clock in the evening. Having planned the trip and not taken into account my lack of ability to calculate miles on a map, we were now about fifty miles from our villa in St. François. I called my friend Marie-Josée and learned that she was about four hours away on the lower part of the other side of the "butterfly." She couldn't possibly pick us up.

My only choice was to hire two cabs to take us to the villa for the price of one hundred American dollars. We did not have much difficulty finding the landlady's apartment, but the taxis could not get us very close to our cottage, so we had to lug our suitcases quite a distance. When we reached our final destination, all we were able to do was to drop into bed and fall asleep.

The next morning we awakened to our surroundings: to a little house that looked just like home. There were two bedrooms, one of which served as a living room or parlor. Paul and I took the bedroom and Nikki, Pauly, and Jackie took the combination. There was also an ample kitchen and large bathroom. The next few days we spent getting to know Saint François, its beautiful beaches, and its expensive restaurants.

As in mainland France, I found *"Bonjour"* is the key to unlocking the three West Indies islands we have visited—Martinique, St. Martin, and now Guadeloupe. One must be able to converse with the market ladies who were dressed in their colorful madras clothing and headpieces. We tried to get into a nightclub one evening, but Paul wanted to see inside before we paid the price of five costly tickets. We weren't allowed to look and see before we paid. We suspected that, in spite of the loud Caribbean music we could hear from the outside, there weren't many people inside having a joyous time. We would probably have been the only ones on the inside.

After a few days in Saint François, we decided to visit our friend Marie Josée René-Gabriel whom we call Marie-Jo. She lives in Basse-Terre, the other side of the island. We also planned some sightseeing as we journeyed toward our final destination. Our first stop was the Rain Forest National Park and La Soufrière.

Pauly parked the car in front of the park's information center. We all went inside where we were greeted by the receptionist. We explained that we were completely new to the area and wanted to see some of the Rain Forest and get a glimpse of the volcano. She said it was all right to leave our car where it was parked, which happened to be almost directly in front of the path leading into the forest. We thought it was quite strange that there were no other visitors in the center.

We set out through the forest pass filled with lush tropical greenery dripping with warm sparkling raindrops, the chirping and other sounds of life, and an unsure footing of puddles, tree bark, and rocks. I had no fear of encountering my deadly enemy, the snake. Marie-Jo had told me several years before that the mongoose had been brought to Guadeloupe by the French. All of the snakes, poisonous and nonpoisonous, had been killed by the mongoose.

After thirty or forty minutes of walking through this no-man's land of dripping trees and foliage we saw a glimpse of sunlight. We rushed toward this ray of light and stepped into the clearing, and what did we see? A parking lot with rows of cars and minivans. The receptionist at the visitor's center had failed to tell us that we could reach the base of La Soufrière by the paved road behind the center.

Anyway we enjoyed the beauty of the rainforest—in spite of the fact that our clothes were dripping wet and our shoes were covered with a thick, sticky, slippery substance. While Nikki and Pauly continued the hike up the mountain to the crater where La Soufrière's throat was belching smoke and ash. Paul took the short walk back to the center to get the car.

Nikki and Pauly returned after an hour or so, and we continued our journey to Marie-Jo's house where she served us a sumptuous lunch. In the afternoon we followed her in her car to a black sandy beach on Basse-Terre. The black sand is the result of La Soufrière's anger.

We stayed overnight for New Year's Eve, and to celebrate the occasion we all went to a New Year's Eve party at a Creole restaurant where the main dish, which I thought was beef, turned out to be goat. After dinner there was the usual drinking and dancing until the stroke of midnight. New Year's Eve was celebrated in much the same way we ring in the New Year.

Pauly wanted to drive back to St. François, but I refused to give him the car keys. He is an excellent driver, but I didn't trust him to drive the narrow and winding roads back to the villa in the wee hours of the morning. We spent New Year's morning at Marie-Josée's cousin's house, and spent another couple of nights in St. François before deciding to go to Pointe-a-Pitre, where we could do some shopping and be closer to the airport. We would be able to return the rental car at the airport.

During our stay in the villa, we were without power for most of a day—meaning no electricity or water. It seemed that there was a group of Guadeloupe's would-be separatists who were demonstrating their desire for independence from France. I am not sure how they managed to periodically interrupt certain government services.

When I went to settle our rent with the landlady, she was nowhere to be found. I slipped the payment that we had agreed on minus the day we were without power. Evidently, she was satisfied, as I never heard from her concerning the way I had calculated the bill for our stay in her villa in St. François.

The airport at Pointe-a-Pitre is very, very small. We had to wait in line for quite a while, as there was only one ticket agent. She was having a discussion with a sweet old lady who would come in every week and ask to extend her departure date for the United States. After the agent gave her what was to be her very last extension, we received our boarding pass.

Once on the propeller plane, we observed that the three people who worked inside the airport were responsible for starting the propeller and guiding the pilot to the correct runway for takeoff. The ticket agent was also the stewardess.

When we finally arrived in San Juan, we discovered that our flight to Dulles had been cancelled. After quite a hassle we were booked on a plane to Washington-Baltimore Airport, with a free taxi ride back to Vienna. The five of us also contracted Montezuma's Revenge after eating the free lunch in San Juan's Airport. Needless to say our post Christmas vacation 1992 in Guadeloupe was one to remember.

> *"A wise man maketh a glad father."*
>
> Proverbs, X: 1

Today, Pauly has joint custody of his two children, Pearis and Paul IV. Our dream, Paul's and mine, is that one day our grandchildren too will see "La belle France" and much of the world's geography first hand. I don't see this dream as ever becoming a reality. Both parents' signatures are needed for a passport application. When there is a divorce, parents often knowingly punish the children by turning the hatred he or she has for the ex-spouse toward the children. It's the same type of hatred that blacks so often have for one another. Richard Wright in his book *Black Boy* makes this observation:

Negroes solve the problem of being black by transferring their hatred of themselves to others with a black skin and fight them.

Sometimes the *others* are our children. But then there are Nikki and Dave!

Epilogue

You Can't Go Home Again
Thomas Wolfe

Having traveled to four continents and realizing that more than half of my life is over, I wanted to go home again. I returned to Drakes Branch the weekend before Thanksgiving 2002. We left Vienna around seven in the morning, headed south on Route 95 and picked up Hull Street in Richmond and onto Route 360. Keysville is only a couple of miles west of 360. We stopped at the Shelton Motor Inn just outside of town limits. As we walked into the inn, we were doubtful as to how we would be received.

Paul and I were now mindful of Trent Lott's "terrible" remark at Senator Strom Thurmond's one hundredth birthday celebration consisting of his now famous forty-five words as quoted in *The Washington Afro American*, January 3, 2003. Months later his tribute to the Senator is still a subject of debate:

> *I want to say this about my state.*
> *When Strom Thurmond ran for*
> *president, we voted for him.*
> *We're proud of it and we- if*
> *the rest of the country had*
> *followed our lead, we wouldn't have*
> *had all these problems over all*
> *these years, either.*

I wondered what problems Senator Lott was talking about. Integrated classrooms? Lunch counters? Neighborhoods? Bathrooms? Water fountains? Paul and I had no intention of causing any problems for the Shelton Motor Inn. We just wanted a place to sleep for a couple of nights.

Paul and I now live in an integrated neighborhood that was once an all black neighborhood. Should we now be the family who moves out? If it were up to Strom Thurmond, this would have been the right thing to do when the whites started moving in back then. Upon entering the lobby we observed a sign saying that the motel was established in 1948, a period of segregation in Charlotte County and in the whole state of Virginia. We looked across the lobby and saw both black and white at the lunch counter. We walked toward the reception desk and two smiling and polite young ladies greeted us with no hint of hostility.

"Do you have any rooms available?" Paul asked.

"Smoking or nonsmoking?"

"Nonsmoking, please."

We were told there was a number of rooms available including non-smoking. Paul, true to form, asked to see the room before we checked in. We found the room in this privately owned motel to be comparable to any of the international chains such as the Holiday Inn, or the Ramada Inn, with the exception of the door opening to the outside elements. We had happened to pick a weekend of bitter cold and a blistering wind.

We took the room, as our only other choice was to drive to Farmville, approximately thirty miles away. Farmville is situated in the county that closed its public schools rather then obey the ruling of the Supreme Court. We found the room more than satisfactory and saw no need to look further.

It had a magnificent view. From our second story window we could see a land of rolling hills, and smack in the middle was a two-story, white wood siding farmhouse. Not far away sat a large barn with an extraordinarily beautiful and tall silo. Grazing on the green hills of grass were about twenty Black Angus cows. This scene brought back memories of Uncle Flood's farm.

After putting our bags in the room and completing our registration, we then headed south to Drakes Branch, my hometown. Our first stop was at what used to be called Wheeler Presbyterian Church. It was here that the Presbyterian Church U. S. A. had sponsored a school to educate the black youth. Mama, Eliza Etta, and Willoughby attended this school.

It is now the newly built Gethsemane Presbyterian Church. A brick church with a pastor's office, ladies and gentleman's rest rooms, and a slightly larger sanctuary had replaced my white wood-sided church consisting of only the sanctuary with a slightly raised pulpit.

I was in the process of taking pictures of tombstones of people I had known. When I used to live in Drakes I never knew anyone who was buried at the old Wheeler Church. I don't remember my old church even having a graveyard. I am sure it did. It was just farther back toward the wooded area. When I was a child, children didn't go to funerals. Mama probably went to funerals without telling me.

Now the burial plots had crept forward almost to the parking area. In a few years the graveyard will reach the road in front of the church.

Back then, I hardly knew anyone who died. I was now seeing on tombstones the names and dates of passing of both my mother's friends and my friends and classmates. Before my mother died in 1996, my sister said that our mother wanted to go back to Drakes. Mama may have wanted to be beside her friends. Even if the logistics of taking her home were possible, I would not have taken her back to Drakes. I wanted her near me. Drakes Branch was no longer our mother's home.

While I was busy taking pictures of the tombstones, a man in a big Lincoln Town Car drove up, stopped, and called out to me.

"Fannie Lillian?"

"Yes," I answer," and you are?"

"Roscoe Eubanks!"

I had attended Sunday school, elementary school, and high school with Roscoe. He was now a deacon in the church where once he had refused to learn a new Bible verse each week, instead repeating each Sunday the shortest verse in the Bible, "Jesus wept." Roscoe gave me a tour of the new church. When people are my age, they seem to begin dedicating more of their time to the church. I just don't believe I can make up for lost time.

Roscoe also told me that our high school was now an early childhood learning center and the old library had been turned into a museum honoring the graduates of the black Central High School.

The next day Paul and I visited the museum. The library, which housed the history of this wonderful school, was actually smaller than many of the rooms at Luther Jackson Middle School and Oakton High School where I now substitute teach. Back then the library seemed gigantic compared to our classrooms.

While we were taking a tour of the church, our high school English and history teacher, Luther Oxendine, showed up. Mr. Oxendine had stayed in Charlotte County and was now also a deacon in my old church. Back then, he wasn't even a member, but Roscoe explained that several Presbyterian congregations in the county had combined under the new name Gethsemane Presbyterian Church

After leaving my friend Roscoe and my teacher, Mr. Oxendine, Paul and I proceeded south to Drakes. As we entered the town limits a colorful sign, "Welcome to Drakes Branch," greeted us. A few yards down the street stood St. Michael's Baptist Church. The white wood siding that used always to be freshly painted was now weather worn. The graveyard that used to be in the back of the church had now crept almost to the street. The front yard of the church had disappeared, replaced by a wider road.

The picturesque sign was a far cry from what we found in the town. Drakes had become a ghost town. It was no longer the place where I grew up. Drakes Branch was now as dead as the people in the graveyards. The brightest and liveliest establishment was a filling station that sold a few necessities. I stopped there to buy a disposable camera; mine had stopped working after my photographing of the tombstones. I didn't buy the camera; it was too expensive. The lady behind the counter said I might find a cheaper one in Charlotte Courthouse.

There were street signs where there had been none. Main Street was no longer the Main Street I remembered on a Saturday afternoon. It once was a street filled with the hustle and bustle of people shopping, meeting, and talking with old friends. Mr. Crouch, "the Grouch's" Drug Store and Dr. Watkins's office above the store, were boarded up; Miss. Minnie's Millinery Shop was closed. The restaurant where Mama used to work was closed; the movie theater where we spent many a Saturday night had been torn down; Mr. Paulette's General Store where Mama bought her live chickens every week was all boarded up; the little grocery owned by Mr. Foster the black man was also deserted; Mr. Canada's supermarket had been turned into a rental hall for weddings and other social functions.

Drakes Branch Fire Department had replaced two businesses on Main Street, the "colored man's" barbershop and a hardware store. I was both delighted and shocked to see the fire station. Perhaps now if a house were to catch fire, it might not burn to the ground like Miss Edwina's house. There was an old lady who kept her life savings in her home, and when her shack burned down, kids went searching for coins for years.

We then headed out of town toward Uncle Flood's farm. The road leading to Uncle Flood's farmhouse was no longer distinguishable from the forest that now covered the land that was once fields of tobacco.

We stopped at my cousins, Franklin and Estella Jennings' house, near the entrance to the farm. They were reluctant to open the door because they thought we were Jehovah's Witnesses. Their home was the fourth house we had visited where people I grew up with had mistaken us for members of this religious group. I then concluded that the Jehovah's Witnesses had replaced, or would replace, the Baptists as the dominant religion.

After visiting with Franklin and his family, we returned to the motel by way of Drakes. My little post office was still in operation, as was the office of *The Charlotte Gazette*. I stopped in at the newspaper office to see if Miss Lucy's husband Mr. Jite and her brother Mr. Sam were still running the county's only paper. Both Jite and Sam were now dead. Sam, Jr. was now the publisher. Miss Lucy had married again and was now living in Richmond.

The receptionist, Nancy Parsons, who said she was the same age as I, greeted me warmly. I left my address and telephone number with her. Nancy said Miss Lucy often came to town. She would have her call me. I was glad the newspaper had stayed in the Tucker family, because Miss Lucy, her parents, and her brother were some of the kindest people Mama and I knew. We begin talking about the good old times. A stranger seeing us together would have thought that we had grown up under the same circumstances, and we were old friends reminiscing about the past.

We knew the same people, both black and white—Ethel and her family, the Gilmores. Our lively conversation about old times and the headlines in the current gazette—*Madisonville Business Owner Murdered, Eighty-year-old Keysville Woman Assaulted*, must have drifted to the back of the building, and two other ladies appeared and joined in the conversation.

There was no discussion of the articles and pictures showing black and white students from the former all white Randolph-Henry High School participating in the marching band, basketball, and the yearbook. There was no mention of Drakes' new mayor Denise L. Pridgen. She happened to be black. This was old news! If a stranger were eavesdropping on our conversation he would think that the four of us grew up in one world rather than two, one black and the other white.

I commented that I wished I had a camera so I could take a picture of the four of us. Later I did return to Drakes and took a picture of Nancy and her husband, Fred. These three white ladies seemed to be oblivious to the quite different paths we had followed. I thought of Robert Frost's poem that I had often read and analyzed with my students, *The Road Not Taken* and in particular the lines:

> *Two roads diverged in a yellow wood,*
> *And sorry I could not travel both*

While engaging in this friendly banter with three ladies, I knew that I had *not* come home, and I am not sure that I ever wanted to.

Looking ahead? To what should I look ahead? A few months ago I thought I had a lot to look forward to. At the top of the list were plans for Nikki and Dave's wedding. For the past forty years I have been living comfortably in Northern Virginia. I have felt safe here, but not anymore. When I go to bed each night I wonder—will I awake in the morning in Heaven or Hell? Will I have been blown to smithereens as I slept, and will parts of my body, like everyone else's on this planet, be indistinguishable? For several months, when I retrieved the *Washington Post* from the mounds of snow, ice and rain, I opened it immediately.

I had to see how the day's headlines would read. Would there be answers to these questions? Have we invaded Iraq? Yes, we have invaded Iraq! Has North Korea attacked the west coast of the United States? Has Japan attacked North Korea, before it is attacked first? Have all the predominantly Moslem countries like Saudi Arabia, Iran, Pakistan, Syria, Somalia, and all of Northern Africa joined forces to fight until death against the United States? Will the United States be able to fight two wars on two fronts—Afghanistan and Iraq—or maybe even Korea, China, Iran, and Syria?

Today, I did wake up and found my body and soul still intact and lying in my bed. I began thinking of the most recent headlines of the past few days and months: *Blix Plans Mixed Criticism of Iraq, Shuttle Probably was Pierced, Schools Boost Preparations for Attack, Forty Thousand Troops Land in Turkey, Special Operations Units Already in Iraq.* The latter indicates that we had already invaded Iraq, before the war actually began. Recent headlines read: *Spoils to the Victor, Thanks for Ousting Hussein, Now Please go Home, A City Freed from Tyranny Descends into Lawlessness, Our Heritage is Finished: Looters Destroyed What War Did Not. Lladró Figurines Appeal to all Types*"...even to Saddam's son Uday. The headline I have *not* seen is *The Stockpiles of Saddam's Weapons of Mass Destruction, Including Biological, Found.*

When I was a little girl my fear was the thousands of snakes, frogs, and lizards around my little house by the Branch. I now realize this fear was nothing compared with that of the children who were in the midst of poverty and war during the 1930s and 1940s and now the 2000s. I have never had a day of hunger, or spent a day without shelter. I didn't realize the danger my brother and other members of my family were facing when they went off to war.

Fear came home to me when I was on the way to New Jersey, and a lady in the Chesapeake Rest Stop looked at my smiling face in the mirror and asked,

"Do you know what has happened"?

"What?"

"America has been attacked!"

"By what country? Russia? China?"

"Not by a country—by terrorists! Washington and New York are under siege."

My trips north concerned the Couliers who were dealing with a dire family problem. I forgot about them at that moment. They were insignificant. I rushed to my car, turned on the radio, and turned around and headed south instead of north.

When I stopped at the Tourists Information Center a little past Baltimore, I was told the beltway was closed. I didn't know any other way to go, so I decided to take my chances and continued on highway 95. After taking off in the wrong direction from the rest stop and being turned around by a policeman, I headed to the beltway. It was not closed. In fact there was almost no one on 495 heading toward northern Virginia.

All government workers, including Paul and Nikki, were confined to their office buildings. Pauly was on work-related travel in Finland. I had only Paul and Nikki to worry about. I thought my family in New York would be pretty safe, because they all live in Brooklyn or on Long Island, and Drakes Branch was a long way from Washington. Anyway, there was absolutely nothing there that terrorists would want to destroy.

Since the new millennium, there had been the September 11, 2001 terror attack, the war in Afghanistan, the Washington sniper of October 2002, and months of talk of a second war. Most people who have been spared the agony of losing a loved one in recent years and in the present war in Iraq will say it is because of their prayers. Am I to believe that the mothers and fathers who did lose their sons and daughters in this war and past wars, lost them because they did not pray to God for the safety of their sons and daughters? I don't believe this is true because no one has the answer as to why some people live and some people die.

Like Mama, I still pray for the safety of my family. I have come to the realization that there is nothing to be gained by living in fear. I have no control over nuclear or biological weapons and neither do most peoples of the world. It is the national leaders of countries like the United States, Russia, China, and Israel who control them. I must live my life the best way I can and no longer continually worry about what terror lies ahead. I know that one day our world is going to be destroyed by the many scientific inventions of man, but I live with the hope that *He will come again someday and I will see Him as He is.* Descartes, the great French scientist and philosopher, questioned how a God who is supremely good can let mere men cause so much destruction. He argues there must be an evil genius that poses a larger threat than God.

There are a lot of things I don't understand, but I will continue to have questions. I continue to read the newspaper, like Mama always did. What about the *Axis of Evil?* For all we know North Korea may already have weapons of mass destruction. Iraq may be hiding all of Saddam's nuclear weapons in Syria or Iran. North Korea admits that they can produce a nuclear weapon at any time.

No one in the Bush Administration or anywhere else has proven a link between Saddam and September 11. In fact, all the hijackers were from our staunch ally, Saudi Arabia, or they came to the United States by way of that country. Recently, the President has admitted that Iraq was not responsible for 9/11. However, over the past few years, he and other members of the administration, especially Dick Cheney have inferred that Saddam was involved.

Let us not forget that none of the hijackers received their flight training in Iraq, France, or any other country that we know of. Every pilot who flew an American plane into the World Trade Center, the Pentagon, or the field in Pennsylvania, learned to fly within our borders. Then there is Zacarias Moussaoui, the French citizen, who was trying to finish his flight training, like the nineteen others, in the United States. Fortunately or unfortunately for him, he wasn't able to complete his flight training here because he was being detained for forgetting to renew his student visa.

We are angry at Germany and France for not sanctioning the war with Iraq. On the other hand, Germany is the only country, so far, which has tried and sentenced anyone charged with the 9/11 attacks on America.

Our American system of justice has permitted Moussaoui to dismiss his federal court appointed defender, Frank W. Dunham Jr., and the standby team and defend himself (pro se). He isn't a lawyer, but he is intelligent enough to use tactics that American lawyers use to set obviously guilty people free—by stalling and misrepresenting the obvious.

The latest *Washington Post*'s, headline May 27, 2003 reads, *Moussaoui is spinning a Legal Web.* Chances are Moussaoui will be granted permission to interview, or even to call as a witness, Ramsi Binalshib who says he, Ramsi, was the planner of the September 11, 2001 attack on America.

Moussaoui contends that this man will say he wasn't the so-called "twentieth Highjacker." Ramsi won't have a problem lying under oath. He will be doing so in the name of Allah, his god. Moussaoui probably will get himself declared innocent, unless his case is transferred to a military court.

In one case, according to a magazine article (June 23, 2003) the United States asked the Saudi Arabian government to send an Al-Qaeda sympathizer, who traveled often to terrorist-training camps in Afghanistan, to Paris, where he would be detained. It was known that a suicide bomber responsible for the attack in Tunisia that killed twenty-three people had called this Al-Qaeda operative.

When it comes to the war on terrorism, France is in the forefront. French laws provide for a looser definition of complicity in terrorism . This allows magistrates to jail probable co-conspirators. Al-Qaeda operatives were not in Iraq before the war, but they are there now, wreaking havoc.

Do we have the right to chastise peoples of the world who do not agree with us on political matters? Nearly six thousand people demonstrated in Paris against possible United States military action in Iraq. There have also been thousands of Americans demonstrating against the war. Should those Americans be branded as traitors like the French?

Both the Americans and the British have criticized and ridiculed France for not remembering Hitler and the Nazis, who invaded France in 1940, and their liberation by the allied forces that landed on the Normandy beaches in 1944.

French bashing borders on the ridiculous, as observed by an eighth grade student, Carly Garrett, in an American History class. When I told the class that I had retired from Luther Jackson after many years of teaching French, Carly piped up and made the following remark: "I now call my French teacher, *'Freedom* Teacher'!" A dim-witted member of Congress had suggested that Americans call French fries freedom fries.

Of course, the French remember who helped to rid their country of the Nazis! Hitler had violated the Treaty of Versailles. According to the treaty, no German troops were to enter the Rhineland, the area along the Rhine River that borders France. No action was taken by France, or any other country, to force Hitler to remove his soldiers from the area. Hitler and his Nazi party, along with their desire to conquer the world, believed that there were certain groups of people that were undesirable in a civilized society. Among those people were Jews, gypsies, and people like me. Let us not forget Hitler's snubbing of the greatest Olympian of all times, Jesse Owens.

While the Axis powers, Germany, Italy, and Japan, planned to extend their power over other countries, including the United States, Congress passed laws aimed at keeping the United States out of foreign wars. When the war in Europe was raging, the United States changed its neutrality laws and began supplying American arms on a "cash and carry" basis to Great Britain. The United States also cut off the sale of war material to Japan. We entered World War II only after the Japanese's surprise attack on Pearl Harbor in the early morning hours of December 7, 1941.

It is true that the Petian Government did collaborate with the Germans. But when France fell, General Charles de Gaulle and other French citizens left France for London. They joined the movement to free their country. A strong French resistance movement developed throughout France, including Paris. DeGaulle and other Resistance fighters entered Paris with the American troops in August, 1944.

The French did not sit around with their wines and cheeses, waiting to be liberated by the Americans. After the allied troops entered France the French did not loot palaces and the homes of citizens, destroy the historical buildings, steal and break irreplaceable artifacts, as the Iraqis have done. Before the Germans were able to steal the great masterpieces, individual citizens went into the Louvre and the other museums of France and took their treasures and hid them in their homes. After the war, every single item was returned to its original home.

Would the Nazis not have loved to get their hands on the most famous painting in the world, *La Joconde*—that's what the French call the lady with the mysterious smile. There are different stories as to the whereabouts of "the lady" while the Nazis controlled northern France. One is that she too was kept in a private home. In 1962, I left my group and went off alone to see this masterpiece in its home, the Louvre. The *Mona Lisa* was hanging on the wall where I could have actually touched the lady. It was not in a bullet-proof enclosure as it is today.

It was through the generosity of the French that I was able to take my students from the all black Luther Jackson High School to see the *Mona Lisa* behind her bullet proof glass in the National Gallery of Art in 1963. France has since said that the *Mona Lisa* will never again leave its shores. How unfortunate for those who will never visit her in the Louvre.

Then there was the *Maquis*. They were a group of French patriots who formed a secret army to fight the German forces occupying France. *Maquis* is a French word for tough vegetation that is found along the Mediterranean. All classes joined the *Maquis* to free France. They conducted intelligence and small-scale operations such as blowing up trains, killing sentries, and sabotaging German military production. Units of up to sixty men hid in the Pyrenees and the Alps mountains in southern and eastern France. The Allies parachuted supplies to them. Jacques Houdaille, a boy during the war, tried to join the *Maquis*. A schoolboy of fifteen was too young even if he were a willing participant.

Lastly, the French did not attack and kill the liberators when they landed on the Normandy beaches on June 6, 1944. I have seen the wreckage of the ships and the man-made piers that brought the Allies to shore. They are a reminder of what happened there.

I know the French remember all peoples who helped to free their country, because I also toured a museum in Caen dedicated to the Normandy Invasion. The story of the invasion and valor of the allied forces and the French is told in this *Memorial Museum for Peace*. I visited this museum in 1989 with a group of Fairfax County students who were participating in a summer Humanities Program that included three weeks in Europe.

The museum had opened the year before. Part of the museum is built on the site of a former German command post. The museum encompasses World War I as well. Its graphic audio-visual presentation shows clips of the actual invasion, and I could only weep as the horrors of war unfolded before my eyes. French Resistance forces inside France who were alerted to the coming invasion engaged in behind-the-lines sabotage and combat against the occupying Germans. The museum is not dedicated to the glory of France, but to all nations who rid their country of despots like Hitler and his Nazi Party.

There are other monuments, streets, avenues, and roadside markers all over Normandy and other regions which are dedicated to those Americans who had helped to set France free. President Bush who continually criticizes President Jacques Chirac never took French history, his being a "C" student at all. Compared to the forty-two presidents before him, George W. Bush is thought to be the least intellectual—that is, the dumbest.

There were also individuals who deserved to be remembered, such as the famous Jean Moulin and Josephine Baker who were active in the French Resistance inside and outside of France. They received the *Croix de Guerre*, *the Legion of Honor*, and *the Rosette of the Resistance*, that are France's highest awards for valor.

In later years Josephine Baker also became active in the civil rights movement in the United States. World War II ended; the Nazis were driven from power, but not by the United States alone. The Museum of Peace at Caen invites visitors of all ages and nationalities to go on a wonderful journey through the history of the twentieth century.

The French have legitimate reasons for opposing the United States' unilateral attack on Iraq, just as some Americans do. The UN inspectors should have been given more time to find the weapons that our armed forces, numbering in the thousands, still have not found. The weapons of mass destruction and biological stockpiles were the main reason that we declared war on Saddam Hussein and his regime. The United Nations was organized in 1945, at the end of World War II for the purpose of working for international peace and security. Just because we are American, we are not forced to agree with President George W. Bush, who wants to get the evil dictator, "who tried to kill my daddy." Those are his words and not mine.

We have no idea where either Osama Bin Laden is at this moment. He may be living right under our noses like the nineteen highjackers of November 11, 2001 and the twentieth one that was left behind. There is no evidence Al-Qaeda was ever in Iraq. But they are there now, probably still under Osama bin Laden's leadership. France, Germany, and Russia opposed the war by threatening to block the United Nation's approval of a unilateral attack on Iraq, so why have President Bush, Secretary of State Colin Powell, and others in the administration singled out only France for retribution?

There are members of the military inside Iraq who are also grumbling about our purpose there. Though all of us are happy to see a madman like Saddam Hussein disappear, we still wonder about the future of that country and the daily loss of American lives. Shouting, "Bring'em on'!" like the schoolyard bully who yells, "Dare you!" was an invitation to the enemy to attack U. S. troops.

President George W. Bush's active participation in the war was putting on a borrowed flight suit, landing on an aircraft carrier, and declaring victory in Iraq. Later it was learned that the aircraft carrier could actually have been in port, and he could have walked on board. But that would not have been as dramatic and all. I don't think President Bush has spent a night in Iraq, though.

I just cannot imagine a candidate for president not having been to London, Rome, or even Paris before seeking the presidency. Mama was more inquisitive and knowledgeable about life beyond the United States than this president. After becoming president his ultimate goal was to bring democracy to all nations of the world particularly the Islamic world. Just what does this mean?

In his 2003 Christmas card Vice-President Cheney used a quote by Ben Franklin that suggests that an empire probably rises by the will of God. Is he suggesting that the president's goal of bringing democracy to the Middle East is the will of God? I think not! I believe that out of the ashes of Iraq another tyrant will rise like the Taliban who replaced the conquering Russians and the Ayatollahs who replaced the Shah.

What about our color alert for terror? The color is continually changed between high and medium alert. No one has really explained what we should do to protect ourselves. Most people pick the most tangible things such as food and water to save themselves and their family from a nuclear or biological attack. Many Americans rushed to buy duct tape and plastic sheeting in case of germ warfare, even though one cannot survive in an airtight room indefinitely or keep germs out. Paul and I have rushed out to buy neither tape nor plastic sheets. We just wait for the next scare!

Because of the problems, the daily attacks on our American military and the mayhem in all of Iraq, President Bush now wants the help of the United

Nations and of countries like France, Germany, and Russia. Recently the president spoke to the United Nations. He received a cool welcome. *The Washington Post*'s headline (September 25, 2003) reads "Bush Fails to Gain Pledges on Troops for Iraq." Below the fold there is "Iraq Weapons Report won't be Conclusive." He wants their help but he still wants to be at the helm. He is still being the ugly American!

Have we Americans gone completely mad? The people of one of the most populous state in the U. S. have elected Arnold Schwarzenegger governor. His claim to fame is based on his playing the part of the *Terminator* and his *Kennedy Family* connection. Arnold's participation in orgies, as described in *Oui* magazine, and the groping of women (for which he has now apologized) rival the orgies of the Marquis de Sade, not to be confused with the *Maquis*. This governor elect is banking on tips from President Bush as to how to solve one of California's biggest problems, the economy.

Schwarzenegger now has his eye on the United States presidency. "I want to shoot for the top." He is banking on the Republicans to change the Constitution, which now allows only U.S. born citizens to become President of the United States. An Islamic terrorist like Osama Ben Laden could then become President. The United States would become a radical Islamic country, and with America's military power Islam would become the religion of the world. All females would be required to wear headscarves. President Jacques Chirac's edit concerning head coverings for students would be rescinded. This theory sounds far fetched, but I am positive Vice President Dick Cheney will see that it has merit. However, President Bush has already said, "We must bring democracy to the Middle East." Dick Cheney just has to bring the President into the "loop."

This is the story of my short but wonderful life, and this is the story of my love for two countries. These are my thoughts, ideas, and beliefs.

In the frontispiece to this autobiography you will find a photograph of my mother, and another of my father.

Please look, really look, at my mother. Then you will find in her calm, warm eyes the strength on which I drew as a child growing up. You will see her firmness of jaw that took the outrages of the South in which she flourished on Earth. And you will see the generous mouth, quick to smile and offer kind words of encouragement, and firm in discipline.

Not seen are her hands, which worked too long in the service of others; loving hands that were always there for her family, to shore them up when spirits were low; hands that were strictly "on loan" to the people she worked for to provide for her family's needs. Hands that could cook and clean for her husband and children.

A deep and abiding spirit, was my mother. Her presence is with me always. Her wisdom echoes through me down to my children, and on to my grandchildren.

Please look, really look, at my father. Look at his quiet stance, the way he looks off to one side, as if looking for company coming, or perhaps in some quiet modesty at having his picture taken. Strength and courage lie in this quiet and elegant man. I was to lose him too soon, left only with a few enigmatic words that I ponder to this day. I wonder what words he would have had for me as I grew into womanhood, married, and bore him grandchildren, and offered great-grandchildren.

Strength he had in unjust times; and the courage to speak for justice when it was not meted out to him. I hold my father close, with my mother.

I hope you have found my autobiography interesting and worthy of your time. I have been so fortunate: good parents have nurtured me; I have studied and learned about this world, especially the celebration of its spirit in times of good and bad. I have enjoyed, and continue to enjoy, friendships and many hours and days of laughter and reflection. And there has been sadness too, and melancholy, and disappointments—but they too are a part of life.

And France. For you to understand me, who I am, you must first know Drakes Branch and where I came from, and the life and memories I hold from that small place in Virginia. To understand my love of France you must track my heart and spirit, through my studies, through the French language, to me the most beautiful of languages. You must catch my excitement as I visit her again and again; each time granted insights into what life is about, by participating in her history, her elegance, her chic luster, and throbbing heart.

If you have been to France—go back. If you have not been there—make the trip. She will enfold you, inspire you, and dazzle you. She reaches even now to me, in my new home in Vienna, not too far from Drakes Branch and the memories of those I love there.

> *Oú sont les neiges d'antan?*
> *Villon, Ballads des Dames du temps jadis*
> *(Where are the snows of yesteryear?)*

LIFE AS A COLLAGE

Our earthly lives are as a stream, seamless and flowing, carrying us forward, at times quickly and glittering, at others a quiet backwater carrying our reflections. We begin our day moving on life's current, exchanging endearments with those we love, we hold tight, we wave, we go about our day, doing what is by turn important and trivial, caring and thoughtful, nurturing and rewarding. And the stream quietly flows, over the smoothed stones of our doubts and worries, hurts and injustice, until again life flows at an eager pace filled with hopes and silent, sometimes hasty, prayer.

But how to catch it? How to catch its glitter and continuous movement? The fact is, we can't. Instead, we can try to catch fleeting moments, passing instants, and interludes that can warm us as we feel the yearning to look back and capture it all.

The following collages offer moments in my life when the stream ran full and clear and sparkling. If you study them, you will catch the laughter, the adventure, the sights, and sounds gone, but **much loved**.

My stream runs on, as does yours, I welcome each bend and turn, each swirling moment, each clear ripple that draws my life exquisitely ahead of me.

Charles de Gaulle

PARIS
1950'S

PAR MON AMI
LEONARD SYNDER

Jones' Hall

Dr. Cole's 1926 Club Reception

STUDENT UNION

50 years

Bennett College

May 8-10, 2003

Bennett College 1958
45th Reunion

Class Meeting "Chez Geneva"

Preference Song

CLASS OF
58

45 Years

Alumnae Weekend

Class of 1958
Greensboro, North Carolina

BENNETT COLLEGE

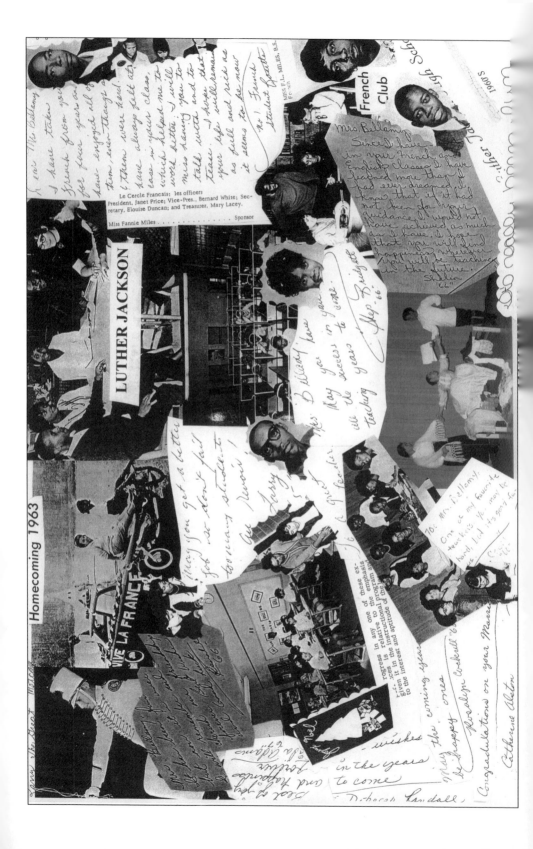

1976 L. J. Students-Paris

1970'S

Marie-Josée at Uncle Flood's

Mrs. Theodora Dusenbury McCauley
March 1935 – September 1994

1990'S

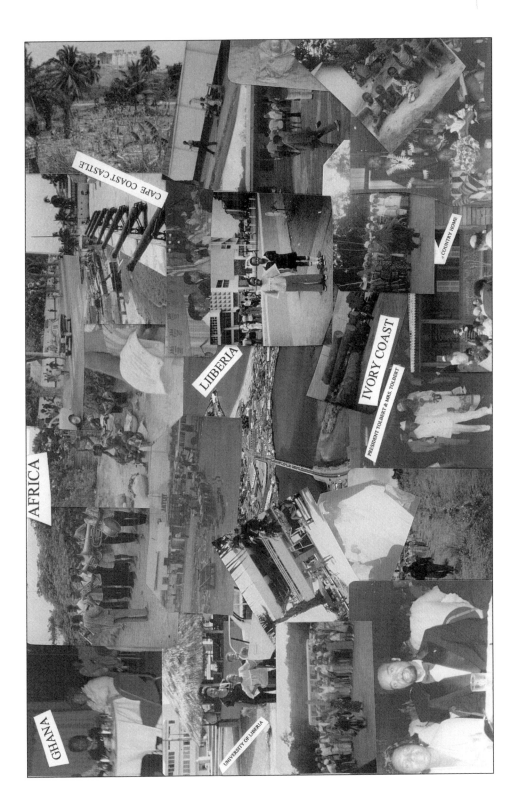

AFRICA

CAPE COAST CASTLE

GHANA

LIIBERIA

UNIVERSITY OF LIBERIA

IVORY COAST

PRESIDENT TOLBERT & MRS. TOLBERT

COUNTRY HOME

CHILDREN

Provençal Wedding Reception

2000's

2003

"Bevor ein Krieg ausbricht, hat er längst in
dem Herzen der Menschen begonnen."
Leo Tolstoi

"THINK NOT ONLY UPON THEIR PASSING
REMEMBER THE GLORY OF THEIR SPIRIT."

«Avant que la guerre s'éclate au grand
jour, elle a longtemps commencé
dans le cœur des hommes»

Bibliography

Agay, Dennis, *Best Love Songs of the American People*, Doubleday, New York, 1975.

Black History Research. compiled by Reginald Washington, National Archives and Record Administration, Washington, DC 2001.

Brown, Linda B. *The Long Walk; the Story of the Presidency of Will B. Palyer at Bennett College*. McCain Printing company, Inc. Danville, 1998.

Bryan, John L. *Little Prayers to live By*. The Stenographic Bureau, Bennett College, Greensboro, 1958.

Davidoff, Henry, Editor, *The Pocket Book of Quotations*. Simon & Schuster, Inc., New York, 1969.

Du Bois, William Edward Burghardt, *The Soul of Black Folk*. New American Library, New York, 1995.

Frame, Donald M., Translator, *The Misanthrope and Other Plays*, Penguin Books USA, New York.

France Magazine. Published monthly, Archant Life, Cheltenham, Glos Gl50 England, 2003.

Oslen, William, *A Way of Life*. Paul B. Hoeber, Inc, New York, 1937.

Michelin, *Guide de Tourism*. Spain, France, Provence, Flanders, Picardy and Paris Region, Michelin et Cie, Artelieurs Typigraphiques, 1987, 1989, 1991, 1993.

44434

Middlemiss, Robert, *A Common Glory*. Iris Press, Oak Ridge, TN, 2000.

Parks, Gordon, *A Choice of Weapons*. Minnesota Historical Society Press, St. Paul, 1986.

Spotlight on Drakes Branch, Virginia. Centennial Committee, Drakes Branch, 1003.

Peter, Clara Hamilton, *A Century's Growth in Teacher Evaluation in the United States*. Vantage Press, New York, 1982.

Peep of the Day. Revised Edition, Thomas Whittaker, New York.

Ward, Bernie, Editor, *Nostradamus, Prophecies You Can't Ignore!* American Media Mini Mags, Inc., New York 2001.

Women's Leadership Institute, *The Bennett College Social Justice Lecture Series*. Bennett College Press, Greensboro, 2000.

Wright, Richard, *Black Boy, A Record of Childhood and Youth*, Perennial Classics, San Francisco, 1998.